Brenda Casey
Texas Oncology
Presbyterian

CREATIVE NURSING ADMINISTRATION

Participative Management into the 21st Century

Tim Porter-O'Grady, Ed.D., R.N.
Affiliated Dynamics, Inc.
Norcross, Georgia

AN ASPEN PUBLICATION ®
Aspen Publishers, Inc.
Gaithersburg, Maryland
1986

Library of Congress Cataloging-in-Publication Data

Porter-O'Grady, Timothy
Creative nursing administration.

"An Aspen Publication."
Bibliography: p. 253
Includes index.
1. Nursing service administration. 2. Management-Employee participa-
tion. I. Title. II. Title: Participative management into the 21st century.
[DNLM: 1. Interprofessional Relations-nurses' instruction. 2. Nursing,
Supervisory-trends. 3. Quality Assurance,
Health Care-nurses' instruction. WY 105 P849c]
RT89.P65   1986   362.1'73'068   85-22940
ISBN: 0-87189-264-2

Editorial Services: Martha Sasser

Library of Congress Catalog Card Number: 85-22940
ISBN: 0-87189-264-2

Printed in the United States of America

4 5

This text is dedicated to
the Father,
who has encouraged me to
participate fully in all the
experiences of my own life.

Special Note

The pronoun reference to ''she'' is used throughout this book. While I recognize that many men are nurses and will be using this text, the preponderance of readers will be women nurses. The use of ''she'' recognizes this reality. However, it is not intended to ignore the fact that there are men in the profession and that they make many fine contributions to nursing. ''She'' is used simply to maintain consistency and to recognize the gender realities of nursing.

Table of Contents

Foreword

True participation in decision-making requires an environment that recognizes the expertise of the participants and allows open interaction among people. In today's tightly constrained environment of health care, such participation is essential in order to engage qualified persons in activities that allow involvement and commitment. Even so, there is a tendency to tighten the administrative reins in times of tight resources and resulting stressors. This tendency negates the importance of participation to gain involvement and commitment. Consequently nurse executives, nurse managers, and others are seeking an appropriate balance between the essential participation and the pressures to act authoritatively.

Tim Porter-O'Grady has captured the essence of participation in this book. The text is particularly pertinent to the experiences of nurses today. It recognizes the evolution of nurses' roles and functions over time and acknowledges the importance of the context in which nurses function. The book provides timely approaches for moving toward participative management and self-governance in nursing. Nursing is a maturing profession and nurses are at varying stages in development of both their willingness and their ability to be participants in decision-making. Developing nursing talents toward effectively participating in decision-making about matters affecting nursing practice is today's challenge. This thoughtfully written text provides assistance for those seeking to meet the challenge.

The advantages of participative management far outweigh the disadvantages. Effective participation is a vehicle for realizing nursing's potential. In the current health care environment, decisions are increasingly made through committees or group work. The "corporate committee" is a phenomenon typical of our corporate society. Nursing's opportunities for participation in health care increase as nurses prove themselves to be capable participants. Learning the fine art of constructive and purposeful participation is thus essential for nurses. This learning can be nurtured within nursing management. Effective participation requires knowledge and skill that can be gained through practice.

Fostering participation among nurses is a key to managerial success. It is also the key to nursing's success in contributing more fully in the broad health care arena. Nurse-power stems from decision making, taking action, and being accountable. Accountability is more likely to occur when there is involvement and commitment. Involvement and commitment are more likely to occur when there is appropriate support for full participation in meaningful activities. This book's importance lies in helping nurses understand how to structure themselves for participation and how to encourage meaningful participation. In the long run, nursing can only benefit by applying the information in this book to its own situation so that true participation is fostered throughout nursing's ranks.

Marjorie Beyers

Preface

Many changes are occurring in health care delivery systems. In preparing for the future, new skills are demanded of nurses in all settings. Nurse managers, clinical leaders, those in both education and service—all will be required to participate fully in the unfolding of a new and challenging health care environment.

The changes are taking place at an accelerating rate. Nurses have hardly learned to deal with one change when another one quickly appears. This tendency will accelerate. Nurses must be prepared to confront these challenges on a much broader basis than they have historically. To be able to cope with such challenges and to be incorporated into the decision-making process that will deal with them, nurses must learn and be ready to participate more fully in the delivery system and with each other.

The delivery system of the future will require that nurses be integrated with other health professionals in making decisions. This interdependence will accelerate and nurses will need to have the skills in group management, group process, and collective decision making if they are to be effective participants in the change process.

For too long, practicing nurses and front-line nurse managers have been excluded from the highest forums of policy making and decision making at national, regional, local, and institutional levels. While certain leaders have been provided opportunities to participate, nursing's input into major decisions affecting the direction of health care has been limited at best. For nurses to make fuller contributions to the system in planning forums and at the policymaking level, they must develop the skills essential to exercising responsibility and participating in the planning and implementation of a true health-based care delivery system.

The script for health care is changing. The business is becoming more and more creative every day. The utilization of health resources for delivering new alternative care services will be a key characteristic of the future care system. By the year 2000, a broad-based health care system will have a profound impact on the delivery of services in the home, in the workplace, in the community, and, of course, in the hospital.

The hospital of today that is based on traditional illness care services will become a health care center serving all such needs of its community through its various programs and services. Nurses must be available to provide leadership in developing these services and to exercise their clinical responsibility in meeting the needs of the consumers they will serve. If nurses are to do so, they must develop the skills essential to incorporate into their practice framework the newer strategies for relating to others and for carrying out their functions.

This book is directed to the nursing leader, be she clinical or management at any level of the nursing organization, who is interested in expanding concepts related to managing and participating. The specific focus is on the development of group and peer relationships within and outside nursing in order to facilitate decision making and ensure positive outcomes. It demonstrates how the practitioner can share in decision making affecting her practice and the delivery of health care services. It presents ideas and strategies that can enhance the role of the practicing nurse in all decisions, including those traditionally reserved for the management process. Some of these ideas may appear radical and may even challenge some of the behaviors, practices, and organizational forms nurses have come to accept, even value. It is designed to assure that all clinical practitioners and managers are working toward the same goal and are collaborating in the process of providing appropriate and meaningful delivery of nursing care services. It is in this context that the future must be confronted.

Old management systems and styles no longer will be effective as the health care delivery system becomes more distributed and broad based. By the year 2000 and beyond, nurses should be involved at every level of the system in major ways. No longer will they merely be the workhorses of the delivery system. In the new mode, they will need to be involved in the decisional process and the group(s) making those decisions. Practicing nurses' ownership in these processes is not optional. However, to exercise that ownership, as noted, nurses must be given the opportunity, must have the requisite skills and abilities, and then must be permitted to utilize all of their resources in developing their practice, contributing to the delivery of health care services, and expanding their own accountability for the work they provide in the system.

This book is designed to aid in the development and utilization of participatory strategies for enhancing the nurse leaders and their practicing nurse peers. It is best used as a reference and as a resource, supplemented by others on specific developmental subjects. The purpose here is to stimulate, encourage, and give food for thought to professional nurses seeking to participate more fully in decisions that affect their practice. It is hoped that once the stimulus is provided, nursing leaders will assume responsibility for their own growth and development and will participate with their peers in providing opportunities for sharing, negotiating, and solving common problems. Through peer participation, the profession can share more fully both clinically and in management the exciting opportunities and challenges that lie before all nurses to provide leadership in the delivery of health care services well into the 21st century.

Tim Porter-O'Grady, R.N., Ed.D.

Acknowledgments

The preparation of a manuscript such as this is never the product of any one individual. Many persons have helped in numerous ways in giving it form and meaning. My thanks to:

Sharon Finnigan, my business partner, colleague, and friend, whose absolute commitment to participation serves as an inspiration to me in the validation of my own beliefs.

Dr. Gary Linz, whose insight and participation with me in my own developmental process has been a source of strength and personal renewal.

Patticolleen Runfola, who has continued to participate with me in the struggle and preparation of all my writings.

To all my nursing colleagues who continue to serve as a source of inspiration and provide many examples of the real contribution nursing can make.

Finally, to those who have shared their love and their patience with me during my own developmental processes—they all know who they are and they know I am grateful.

Participation as a Social Mandate

Discuss the historical context for current nursing practice.

Outline the social and work characteristics mandating participative management strategies.

Identify current changes in the delivery of care and relate them to the development of technology.

Clarify the issues related to creating a professional workplace in the health care system.

Describe the social changes in women's roles and the impact of that process on the growth of nursing.

Review the skills and abilities the nurse manager will have to incorporate into her role to be effective in the future.

1

The transformation of the American workplace since the turn of the century has been breathtaking and in many ways overwhelming. The nation has moved from a largely agrarian culture, through a dynamic industrial phase, into a new information age that depends upon high levels of technology. The changes have altered the workplace considerably, with a dramatic impact not only on the work to be done but also on the workers affected (Figure 1–1).

Now, a new and powerful social and technological change is rolling across much of the nation. It is creating a new environment in which work will have significantly different characteristics. The changes in society and thus in the workplace will occur at a radically accelerated rate. Many of the changes will be unplanned and destabilizing. Stability will be perhaps one of the most illusive

---

Figure 1–1 Social Transition Affecting the Workplace

Pre 1900	Early 20th Century	Mid 20th Century
Slavery	Industrial Formalization	Rising Technology
Child Labor	Management Science	Nuclear Age Society
No Employee Rights	Formalization of Nursing	Technical Trades Development
Industrial Expansion	Universal Basic Education	University Education for Nurses
Postmedieval Health Care	Mechanical Trades Development	Human Relations Management
		Growing Labor Unions
		Industrial Expansion

Contemporary 20th Century
Proliferation of Computer Technology
Declining Industrialization
Growing Middle Class
Professionalization of Nursing
High-Tech, High-Touch Integration
Humanization of the Workplace
Worker Participation in Management
Constraining Resources: "Tighter" Economy

3

conditions of work. Instability, breakdown, building up, alteration, excitement, and encouragement are words that can be applied to the workplace of the future.

It is important to recognize that many of today's changes are not independent of one another; they are not unreasonable or random. All of the variables that make up society have a dramatic impact on each other so any change in one has an effect on others. Individuals who seek to be leaders in this environment must sort out the variables that affect the change process in their workplace.

Leaders will have to give direction and support to those who will undertake the changes. Leaders of today no longer can be idealized as the St. George who fights the dragon or Teddy Roosevelt who leads the nation single-handedly into victory. Isolated, self-identified leaders seldom can be successful in the current social environment. The interaction and relationship of all the variables in the workplace, including those of the workers themselves, will require an entirely different format for leading.

HISTORICAL PERSPECTIVES IN PARTICIPATION

In the years since the Depression, research has demonstrated clearly that management that consistently involves participation and participative practices improves relationships, productivity, environmental circumstances, and outcomes. Historical research in the behavioral sciences from Frederick Taylor[1] through Elton Mayo[2], Herzburg[3], Maslow[4], Argyris[5], and others suggests that the behavioral component is one of the core elements of work that must be addressed carefully and scientifically. While there has been much research on these issues, there have not always been subsequent changes in behavior in the workplace. Changes in knowledge about work are easy to make; the hardest elements to alter are attitudes and behaviors. However, it is essential in the workplace that the structuring of leadership focus on altering behaviors, especially in the managerial role. This transition will result in the positive outcomes indicated by the behavioral research on the management role and leadership behavior (Figure 1–2).[6]

One of the most difficult areas in which to see altered behavior in leadership has been in participative management. Since the early 1930s, human resource research and development has indicated that individual participation in decision making in the management process, when spread among those in the workplace, improves both process and outcome. What is necessary to consider in regard to work and to leadership is the impact of this research on the workplace in light of today's technologically driven social transformation.

Any managers, well informed and educated in their role, recognize the value of participation. It is not often apparent, however, that they have a full understanding of that role in relation to participative practices, or perhaps even in the process undertaken to assure that participation occurs. The ''high-tech–high-touch'' social transformation being experienced today and that can well continue for much

Figure 1–2 Transition to Participation

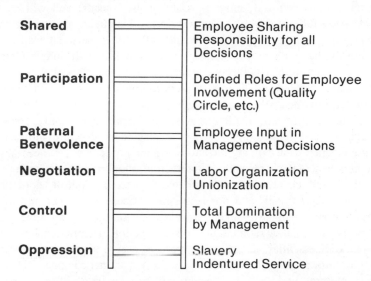

Shared	Employee Sharing Responsibility for all Decisions
Participation	Defined Roles for Employee Involvement (Quality Circle, etc.)
Paternal Benevolence	Employee Input in Management Decisions
Negotiation	Labor Organization Unionization
Control	Total Domination by Management
Oppression	Slavery Indentured Service

of the next two decades, indicates the need for an entirely different belief system that results in a different set of relations and behaviors in the work environment.

The New Types of Work

Work in the future will become less repetitive, narrow, and timebound. Workers no longer will be the obedient, subsequious employees who have no stake in role, function, or outcome or sense of ownership regarding their jobs. Industrial society beliefs that enabled those concepts to develop are passing, to be replaced by worker values based on accountability and responsibility.

In the society of tomorrow, as technology provides a stronger baseline, work will become less routine, less structured; instead, it will become more integrated, more uniform, more interrelated with other aspects of work. Work will be less "massified" and will be broken up into smaller and smaller components, each having some impact on other components being done by other workers. Workers of the future will need the freedom and the ability to accept broader responsibility, to understand how their work relates to others', to share roles, to expand the basis of work, and to be able to interrelate and interchange creatively with other individuals. A systems process of work, and its outcomes, can be interrelated and understood by those who participate in it.

Because workers will have a stake in their jobs, they will demand more responsibility, more interest in the job, more communication, more commitment, and an expanded sense of control over decisions that affect outcomes. Workers will be more individualized, more separate in their needs, and will want to participate more fully in selecting wages, salaries, benefits, and working conditions that more systematically and significantly affect their personal needs. There will be both individualization and integration of work, with unique elements defined and structured clearly. Pieces that relate to other elements of work also will be defined and integrated with them to provide complementary work and services.

Traditional ingrained ideas and concepts of authority and control will pass; workers of the future no longer will look at the boss in the same context. There will be a strong move to reduce high levels of management structure and facilitate shared governance kinds of organizations where group process becomes the central component of decision making. Interaction, support, and relationships will become the major characteristics of the work process. Control, domination, authority by force of will, and nonnegotiable processes will become foreign elements. Workers will have higher expectations of those who have greater responsibility. Information, communication, interaction, and relationships will be valued—indeed, essential—elements of work to assure appropriate outcomes. The need for information will expand and will have a dramatic impact. The ability to collect, interpret, and share information will be a key mark of leadership.

Technology's Impact

A high level of technological understanding and awareness of the impact of technology on human resources will be an important characteristic of both workers and managers. Technology has a tendency to alienate and isolate people from the relational and emotional issues essential to human interaction. Managers of the future will be integrators, communicators, facilitators, and experts on the human and humane aspects of work. Clearly, a new set of behaviors and management rules will have to be applied to integrate technology with human needs (Figure 1–3).

In health care this will be no less true. If anything, a new management style will be even more important. This is one of the most people-intensive of industries. However, its people intensity is offset by an almost overwhelming reliance on technology. As the technological applications of health care grow, the need for intense human relationships also will grow. The high-tech, high-touch balance outlined by John Naisbitt will need to be identified clearly by managers of the future.[7] Health care managers will have a special responsibility for maintaining the balance between technology and human relationships. If health care is to retain its human focus and harness the generative and healing processes within every individual, skills in technological and relationship integration will be essential.

Figure 1–3 High-Tech, High-Touch Integration

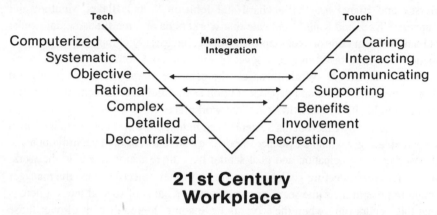

**21st Century
Workplace**

The Participative Mode

It should be apparent that participative strategies for the future are not optional but are absolutely necessary. Successful managers will have entirely different behavioral characteristics from the traditional traits. (Those characteristics are explored in detail in Chapter 3.) The transition to these new sets of behaviors and workplace rules, when incorporated into leaders' behavior, will produce a radically different sense of satisfaction and of outcome in both workers and managers.

While the focus here is on participation, it is looked at differently from historic perceptions, with the concept developed in a manner well removed from the predominant conception. At the outset, processes that will be essential to the management of participation in the workplace are analyzed.

Participation needs to be defined clearly to provide a frame of reference within which to operate. Shashkin[8] offers perhaps the most practical and meaningful definition, describing it as worker participation in setting goals, making decisions by choosing from among alternative courses of action, solving problems through definition of issues, generation of alternative courses of action, and making changes in the organization. This definition is somewhat broad, yet it includes the key elements in the workplace over which employees seek to have some influence or control. While these elements may have varying degrees of influence, depending on the circumstances and objectives of the organization, they constitute the characteristics essential for the participative process in the workplace.

Research over half a century has demonstrated consistently that participatory management has been effective. Much research has been undertaken in this area, especially emphasized in the work of Kurt Lewin[9] in the 1940s and 1950s. Much of that work has been expanded in the 1970s and 1980s by researchers such as Hersey and Blanchard,[10] Blanchard and Johnson,[11] and Blake, Mouton, and Tapper.[12] Katz and Kahn[13] indicate that workers have three fundamental needs: (1) autonomy or control over their own work behavior, (2) completion or achievement of a whole task, and (3) a level of interpersonal contact within the work activities themselves. While these can be separate elements, they actually are thoroughly interrelated and dependent upon each other and, indeed, are essential to the joint health of the worker and the workplace.

As identified by Likert in his Systems Four management model, participation in the workplace gives ample evidence of positive outcomes for both the institution and the worker.[14] Participation and goal setting have three major effects in the workplace. Workers selecting goals tend to choose higher objectives than the manager might impose in the same set of circumstances. What is of special interest here is that this occurs only when the workers have some degree of control over those choices. With such higher goals, the workers tend to be more willing and able to achieve them because of their ownership in having selected them. This kind of participatory strategy also builds a more acceptable and a longer lasting climate of trust and security, as identified in Likert's System Four process.

When workers select goals, they have a stronger commitment to understanding the efforts, activities, and knowledge involved in implementing them. They feel and demonstrate more control over task activities and selections. They have a stronger knowledge base regarding what has to be done because they have participated in defining those activities themselves.

Jackson indicates that participatory decision making gives workers an increased sense of control and influence as well as autonomy in relation to the task.[15] Behaviors related to participatory performance have a positive impact on reducing absenteeism and turnover.

What is not always clear, and is not discussed generally, is the effects on the workers and the workplace when participatory management strategies are not used. There is substantial evidence that when workers' human needs are not fulfilled and when the organizational environment and working conditions reflect this, there is direct harm to both the institution and to the workers.[16] The tradition of employer dominance and control over employees has a long history of negative social manifestations. The development of unions and the model of problem resolution based on antagonism and conflict are evidence of the traditional employer-employee relationship. Such conflict clearly has had a deleterious effect on that relationship and its impact on productivity has been much discussed for several decades. For example, the failure of unions to provide higher levels of productivity consistent with the higher standards of living that they have negotiated is a key element of the conflict theory of management-labor relations.

THE WORKPLACE: A HISTORY OF SUPPRESSION

It is curious in a country that espouses the democratic principles of responsibility and participation that its workplaces historically should be so devoid of either of those characteristics. In a democratic society, responsibility, individual accountability, compliance with legal mandates, and full participation in its activities are among the expectations of citizenship. Without these behaviors the social system in a democracy would soon collapse because participation, involvement, and social responsibility are basic characteristics. Because the democratic system is so dependent on these processes, a failure of a large element of the populace to undertake activities directed toward assuring democratic survival would result in total governmental and social collapse.

An important difficulty arises when the individuals who are expected to be responsible, capable, mature, able to participate within the legal framework of society, and make judgments regarding privilege, process, and voting practices enter the workplace and confront a whole new set of rules. It appears as if the democratic expectations for responsibility are not validated or supported in the workplace; indeed, the structure of the work environment is such that those basic characteristics are absent. High levels of structure, authority, and control are fully defined in the organization, with the intent of limiting the power centers to individuals who have been identified as the controlling forces in the entity.

Policy determination, decision-making systems, implementation strategies, and evaluation mechanisms all reside in the power levels and are defined in terms of the individuals who hold those roles. Participation in the process and its outcomes is not expected, yet employees are expected to do the organization's work. Their ownership is not generally supported in determining, defining, and evaluating the process, its content, or its outcomes.

This dichotomy between the beliefs of a democratic society and the practices of the workplace have produced many negative results for both workplace and workers. Because there is a fundamental human urge to be responsible, to be accountable for one's own affairs, and to participate fully in elements over which one can exert ownership, entry into the workplace confronts a set of circumstances that operate at odds with basic human needs. Historically in this country, where the democratic principles of responsibility and social participation are at odds with workplace practices that are authoritarian and nonparticipatory, significant social implications have emerged.

The introduction of conflict as an element of work appears to be consistent with the behavioral incongruities between society and the workplace. Individual workers begin to examine the workplace in the context of the greater freedoms represented in society at large. When they recognize the dissonance between the workplace and the expectations of their role in society, they begin to question the workplace's commitment to their individual needs and, conversely, their own need to commit to the workplace.

As workers begin to reflect on their lack of ownership, participation, and significance in work relationships, especially in those that represent authority and control over their ability to do work, they become less committed and less involved. Ultimately, over a long enough time, this process also affects productivity and output.

Quality of Work Life

Efforts to improve the quality of work life have been directed toward addressing worker satisfaction and participation. For the last several decades, evaluation of that satisfaction in relation to corporate culture, corporate goals, and organizational strategy has been the basis of numerous studies.[17] These have shown that sound relationships are essential for any basic measure of a group's success.

Workers tend to feel a sense of powerlessness. Decision making, responsibility, and authority for the establishment of policy and of the nature and content of work occurs primarily at the highest levels. Individual workers are divorced from this significant element of the enterprise and feel that their participation is limited to task completion. Even the mental processes needed to carry out the work do not offer significant meaning to workers. They are segregated from the major decisions that define the work process itself.

The significant concern thus is that workers essentially are separated from the very elements of work that are essential to its understanding and to the employees' commitment to the job. They are involved solely in the "things" of work and in the production of the element assigned to them. They have no sense of wholeness, no feeling of identity, no knowledge of the constraints and possibilities essential to establishing meaning in their work.

The Meaning of Work

No part of a job can have meaning for workers if it is separated from its more meaningful elements. As noted, if workers undertake only a specific portion of the job, their understanding of their role is limited to the tasks they are performing. In other words, if they do not understand the other elements of work that have an impact on their function, then they begin to look at the job solely in the context of that function. In that process, they become self-alienated and isolate themselves totally within their own function, with but limited understanding or interest in how the process affects the whole. The result of this kind of alienation is fragmentation and a breakdown in communication and the relationship essential to integrate the work in such a way that it assures meaning and value for the employees.

Meaninglessness in the workplace, obviously, has psychologically distressing outcomes for the employees. Such work is unpleasant, unfulfilling, purposeless, and terminal in nature. In nursing, examples of this kind of behavior abound. Much of what is involved in nursing relates to its functional elements: doing medications, doing treatments, doing charting, doing processes. Everything in nursing becomes procedurally oriented and functionally based. As a result, nurses become fragmented in their role to the extent that the doing of things becomes the total scope of their frame of reference. This soon becomes the whole context of the role itself.

Managers' major difficulty in this process is in overcoming the fragmentation of the role so that, instead, they can develop a holistic perspective. Managers must help the members of the professional staff who have been thus limited to begin to look at nursing's broader role. Staff members are slow to realize the full and real impact of all of the nursing activities and their outcomes in relation to patient care.

Since most nurses look at their work in terms of their own role, it is those functional components that create the most difficulty in righting the staff's perspective. The problem stems from the traditional hierarchy organization in which the medical staff writes the orders for care and nurses simply carry them out. Nurses look at their role as subservient to the predominant medical staff. Regardless of how hard the nursing division works to enhance the professionalism of practice, if the character of the organizational mandate is not altered, then the behavior it produces will not change.

Meaning in work cannot be provided unless work is made worthwhile and factors that create meaninglessness are removed. Unfortunately, in the case of nursing, the focus on functional components and all the elements that support it can only facilitate meaninglessness. On the other hand, organizing and structuring work so that its integrated processes are designed in the workplace (rather than by top management) can make it meaningful and begin to relate the process to its results. In making this connection, professional nurses can begin to view all of the functional elements of their work in the context of its purpose. It is in purpose that meaning can be found.

As nursing practice expands and technology's influence grows, the integrative relationships of nursing practice will have to be encouraged. Technology by its very nature tends to be mechanistic, objective, systematic. Many of the elements that go into the management and use of technology support those characteristics. However, workers must have relationship—a sense of connection to the work, the workplace, and their peers. These factors are not often consistent with the circumstances associated with the management of technology.

As a result of this dichotomy, managers of the future must be an integrating element. They must strike a balance between the needs of the objective management of information and technology and the subjective application of the human elements in the workplace. If this integrating process does not occur, then the environment in which work is performed will be affected radically. Without the manager as balancing agent, the workplace becomes unbalanced and the workers become isolated and segmented, with the resultant impact on their health and environmental stability.

Feelings of Isolation

Another major impact on workers is the result of the traditional management practices that have led to feelings of isolation. The management-dominated system alienates and isolates workers. Because the work becomes highly specialized and functional in nature, the employees' focus is specifically on the work they do. Further, because that work is prescribed through the institution's authority structure, the functional elements of the role become fixed. As noted, employees' whole world of expression becomes the work they do. Their isolation results from this separateness, caused by functionally defining work in the context of the elemental factors that must come together to accomplish the job.

In nursing this is demonstrated by the diffusion of functions as a result of the increasing use of new technology in patient care. Many institutions have IV nurses, renal nurses, nutritional support nurses, rehabilitation nurses, and many other classifications divided by their functional capacity. While this may be essential in responding to the technological changes, it also divides nursing into subcomponents. Those who practice in such subcomponents begin to see nursing only in that context. As a result, their perception of the world becomes differentiated from that of other nurses who have different functional frames of reference. It should come as no surprise that out of this emphasis on specialization comes an array of highly individualized biases regarding the practice of nursing based on which functional perspective is being advanced on any given issue.

This is not to suggest that there is no need for highly technical specialization. What is indicated is that there is a parallel need for integration and communication between and among the members of the nursing profession in the institution—and this concept has not received equal attention. This has created a disequilibrium both within nursing and with other professional groups with which nurses interrelate to serve patients.

Physicians constitute an excellent example of the ability to successfully provide specialty differentiation yet maintain professional integration. This specialization/integration clearly shows how professionals can focus on the diverse technical aspects of medical work yet maintain the need for a uniform image and position on issues affecting medical practice in general. In nursing, emphasis on specialization, without a strong effort to maintain professional solidarity, has contributed to a sense of isolation and the resultant conflicts, as described.

In the traditional management system, control of both function and relationship rests with the organization through those identified in its hierarchical power structure. They may be committed or not committed to the goals of the profession, but by virtue of their position they must be committed to the interests of the organization and represent its predominant values. Workers subject to the rules and controls of this traditional framework do not have the same opportunity to influence both the institution and their work in the profession.

The Nursing Administrator

This conflict is especially apparent in the role of the nursing administrator. While this individual often is perceived as the highest level operating nurse in the organization, in reality the person may be one of the highest level officers in the organization. While perceived as representing the best interests of the nursing profession at the executive level, this individual also is positioned to act more within the administrative context of the institution than in the nursing frame of reference she is supposed to represent. To peers on the nursing staff, she frequently appears as a part of the "them," not the "us," framework. In her role as administrator, she is charged with the responsibility of fulfilling the institution's mandates through the nursing staff, which in turn performs the functions essential to meet the needs of the institution and its major client, the physician. Most often, the professional, social, practice, and policy directives that determine the professional nursing role in the organization are subordinated to the rules and mandates of the institution as provided by those who control it.

In reality, the nursing administrator becomes administrator first and nurse second—a "Catch-22" position. She is responsible for interpreting the professional mandates of nursing to the organization, creating a climate that best represents the profession's practice characteristics. On the other hand, as an administrator, she has a dual role: (1) she is responsible to the chief executive officer and plays an important part in the institution's policy framework; (2) she is viewed by the facility's officers as their agent, interpreting to the nursing staff the institution's mandates, goals, and objectives. Because it is as the nursing administrator that she receives her power, she must maintain an institutional perspective. This is the perspective that is held by both administration and staff. The message of where she "really" stands when all is said and done becomes clear to all.

In the traditional organizational system, the practice of nursing becomes institutional, rather than professional, in focus. For most health care institutions, nursing's response to the demands of the facility emphasizes the functional. The professional issues that theoretically are essential to safe and competent nursing practice tend to take second place, if and when they do not interfere with the hospital's predominant functional values and mandates. It is no surprise, in this context, that feelings such as isolation, alienation, and burnout are common in nursing.

Satisfaction and Relationships

In nursing, professional and personal satisfaction are linked inextricably. Satisfaction in work is a major contribution to the individual's sense of values regarding that work. Organizations must be especially sensitive to allowing individuals to influence their circumstances and control their lives. Professional workers demonstrate fundamental values in their role, and nursing is no different from others. However, the problem is that the demands and expectations of the traditional workplace often are not in concert with the demands, expectations, and performance characteristics of the professional workers. The workplace must establish authority, accountability, a clearly delineated policy structure, and associated administrative mandates; however, that does not necessarily integrate well with the characteristics of professional practice.

Professionals need room for decision making; a strong lateral communication network; and the ability to make independent judgments, to consult and collaborate, and to alter decisions where necessary. They need a flexible organizational structure to support professional practice—a structure generally not present in the environment in which nurses practice. As a result, the team that functions as management's controlling agent often becomes the sole frame of reference for the facility's operation.

The professional work of nursing demands a different set of relationships not apparent in an organization with its focus on managerial authority and a controlling network to meet its goals. At this point, the first issues of basic dissatisfaction begin to emerge. Because nurses need to be involved in decisions that affect their practice—and they often are not—they become disassociated psychologically from the processes set up by the institution, turning instead to the functional elements over which they have specific control. They find their satisfaction in delivering the functional elements of nursing, since they are not involved in the decision-making processes that determine their work.

Functional roles are lower on the satisfaction scale than those associated with achievement, decision making, influence, communication, and defining performance expectations. Since nurses have but limited opportunity for satisfaction above the functional level, management only creates dissonance when it raises their expectations for defining self-responsibility but does not provide an environment structured to support it. This in turn results in even greater dissatisfaction.

Nurses hear their manager call for accountability and responsibility in delivering care yet have no realistic opportunity to determine what those characteristics are. Often, the manager will define what nurses will do in the hospital, and the decision frequently occurs in isolation from nurses. They must implement new managerial decisions without an opportunity to participate in any of the processes that went into arriving at the decision and determining its direction.

For example, many institutions across the nation have career ladders or levels programs developed for the staff by management, sometimes with little input from those affected. The same thing occurs in the development of primary nursing. Many institutions have attempted to establish primary nursing as the mode of operation, only to find various degrees of staff conflict and nonsupport. Some of this results from the mechanisms used to reach these decisions. Management individuals assume responsibility for determining what they believe is the most appropriate practice modality. They develop systematic approaches to implementing it, only to find that the commitment of the nurses essential to making it work is missing and seems difficult to generate because the staff lacks a sense of ownership. This approach is incongruent with the intent of the system. It is only logical to involve, from the outset, the practitioners accountable for the implementation of primary nursing processes. To be successful, such programs must derive from the staff's interest in participating fully.

Traditional management approaches to professional nurses that omit active participation in the process can expect minimal success. Much of nurses' interest in collective bargaining has resulted from such management tactics. Collective bargaining almost always results from management's failure to do its job effectively. Nursing management has a special need to push participative strategies, which represent all of the characteristics essential to professional practice. What nurse managers' most often lack are the abilities to undertake the processes that facilitate participation.

Gordon Jackson, a labor relations attorney representing many institutions in the labor relations arena, suggests that the best way to deal with unions is to stay union free. He has indicated that once the union is on board a whole new set of relationships develop that demand responses which will hinder a positive and open environment.[18]

Since union activity is confrontational and competitive, it does nothing to bring all participants in the organization together on an equal and balanced footing. Each side has its own agenda, and the name of the game is to assure that one's own agenda is met—regardless of what might be best for all parties concerned. Investment by either side is in their own concerns. It is rare that their interests and concerns are the same, or reflect the same values. It is an "us–them" environment.

In order to protect each other's issues, each side has its protective and monitoring clauses in the contract. The union must have stewards, there must be an arbitration process, contract provisions for problem solving, and a system for negotiation and problem resolution. Such design and content sound more like the processes for dealing with human conflict than for creating an open and committed workplace. Indeed, many of the characteristics for labor relations management model the rules of war.

Creating a highly participative and involved organization, where staff is committed to and plays a major role in the work and the decision processes, is the best defense against a union. It is the intent of this book to outline just such strategies. If properly applied, no organization using these processes need be concerned about union organizing and/or union behaviors.

Responsibilities in the New Era

This book is designed to help nurse managers meet some of their needs in acquiring skills and insights required to develop the participative management process. While professional nurses have a responsibility to carry out their practice and to participate with their peers, managers as integrators of resources and as facilitators of outcomes must have the skills to bring together all of the processes essential to implementing nursing practice. The strategies defined here as necessary for management approaches may be in conflict with the institution's philosophy (such as the need to control, management rights versus employee obligation to obey, policy and rule orientation, etc.), so nurse managers must take responsibility for the ethical and professional considerations they bring to the management process. There is room for ethical decision making as to the most appropriate and meaningful approach to managing human resources, especially the professional nursing resource.

Nurse managers have a special obligation to carefully review their approach. As indicated, technology and all it implies has grown dramatically in the last two decades. The ability to understand it and interpret its impact on the workplace is fundamental to its successful application. Managers thus must be cognizant of the human relations needs of professional nurses in the work environment. The nursing managers' role is different from almost any other kind of manager in industry or health care. They manage large numbers of professional workers who have a unique set of skills, needs, and interactions of which managers always must be aware. Traditional behaviors and rules governing superior-subordinate relations do not always apply where professional workers are the managed.

The Female Factor

Managers also must realize that the staff in the nursing workplace is predominantly female. In a female organizational system, the kinds of relationships and interactions can be different from those where the workers are predominantly male. The socialization process involved in the growth and development of female workers is significantly different from that with males. Females' historical experiences and relationships are different and require a different set of behavioral responses from managers. The interfemale relationships have a tremendous impact on the role of the manager in integrating nursing professionals in order to achieve a relatively uniform outcome. Women nurse managers also must adjust behaviors in their management style in a role that has been developed in the context of male managerial definitions.

In recent years, much has occurred to change the role of women in the workplace and to reduce discrimination. This discrimination is no less important for the manager. Most women managers must look at their role in the context of the relationships established, not only with other women who are nurses but also with other department heads and specifically with the men who tend to hold key positions in the organization.

Society defines what it deems to be desirable female behaviors. Women who demonstrate such behaviors in their roles with men are perceived in a specified way.

The behaviors said to be desirable for women, such as femininity, deference, gentleness, and nurturance, are not always the characteristics essential to strong management. When women are placed in positions of authority, they may find substantial differences between their learned social/cultural roles and the roles demanded and expected of them as leaders and managers. Women who present the behaviors associated with managerial expectations and attitudes may be labeled as cold, hard, calculating, and unfeeling when evaluated by other managers. Comparable desirable behaviors in male managers may be firmness, determination, strength, courage, and forthrightness. The difficulty caused by such distinctions is obvious.

However, women need not give up traditionally defined female behaviors in order to become effective managers. Nurturance, gentleness, sensitivity, and caring are important components of human resource management. The fact that they are associated primarily with women is not necessarily a disadvantage for managers. Women who have these characteristics as managers should develop them and refine them. To the extent that they are refined, the managers' roles may be improved significantly, especially in management participation.

Indeed, the behaviors commonly identified with women may be precisely the ones essential to humanizing the workplace and obtaining results in commitment and job ownership. All are requirements of the participative environment. This means, however, that some of the traditional "game-playing" behaviors commonly associated with women (especially women managers) will have to be adapted to newer, more appropriate conduct in the workplace. Today's women leaders and managers must be concerned with the need to be direct, straightforward, honest, and problem solving in their roles. Women have grown into a subcultural norm where learned social behaviors with each other have not necessarily been beneficial in the workplace. They have learned that ladylike behavior is different from managerial behavior.

Women managers of the future must change their operating styles to newer, more direct forms. These include assertive skills, the ability to negotiate, being straightforward, and confronting situations. The corporate and management culture requires a sense of self; an ability to utilize personal authority; knowledge; and the ability to interact, negotiate, confront, and manage conflict. Managers must possess all of these characteristics if they are to be effective. This role will be significantly different for the manager who is both nurse and woman.[19]

THE MANAGER-PRACTITIONER RELATIONSHIP

The relationship between managers and practicing nurses has evolved through a long exposure to the bureaucratic environment. Hospitals have always been primary employers of nurses and have always viewed nurses solely as employees. Much of the development of nursing practice thus results from the employer's view of nurses in the framework of the management structure.

Obviously, managers and practitioners are closely interdependent. The hospital depends on practitioners to meet its needs and those of the patients it serves. Practitioners demonstrate to the hospital that nursing is essential to achieve the facility's goals in patient care.

Nurse managers, on the other hand, represent the institution's goals, objectives, policy, and authority. As nurses become managers, they apply the institution's values, needs, and structure on behalf of the facility toward the nursing staff. This has tended to separate nurse managers functionally from the nurses. The nurses see their managers as agents of the institution and therefore do not relate to them as an integral part of their clinical practice. Nurse managers are further distanced from staff because the processes of maintaining nursing discipline fall within their purview. Staff members may position themselves on one side of an issue and the nurse manager on the other.

In tomorrow's environment, an entirely new set of relationships must exist between managers and practitioners. Since practice is the focal role of nursing, it should be emphasized at all levels of the organization. While newer kinds of structures can be designed to support this status, the relationships at the unit level are the essential components that either validate or invalidate the central value of practice.

Nurse managers must involve staff members in terms of their interest and expertise in assessing and deciding issues that relate to their practice and in developing mechanisms to identify and resolve strategies for work-related issues. Managers of the future therefore need a whole new set of behaviors significantly different from their traditional ones.

In the participatory approach, nurse managers may need to focus on their role as facilitators and emphasize the integrating nature of that role. To work successfully with professional peers, nurse managers must assure that nurses play a central role in the responsibilities traditionally assigned to managers. In such circumstances, managers must act as coordinators and facilitators in decision making. This will involve more than their own skills and abilities in problem identification and resolution.

TRANSFORMATION TO PARTICIPATION

All institutions are designed to provide a mechanism for meeting their corporate purpose. In health care, most institutions are service oriented, so their purposes arc to implement such services. Nursing is a service profession. In meeting its purpose, nursing's actions must be consistent with the overall goals and objectives of the institution and its desire to provide specified professional health care services. The differences between the profession and the institution are the mechanisms, perspectives, and processes intended to achieve that end.

From its perspective in relation to its resources and constraints, the institution may see the provision of services within a narrow set of parameters. The nurses may see the same factors with an entirely different set of parameters and responses. What is needed, then, is a mechanism for correlating the needs of the institution and those of nursing so that the purposes of both may be fulfilled. In providing patient care, the goals of both must be addressed in order to meet the projected outcomes. It is at that point that the traditional conflicts have become fixed and, to date, remain unresolved.

The institution sees as one of its predominant roles the defining of the policy and processes essential for meeting its service needs. Indeed, it has held the prerogative for doing so independent of and often above the service professionals. While nursing is changing, most institutions still maintain that stance. They insist it is administration's responsibility to establish policy and to undertake activities that support the mandates of the board of trustees' overall goals and direction. This includes implementation of programming, structuring of relationships, organizational strategies, and the management of work.

Those responsible for offering the services—the professional workers, including nurses—then implement in their practice the goals, objectives, strategies, and processes approved by administration. This often serves to entrench the already strong dissonance between the character of nursing practice and administration's mechanism for providing services. This conflict can have a strong impact on the practitioners' roles and can even influence the very nature of nursing practice.

Nursing traditionally has experienced such conflicts more than most other services. Nursing has a history of independent development as a profession (educational) yet has maintained a dependent role in practice (service).

Since the turn of the century leaders in the profession have attempted to establish parameters for education, competency role, ethics, and responsibility to the consumers that use nursing services. This has often been complicated and hampered by two considerations: society's prevailing view of the role and position of women in work, organizations, and the home; and the fact that non-nursing leaders in health care (physicians and administrators) sought and have maintained control of the use of nursing services. Nursing is primarily institution-based. Therefore all practice mandates that may come out of the profession often are subordinated to those in administration. In that way, the organization's administrative structure actually determines the character of professional nursing practice. This obviously leads to continual conflict.

Those responsible for professional practice soon come to understand that their activities are subject to review and approval by administration. This can both discourage the practitioners and lead to a working relationship that does not achieve the best results. This has produced a long-standing conflict between nursing and many health care agencies around the world. The traditional expectation of direction from management and obedience and compliance from nurses has created its own obvious set of difficulties in the health care workplace.

Professional and Institutional Goals

Professional roles and activities in institutions have grown more complex, more involved, and thus more vital to the facilities' achievement of their overall goals. Nurses' contributions to the success of those objectives are becoming more and more important. As the profession has become more technically complex and more involved in every element of patient care, nurses have developed a strong expectation of playing key roles in decisions that affect their practice. As a result, they look for opportunities to participate more fully in processes that will influence their practice and enhance their contributions.

Changes in the role of women and in their expectations have an impact on the ability of the organization to fulfill its objectives. Stronger emphasis on the relation between practicing nurses and administration has become essential in the current health care marketplace. A closer collaborative, participatory relationship between institution and nurses is essential for achieving optimum levels of productivity and satisfaction, as well as fulfillment of the objectives of the institution and its services.

Nurse managers of the future will have to provide a different framework to ensure that ethical, meaningful, and valuable participative strategies involve all practitioners. These managers must be able to share with professional colleagues more control and responsibility over the work itself, including defining its work parameters. Along with control goes responsibility; along with responsibility comes accountability arising out of the professional workers' commitment to their role.

This means that professional nurses also must be managers of their own work. The managers must assist by establishing and maintaining a framework that permits collaborative activities with the nurses. This will affect performance and care outcomes as well as the degree of nurse satisfaction at all levels of participation. This new kind of manager must be able to offer professional nurses the alternatives, strategies, and processes that will enhance decision making in the institution. Directives from above will have less significance as the role of professional nurse expands its influence in the organization's processes.

When the institution undertakes policy formulation, managers must insist on involving all those who will be affected. Managers must have the ability to solicit, negotiate, support, and modify the nurses' ideas for changes and for new policies. Through the use of participatory strategies, managers can provide nurses with opportunities for increased control over their own practice, thus satisfying nurses' basic needs, not only of work, but of life; developing the ability to influence their own circumstances. The ability to move the profession to higher levels of autonomy and accountability in an institutional context, so that the control of work generates out of the exercise of work, will be required of managers of the future.

Human Needs

Nurse managers must be aware of the basic needs of everyone in the workplace. They also must understand human needs and relational characteristics and undertake strategies to meet them in a different framework. Participatory management in this context also requires understanding the needs evidenced in work groups and other relationships. The managers must help nurses set goals and provide feedback as to their achievement. Effective feedback is essential because the critical nature of work depends upon communication and completion of the feedback loop. This assures that all aspects of work are addressed.

Nurse managers of tomorrow must be able to encourage nurses' participation in problem identification and resolution. These include problems related to interpersonal conflicts, concerns between professional practice and the rules of the institution, and constrained resources. The ability to work in a way that emphasizes relationships and the interaction of individuals is essential to the success of both managers and nurses.

The implications of increasing external influences on hospitals will demand a closer relationship, stronger communication, and a sense of full ownership and participation in the processes that govern the work of nursing. The ability of nurse managers to extract ideas and creative processes from the work environment, and to develop programs to implement them, will be essential. An understanding of the psychology of work groups, group dynamics, interactional elements, socialization, and corporate acculturation also is important.

These skills clearly are different from those traditionally expected of nurse managers. The bottom line is that in an environment that demands interactional and participative roles, nurse managers of today are unprepared. Practicing nurses also are not prepared to operate successfully in such a health care environment. The skills that nurse managers must develop are those that build and enhance the relational elements of the workplace. In the high-technology environment of health care, managers will need a high level of skill and preparation to utilize strategies and processes that emphasize the holistic aspects of patient care and the delivery of nursing services.

It should be clear by now that participative management strategies no longer are optional in the management of health care delivery in this country. Managers' ability to utilize all of their resources in this role in health care entities will be essential to their success as well as to that of the facility. An understanding that there are different kinds of emphases that must be developed consistent with the role of the nurse manager is the beginning place for change. Also essential is awareness of the human relations elements involved, and the ability to mobilize such resources.

One of the greatest failures in the delivery of health care services has been the lack of emphasis on the human relations factor in the management process. In so many ways, many places across the country still lack a full understanding of the working relationships and requirements of managing the human resource. The ability to implement high levels of technology in this century frequently will depend on an ability to utilize those human resources appropriately.

Nurse managers are at the cutting edge in these complex processes.[15] These systems will demand close working relationships among all members of the medical care team in meeting patient care needs.

A major consideration affecting all health care services is the impact of technology on the patients the nurses serve. The patients will feel ever more isolated as more and more technology is used to facilitate the healing process. This sense of isolation or "objectification" can alienate patients from their resources and from themselves. Both the relational and self-generating elements are essential to facilitating the healing process. Patients need and demand that the subjective and objective care elements necessary to facilitate their own personal growth and transition as they move from illness to wellness or accommodation be connected. The ability of nurse managers to create an environment and an atmosphere where everyone involved in meeting patients' needs can share in the responsibilities for care often will be the major influence for success or failure.

As organizations become increasingly decentralized and as women professionals become more and more accountable for their own practices and the decisions that affect that practice, the institution will need a facilitating and interactive leadership structure if it is to meet its needs. Nurse managers must be key leaders of this environment, pulling all of the elements together into a meaningful whole. It will be their responsibility to provide the resources, support, and material supplies necessary to assure that nursing is practiced in as efficient and effective a manner as possible.

To facilitate the professional relationships and to encourage the development of accountability, nurse managers must be able to develop the skills and strategies essential to assuring interaction, collaboration, sharing of knowledge, and providing of appropriate and meaningful judgments that will have a positive impact on the delivery of patient care services. Managers must realize that much of what unfolds over the next two decades will depend on the ability of nursing professionals, both managers and practitioners, to interact successfully with the complexity of services and to relate on an equal footing with all participants who make decisions related to health care delivery.

Interdisciplinary Relationships

Professional interaction will be highly interdisciplinary. If nurses are to communicate effectively with other disciplines, they, too, must be well educated and well prepared. Communication, problem solving, negotiation, and the ability to collaborate at a high level of interaction will be essential to the practitioners' role. The managers will be responsible for assuring that the organizational structure supports this interaction. Professional relationships among practitioners will be dependent on the environment. Providing the right environment, undertaking the appropriate strategies, interpreting the signs and symptoms of variances in the workplace, and understanding the complexities of interaction will be key functions of nurse managers.

Is participation optional? Is it an ethical imperative? Whether it is one or the other, it is clear that participative strategies will be essential in the structuring of work relationships for the future. The most successful nurse managers will have mastered the skills and techniques essential to facilitate interaction and participation. Those who can provide leadership and guidance, rather than just control and direction, will be the ones most able to meet successfully both the needs of the organization and the people who serve it. Management skills directed toward that end no longer are optional. Participatory strategies, regardless of the extent to which they are implemented, are, at a minimum, a baseline for managerial behavior of the future.

The ability to mobilize the resources of the institution—human, fiscal, and material—and to integrate all of the elements that facilitate that process, will be a central factor in nurse managers' success. So, too, will be the ability to generate human relationships essential to assuring a high quality of practice in achieving the institution's goals. New insights and different skills will be essential. This and succeeding chapters provide a baseline for addressing these issues further.

NOTES

1. Frederick W. Taylor, *The Principles of Scientific Management* (New York: Harper & Brothers, 1911).

2. Elton Mayo, *The Human Problems of an Industrial Civilization* (New York: The Macmillan Company, 1933).

3. Frederick Herzburg, *Work and the Nature of Man* (New York: New York World Publishing Co., 1966).

4. Abraham H. Maslow, *Toward A Psychology of Being* (Princeton, N.J.: D. Van Nostrand Co., Inc., 1962).

5. Chris Argyris, "Leadership, Learning and Changing the Status Quo," *Organizational Dynamics,* (Winter, 1976): 29–43.

6. Warren G. Bennis, Beyond Bureaucracy: Essays on the Development of Human Organizations (New York: McGraw-Hill Book Co., 1973).

7. John Naisbitt, *Megatrends: Ten New Directions Transforming Our Lives* (New York: Warner Books, Inc., 1982).

8. Marshall Shashkin, "Participative Management: An Ethical Imperative," *Organizational Dynamics* (Spring 1984): 4–22.

9. Kurt Lewin, "Group Decision and Social Change," in *Readings in Social Psychology,* 3rd ed. E.E. MacAbee, T.M. Newcomb, and E.L. Hartley (New York: Holt, Rinehart & Winston, Inc., 1958), 197–211.

10. Paul Hersey and Kenneth Blanchard, *Management of Organizational Behavior Utilizing Human Resources* (Englewood Cliffs, N.J.: Prentiss-Hall, Inc., 1982).

11. Kenneth Blanchard and Spencer Johnson, *The One Minute Manager* (New York: Berkeley Books, 1983), 11–23.

12. Robert Blake, Jane Mouton, and Mildren Tapper, *Grid Approaches for Managerial Leadership in Nursing* (St. Louis: The C.V. Mosby Company, 1981), 18–113.

13. Daniel Katz and Robert Kahn, *The Social Psychology of Organizations* (New York: John Wiley & Sons, Inc., 1978).

14. Rensis Likert, *The Human Organization* (New York: McGraw-Hill Book Company, 1967).

15. Susan Jackson, "Participation in Decision Making With a Strategy For Reducing Job-Related Strain," *Journal of Applied Psychology* (January/February 1983): 2.

16. Richard Hackman and Greg Oldham, *Work Redesign* (New York: Addison-Wesley Book Co., 1980).

17. Daniel R. Denison, "Bringing Corporate Culture to the Bottom Line," *Organizational Dynamics* (Autumn, 1984), 5–22.

18. Gordon E. Jackson, *How to Stay Union Free* (Memphis, TN: Management Press Inc., 1983).

19. Kathleen McCullick and Rosalee Fernandez, "Reaching for the Stars," *Nursing Management* 14, no. 1 (January 1983): 24–26.

The Needs of the Managed

Chapter 2

The Needs of the Managed

Objectives for Chapter Two

Explore the inadequacies of the current organizational systems in preparing for the future.

Review the power equation operating both historically and currently having an impact on nursing practice and management.

Describe the professional character and needs of nursing in an organizational context.

Outline the organizational characteristics necessary for participative strategies in both management and practice.

Discuss the relationships essential in the professional environment in order to share decision making and accomplish the work of nursing.

List the organizational supports necessary to obtain individual commitment to the purposes of nursing practice and the objectives of the institution.

2

We are people first, workers second. That sounds like the last thing individuals would ever forget. So, it is not unreasonable to believe that basic human needs must always be addressed as a part of meeting employee needs in any work environment, specifically including nursing. Work usually is accomplished through the utilization of human resources and much of its impact, whether successful or unsuccessful, involves the ability to manage the human resource effectively.

Since the Industrial Revolution of the 19th century, work has been increasingly analyzed in fragments. As it has become more specialized, especially among professions, it has been refined further into many subspecializations. This of course is especially true in nursing practice. Unfortunately, as work has become more specialized, it has become even more segmented into smaller and smaller types of activity. The result is that each of the activities essentially has been isolated from its other parts and from the whole.

Participative management seeks to reverse the effects of these highly specialized aspects. Specialization has resulted in three common characteristics, especially in health care: powerlessness, meaninglessness, and isolation. Each has an impact on workers' effectiveness and health.[1] Each also needs further analysis, especially in regard to its impact on nursing.

POWERLESSNESS

The Industrial Revolution contributed to the creation of a new class of relatively powerless workers—and of a class of powerful managerial or administrative individuals. It was not until the middle of the 20th century that behaviorists began to explore the relationships between these two classes, their organization, and their environment.

While nursing paralleled much of the era of powerlessness, it had unique characteristics that developed out of its own history and relationship with the health care industry. Much has been written on the development of nursing and nurses and the role of women since the mid-1920s.[2] However, little has been researched on the social and personal impact of women's roles as nurses. It is in that context that the powerlessness of individual nursing workers becomes clear.

During the formative years of the health care delivery system, the role of women (specifically nurses) was underrated and generally not even addressed. Most often, they fulfilled the functions and mandates decreed by physicians or administrative superiors in the rudimentary levels of patient care. This was not inconsistent with the perceived role of women during the Victorian era. Women were not looked at then as full participants in decision making and in responsible roles. Rather, they were regarded as subservient individuals subject to the predominant men in society and, thus, in health care. Most of them were perceived as nurturing.

As a result, they were not able to move into roles that would establish them as professionally accountable, responsible, independent, and decisive. Because of their positioning in society, they were not equipped to function at the levels of responsibility associated with decision making and judgment in collaboration with peers. Simply put, women's roles in hospitals became clearly sex defined.

Women nurses were less independent and less opportunistic, intellectually lacked initiative, suppressed their drives, and had limited direction and support for independent activities. Their social status (less skilled and less exposed to education) tended to make them less creative and less developed intellectually than men. As would be expected, they generally were subject to male guidance, direction, and support. In relation to the medical profession, the development of nursing reflected women's social positioning at the time.

The Impact of Education

As schools of nursing emerged in association with hospitals at the turn of the century, their functional arrangement further evidenced the predominant social relationship between men and women. Physicians, then as now, were the chief decision makers and determined nurses' care of "their" patients. Physicians and hospital administrators, primarily male, by virtue of their positions in the health care delivery system had the right and power to determine the direction, policy, process, and function of nursing. The role of the women nurses was to carry out the directions of the physician and administration. What relatively little education was provided to support nurses in hospitals focused on the role of assisting the physicians and thus the institution in delivering medical care. Patients' responsibility was primarily the physicians' and the control of all care rested in the physicians' hands.

Physicians and administrators at the time expended a great deal of time in determining the appropriate curriculum for nursing. Physicians assumed responsibility for assuring what was the most appropriate health care delivery to meet the public good. They looked at nursing as a part of their responsibility in fulfilling the obligations of patient care. Education of nurses became a key element in helping to control them in the exercise of their responsibility. There were strong arguments against having women too highly educated for delivering nursing services; there was some fear that if they were, they would attempt to operate beyond the established level of dependence, thus altering the degree of control over them by physicians and the administrator. It was emphasized that the major role of nursing education was to provide only enough information so nurses could assist physicians in doing their work.

Nursing education obviously changed over the course of the century. Nursing schools became more and more independent in terms of their curricula and program content. What did not occur, however, was an increase in the freedom necessary to practice nursing consistent with the emerging information and knowledge base. Even as nursing began to move into the academic mainstream, the function and relationships of women in the service sector was not altered substantially. Even as the industry grew and changed, the limited social perception of the role of women in the workplace was the primary determinant in how they were utilized.

Hospitals developed rigid, structured, organizational designs to control their operation and to guide nursing practice. These relationships were described clearly: the physician was at the top of the clinical hierarchy and the administrator at the top of the institutional hierarchy. Nurses' positions as managers, historically were, as noted, to interpret and support the physicians and the administrator in decision making affecting clinical practice. For most of this century, nurses' primary role has been relatively unchanged.

The rigid nature of the hierarchy clearly mandated the powerlessness of nurses. Since authority rested solely at the top of the organization, nurses had only limited decisional roles. The hierarchy of command established its relationship to the medical staff: physicians wrote orders, nurses carried them out. If physicians' orders were not appropriate, nurses could question them and call them to the doctors' attention, but the final decision always rested with the physicians.

Even in the more enlightened age of the 1980s the same basic structure and relationship of nurses and physicians shall persist: physicians predominate, they still write the orders, and nurses still implement them. Clinical care decisions still are made by the medical staff in most institutions. Nurses fulfill their tasks within that context. While this relationship now is less rigid, physician supremacy still is strong and clear.

Bias Based on Sex

While the system may not necessarily intend any longer to allocate role and responsibility by sex, the differentiation still reflects sex-based bias: Most nurses are female, most physicians are male. Much of society is changing, as are many health carework places, but the fundamental structure still perpetuates the discriminatory and hierarchical relationship. Its impact on feelings of powerlessness in nurses is significant.[3]

Since powerlessness is one of the greatest complaints of woman, especially nurses, it is a core consideration in analyzing the relationships for accomplishing the work of nursing in the institution. Overcoming powerlessness is essential to expanding the practice base and the relationships of nursing. Nurses' ability to feel a sense of control and influence over their lives and practice is an important consideration as they develop as full members of the health care team. This factor will be central to the growth of the nursing profession over the next two decades.

Nurses today are anxious to become equal participants in the delivery of health care services. As nursing education and academic preparation improve, significant changes in the sense of control, power, authority, and autonomy will be important considerations.

Feelings of powerlessness work to stimulate nurses' demands for an altered work structure. The relationships they seek require that their responsibilities and tasks be advanced to parallel those of other primary providers. Nurses seek a more open, responsive communication with physicians. They want the nursing impact on patient care to be viewed in the same significant context as is the medical impact. While it is essential that nurses be viewed as parallel with physicians, they want that parallel to be clearer so that the impact of their practice is recognized as a part of physicians' behavioral frame of reference. Through their new sense of self and their ability to interact and communicate freely with other members of the health care team, nurses begin to confront the issue of powerlessness in their relation to the delivery of their own service and of patient care provided by other disciplines.

MEANINGLESSNESS

One of the most profound human emotions is the need for a sense of purpose and meaning in work and in life. Meaninglessness in work is one of the most frustrating of human circumstances. People need meaningful work; if they do not get it, they develop feelings of meaninglessness and their work may fail to serve their needs or purposes. It is this sense of purpose that is vital in the workplace.

Nurses come to the workplace with a high sense of purpose. They hope and desire to participate in a concrete way in the delivery of patient care services. They believe their work can make a difference and that that difference can be important. Nurses also believe that through their special skills and abilities they bring a systematic approach and knowledge base that can improve patient care. Nurses' other important considerations include the ability to facilitate patient outcomes, to see the healing process at work, to be a part of that process, and to assist others in achieving their highest level of wellness.

In the current health care environment, much of nursing is focused on specified tasks that often are divided into subfunctions. Nurses concentrate on the subfunction to the extent that it may be the sum total of the work performed. The ability to connect function and task with outcome often is diminished to the point that work is reduced to smaller and smaller functions and more and more specialized tasks. Their connection to the work as a whole becomes less and less clear. Patients, instead of being whole persons involved in the process of achieving wellness or accommodation, are relegated to being a particular treatment, a particular process, a therapeutic undertaking, a functional element for nurses. The patients become an amalgam of fragments never fully involved in the healing process.

While newer holistic strategies such as primary nursing have been introduced to offset this kind of behavior, in many ways the functional elements of the hospital force the division of patients into a series of disconnected, specialized, organic functions. This diminishing of the wholeness and the humanistic aspect of the healing process creates significant problems not only for the patients, but also for the nurses who deliver services. Patients come to be seen not as human beings, but as a series of functional processes that collectively move to a cold, objective continuum of health or illness rather than to a personal valuing of the individual who is sick or is whole.

Meaninglessness also is evident in a sense of unfulfilled purpose. As do all people, nurses seek to have their purposes fulfilled. The ability to control circumstances and variables that influence their work is central to that sense of purpose. When practitioners feel that ultimate control of their work rests in the hands of someone else, this feeling of second-hand purpose further reduces their commitment to the ideals of their work. Work then becomes a series of processes and functional elements over which nurses have no ultimate control. The functions and the tasks themselves define the total scope of work and become the whole picture of the nurses' sense of work and self, so that purpose becomes function.

In the context of function, outcomes, change, the difference work makes, and its impact on recipients become factors that are influenced and controlled by others who have the power to change such variables. Nurses often feel as though they have no influence over those variables, so doing medications, giving treatments, starting IVs, putting down NG tubes, inserting Swan Ganz become not only the function but the purpose of the work as well. The impact of function-based purpose, meaning, and value becomes more manageable, but less significant, to nurses. They become locked in the safety of their role and insulate themselves from its impotence. They then become reactive rather than active, and all possibility for change and growth diminishes and eventually dies.

If the perception of the meaning and value of work resides solely within the functions that are performed, rather than in their purposes, the workers become externalized to those functions. In other words, they become the function themselves and see their role solely in the context of those functions.

Control and influence over the delivery of service become the territory of those with the power to deal with them. This can include attempting to enhance the role by developing accountability, improving judgment, having an impact on policy, exerting social influence, participating in role determination, and establishing relationships with other disciplines. These are legitimate issues in the territory of practicing nurses. Their only power and authority, however, is over the immediate, short-term functions for which they are responsible.

Practicing nurses' meaning and value begin and terminate with what they do in the time frame allotted to do it. It should come as no surprise that many front-line nurses are disinterested or unconcerned with the broader national and regional social and political as well as professional issues that have an impact on successful practice. They merely live with the perception of their powerlessness. For the professional, this clearly is meaninglessness at its height—or depth.

ISOLATION

The current structure of the workplace often is based on industrial models. Segmentation of work is an industrial concept. Applied to health care institutions, this produces divisions of work: a disease, a procedure, or a major human system. This classification is especially evident in hospitals, where such services as ophthalmology, orthopedics, and oncology all are described in terms of their clinical parameters and of the responsibility of delivering such care. While some of this may be essential, it does define a relationship in the work environment that by its very presence is isolating.

Nursing practice also has been based on these clinical delineations. The predominant ones obviously are developed for the primary participants—the physicians. On that basis, services in hospitals and other facilities are designed for the convenience and schedule of doctors. The isolation that this creates, however, results in limiting the exposure of one group of practitioners to others on issues of mutual concern to all. A mechanism must be established in the organization that integrates all nurses so that there is a common sense of the work they do and its purposes. Frequently, especially in hospitals, that isolation is never overcome.

An ophthalmological nurse remains an ophthalmological nurse and deals only with other ophthalmological nurses. The same can be said for the neurological nurses, cardiovascular nurses, oncology nurses, etc. They conduct their nursing practice strictly within the confines of their clinical delivery system. Issues of mutual concern to nursing as a whole often are relegated either to management or other support persons not directly connected with the delivery of clinical services. The nurses' concept, perspective, and value system is developed solely in the context of the unit of activity within which they function. Their isolation decreases their ability to have an impact on the total professional practice of nursing in the institution.

Thus it is up to nurse managers to be responsible for concerns about the practice of nursing in the institution. Unfortunately, clinical integration and its impact on practice receives little attention when it is solely the responsibility of nurse managers to undertake the interactional communication and relationships for influencing the nursing service. This clinical isolation of nurses from peers other than those in their own service adds to the alienation and disintegration of professional relationships in practice. (Figure 2–1.)

It is these major workplace characteristics that nurse managers must confront. They must understand the impact of these characteristics and their concomitant needs on both practitioners and managers, and how best to respond to those needs.

These first three sections have described the situation in which practitioners most often find themselves in health care institutions. The managers' responsibility is to look at the environment and the system, understand it, modify it, and adjust their behaviors to facilitate the best possible outcomes. Managers can best begin by understanding the basic needs of professional nurses in the workplace, then developing strategies and mechanisms to respond to those needs, and finally mobilizing the practitioners to meet not only their needs but also the goals and objectives of the institution.

THE NEEDS OF THE PROFESSIONAL NURSE

Professional workers obviously require something different in their environment from what vocational workers seek. Much of vocational work is focused and

Figure 2–1 Social Failure Equation

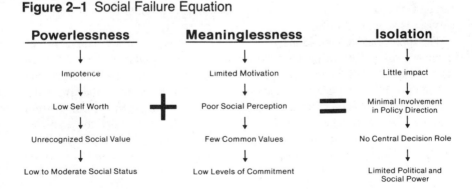

task based, requiring a highly centralized organizational structure that reduces or eliminates the opportunity for misjudgments and errors in the process. While there are varying degrees of control and superior-subordinate relationship, much of the responsibility for task-based activities in a vocational work environment must rest with those who establish the sets of tasks for meeting specified outcomes. In a telephone assembly line, for example, it would be inappropriate if each of the component parts of the telephone did not integrate with the other parts. Therefore, a well-defined mechanism for putting telephones together is essential. The individuals responsible for each specific component must focus on the roles and obligations involving that unit.

Professionals, however, must operate in an entirely different frame of reference. Professionals have characteristics that are unique to the activities and the services they offer. Blane identifies six characteristics common to professional workers:[4]

1. a defined body of knowledge with specific skills that are acquired through an educational process
2. an orientation that is service based rather than productivity or financially based
3. discipline, peer review, and a supporting code of ethics
4. autonomy in practice with appropriate legislative and legal sanctions for workers who practice the profession
5. an organized system composed of professionals recognized by society to carry out the mandates, roles, and responsibilities of the profession
6. a culture that supports the professional activity.

Obviously these indicate that nurses are involved in a different kind of work relationship from other kinds of workers (see Figure 2–2). For example, they have a set of expectations unique to the characteristics of their professional role. They utilize a number of variables and needs different from those in other work-based structures. There must be mechanisms, supported by the system, that assure that the professional character of practice is met and its product (nursing care and service) is supported fully.

The appropriate organizational design that can support professional practice of nursing is discussed in Chapter 4. Meanwhile, effort should be directed toward nurses' basic needs in the workplace if they are to fulfill their professional obligations. It is important to look at these basic needs from the perspective of the practitioners. Provision of professional nursing is the obligation of the institution offering care. That means that the facility must clearly identify the activities essential to support that work. In addition, elements that professionals require to practice nursing, such as autonomy and an ''open'' structure, should be clarified and developed. Everyone in the workplace should know nurses' basic needs, and

Figure 2–2 Workplace Behavior Patterns: Vocational vs. Professional

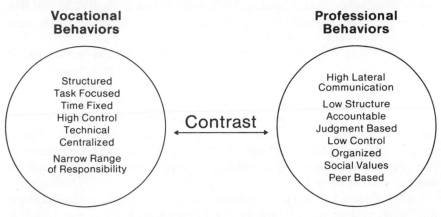

Vocational Behaviors		Professional Behaviors
Structured		High Lateral Communication
Task Focused		
Time Fixed		Low Structure
High Control	Contrast	Accountable
Technical		Judgment Based
Centralized		Low Control
		Organized
Narrow Range of Responsibility		Social Values
		Peer Based

management processes should be adjusted specifically to meet them. A participatory style along with a shared, self, or open organizational system are beginning places for providing this support.

Everyone has basic needs that must be addressed in the work environment. Individual needs identified by workers somehow can assure their integrity in carrying out their jobs. Managers must be aware of some of these basic needs. They fall into five broad categories:

1. respect
2. trust
3. appropriate information
4. human and material support to accomplish the work
5. meaningful rewards, both economic and personal, sufficient to maintain acceptable levels of personal and economic security.

Respect

All individuals require some degree of respect. They recognize that under society's value system they are asked to be responsible and mature—accepting responsibility for their own behavior and sharing in the social responsibility to maintain stability, keep the peace, and maintain the vitality of society. Certain relationships must be in place to facilitate this.

Mature individuals as identified by Argyris are those who accept the primary responsibility for their actions and are involved in things of primary interest to them.[5] They understand the nature of their interdependence with others. The ability to communicate and interact successfully is a key characteristic of maturity.

Such individuals are capable of behaving in many ways, depending on the situation. All behavior can be modified by the situation, and can be expressed in an appropriate and meaningful manner, without resorting to characteristics normally recognized as immature and childish.

The ability to discuss, to venture points of view, and to be involved in mechanisms for self-expression all are characteristics of mature individuals. Their ability to look at themselves and others over the long term, to develop perspective on both past and future processes and their relationship to the individuals' activities also are characteristics of growth and maturity. Mature individuals can control their own behavior, to understand behavior's nature impact, and recognize its constraints and obligations. Mature individuals exercise appropriate behaviors in given circumstances to achieve balance between the demands of the situation and the needs of the self.

Mature individuals expect to be respected for their contributions and participation in the workplace, regardless of how extensive such involvement may be. Respect demands acknowledgment of individuals' contribution to the organization and full understanding of their participation in meeting the institution's goals. Respect demands recognition that individuals play an integral part in efforts to meet the facility's goals and objectives. Respect also demands the opportunity to be heard, to have a voice, and to communicate feelings, thoughts, ideas, and processes that may have an impact on relationships as well as on the outcomes of work.

Workers must be able to recognize the quality of relationships in the institution. Differentiation in relationships based on role definition has a significantly different impact than differentiation in relationships based on the perceptions of individuals. Individuals require a management perception that equates them with all participants in the organization and a respect that acknowledges that in their individuality they share fairly with all workers. Differentiation by role is acceptable; differentiation by personality, by position, or by function, with subsequent social and political discrimination, is unacceptable to anyone. The activities, processes, relationships, and behaviors that support the valuing of workers as equal contributors to the institution's processes are key components in providing the respect essential to maintaining worker involvement and commitment.

Trust

An important component essential to worker satisfaction is the building of trust in the workplace. Trust is an element central to any relationship. These relationships, whether they be on an individual or group level, require some sense of belief, of understanding, of faith. All human beings are social creatures. Social interaction demands a certain level of belief and trust. When social relationships are built on mistrust, they actually provide barriers to the development of interaction and social affiliation essential in addressing any common objectives. In fact, mistrust works against the achievement of common goals. A mistrusting environment breaks down the social milieu essential for interaction, communication, and the sharing of responsibility. Interaction, integration, collaboration, discussion, and problem solving all are processes that demand a high level of trust.

Trust is one of the easiest components of work to discuss but one of the most difficult to achieve. Much of the structure of the workplace is designed, intentionally or unintentionally, to interfere with the building of trusting relationships. The stratification of decision making and the limitation on participation in policy development, often excluding those responsible for carrying it out, are more obvious symptoms of this environment of mistrust. In health care, the opportunity for establishing mistrust is evident in the conflict between roles in decision making: there is trust in the management role but only limited trust in the clinical role. Many organizations seek a trusting environment but often work against a trusting environment by the very nature of their structure.

The elements that build trust in an organization are those that emphasize relationships. Since humans are social creatures, all individuals in the workplace demand an emphasis on relationships. It is through relationship that work is accomplished. It is through relationship that human social actualization occurs.[6] Institutions that can best establish an emphasis on relationships, trust, and honesty are bound to create an effective working environment.

Individuals seeking trust look for opportunities to be involved and to be asked for their views, which are accepted equally with those of others. Individuals in a trusting environment have to feel a part of the group and all of its processes and activities. The trusting environment demands mutual commitment, a sense of belonging, a sense of familiar or relational interaction. Trust requires a sort of egalitarianism in the organization. Egalitarianism simply indicates that everyone utilizes discretion, sense of autonomy, and self-trust without the need for overriding detailed supervision and direction.

Trust underscores a strong belief that what is going on in the health care institution corresponds closely to the commitment of the people who are carrying out the organization's goals. There is a belief (1) that individuals are committed not to create harm for themselves or for others, (2) that they therefore act out of the urge to be supportive of self and others, and (3) that they want to build a working relationship that not only will meet the facility's goals, but also will provide support for themselves and each other in relationship. Such trusting characteristics obviously represent individuals' basic needs as they apply themselves to the processes of work.[7]

The Need for Information

Certainly no one can undertake to meet the demands of any given responsibility in work without the information necessary to perform the task. It is not an overstatement to say that people today are products of the information age. Work cannot be accomplished without meaningful information. If trust and respect are to be present in the workplace, and sufficient information is not generated to enable the workers to accomplish the job, a high level of frustration and self-doubt will result.

Information is central to the successful role that anyone performs in an organization. The networks that the institution provides to assure that meaningful information is provided to the appropriate people is an important corollary to the responsibilities for meeting the facility's goals and objectives. If high levels in the structure and systems support decision making but fail to provide the appropriate information bases for reaching those decisions, the quality and effectiveness of the decisional process will be hampered significantly. This is no less true for individuals. They all require support and the information essential to doing their job. They have a right to expect that the system will provide the opportunity to obtain the orientation, information, response, feedback, and resources appropriate to their functions. If those who control or manage information fail to provide the pieces workers need, the decisional process will be harmed.

Information missing because the system did not recognize workers' need for it is just as damaging as misdirected information. Workers' decisions often are based on intuition, assumption, and supposition. As a result, much of their work product may reflect that same kind of deficit in decision making. Workers must have information that is appropriate and meaningful. If the meaningful component is missing, it does not matter how much other information is provided because it still will not meet the needs of both the workers and the work to be done. Workers must determine that the information is sufficient to allow them to make the kinds of decisions and undertake the kinds of action appropriate to their role.

Information generation is a process that moves both directions. The ability to receive and impart information in order to complete the communication loop is essential to the work and the work system and is as important to nurses as it is to the institution.

The process and attitudes favoring the free flow of communication both to and among workers are necessary to make information meaningful. An environment that supports this free flow will assure workers that information is not withheld, managed, manipulated, or based on the will of the organization or the whims of its executive or others. As with all of the other components of workers' basic need systems, the need for information is related closely to the need for respect. There must be faith that the information will be handled appropriately and trust that it is meaningful and can be applied by workers to the accomplishment of their tasks.

Human and Material Support

No persons can feel comfortable in the work environment unless they feel there is support, not only for their role and function but also for them as individuals. The health care institution must believe that its workers are worthy of involvement, of commitment, of belief, and of all the systems support necessary to facilitate their performance and their function. This support amounts to more than providing the material and fiscal resources; it also involves a sense of communion and relationships among the individuals responsible for the institution's output (health care services).

Workers properly expect the trust of administrators and the nurse manager's availability when there is a need. They expect the nurse manager to understand that need and be willing to spend time and resources to help meet it. When workers feel supported, especially by the nurse manager who is their leader, they are involved and are willing to make commitments to the facility. This generates a sense of unanimity with the organization and its goals. Workers clearly understand that these relationships facilitate work, can be trusted, and bind them not only to the processes and activities involved in accomplishing the job but also to the institutional leadership.

Workers get support from people, not from inanimate systems and a faceless institution. Workers recognize the institution and the faces of those most responsible for its work. Workers look to those individuals to best articulate the needs of the organization, to support them, and to help fulfill their needs. Workers constantly weigh and balance the connection between these two entities. They feel a sense of trust, commitment, and support when the environment is open. The open institution provides an opportunity for these interactional commitments to enhance the workers' sense of safety, involvement, trust, and ability to accomplish the expected tasks.

Support is manifested in a number of different ways. Workers need to know what is expected in the way of job performance, their obligations and expectations, and factors essential to carrying out their work. After these points are clarified, individuals want to be assured that the relationships, roles, responsibilities, and processes will be consistent. Without such assurances, they quickly develop feelings of fear and mistrust, of reduced commitment to the job, and of a need to complete only the basic requirements of the work.

To the extent that the value of the work is divorced from the valuation of the workers, there will be a clear lack of commitment to full ownership of the job by those responsible for its completion. The need for support and encouragement and for human connection is basic to workers' commitment and full participation in all aspects of the job, consistent with corporate expectations for it.

Meaningful Rewards

All workers expect to be rewarded consistent with their roles, responsibilities, the demands of their jobs, and their productivity. While no system of rewards fully meets any individuals' total expectations, workers are looking for some evidence of fairness and appropriateness in the application of recognition for their performance. Rewards can be divided into two basic categories: economic and personal, although there is some overlap.

All workers expect some economic reward at essentially the same level with those who perform like or similar functions. Management must clearly explain the institution's salaries and wages, benefits, and other reward factors before workers accept responsibility for a job.

Workers begin to build trust immediately upon joining an organization, expecting a sharing of the information that affects their personal and economic welfare. When the hospital does not honestly and freely supply all of the information workers need to do their jobs and to make judgments about their future there, a feeling of basic mistrust insidiously begins to undermine all other supports.

Those who represent the institution's human resource process should understand that no secrets remain so for long in any enterprise. Attempts to maintain confidentiality on a wage and benefits program for workers constitute an exercise in futility. Health care administrators who believe confidentiality is a legitimate basis for nondisclosure of full information on economic issues can create a hotbed of dissatisfaction among nurses and ultimately throughout the institution. Official policies and rules notwithstanding, workers tend to share information on their personal and economic benefits. If management does not explain at hiring that disparities may exist or develop, worker distrust will appear when differences in salaries or benefits become known. Lack of advance discussion of differences, similarities, weaknesses, strengths, potentialities, and drawbacks of a salary and benefits program, and of their relation to the long-term goals of the institution, prevents workers from feeling fully involved and from believing in the hospital's trust and commitments. As a result, seeds of separateness from the values of the institution are sown at the beginning of the work relationship and is difficult to alter or eliminate once it has been entrenched in workers' minds.

Nurses also look for personal rewards as individuals: the feedback that supports and encourages their work and the strength that comes from establishing close relationships with co-workers. The ability to relate directly, openly and honestly, with the nurse manager, and to influence, make decisions, make recommendations, and be heard—all of these constitute a basis for the establishment of personal rewards. A sense of accomplishment and of satisfaction, plus encouraging words of support from peers and managers, provide a system of rewards equally as valuable to workers as those in the economic area.

When a sense of well-being can be generated from the workplace and an understanding that they are desired, appreciated, and valued is attached to economic rewards, workers feel valued and comfortable with the interactions in accomplishing work. Workers in turn appreciate it when the nurse manager takes the time to understand, to listen, to be concerned. Nurses have feelings of satisfaction when peers or managers show an interest in their personal affairs. Of course, this does not refer to an interfering or meddling interest; rather, it means one that is supportive and caring.

It is important for individuals not only to sense the commitment that comes from relationship but also to receive the rewards that come from the work itself. As Herzburg indicates, workers are encouraged and motivated by processes that they experience in the role of performing work itself.[8] Processes that bring such high levels of satisfaction are identified as work-related motivators. They go beyond nurses' relationship with their peers and managers, satisfaction with working conditions, and economic framework.

Workers are motivated when they have the opportunity to exercise initiative and creativity, to make decisions that have an impact on the job, to handle problems in relation to the work and to take responsibility for resolving them, and to improve ways of performing tasks. When nurses are recognized and challenged in their work, growth and development can result, producing high levels of motivation and satisfaction.

Nurses operate in conjunction with others yet also must generate out of their own "space" rewards that come from a satisfying experience in their work. This can produce personal satisfactions of the highest level. The truly open organization provides the relationships, supports, environment, and opportunities to the fullest extent possible for this kind of personal reward system. (See Figure 2–3.) Here, and as previously discussed, a trust process must operate in the work

Figure 2–3 Cycle of Trust

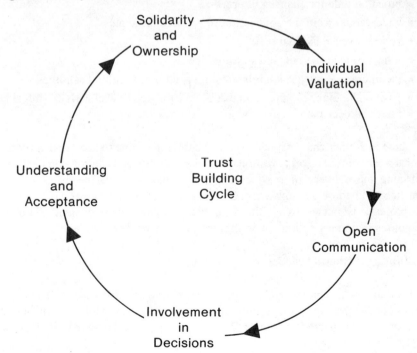

environment; valuing the individual nurse's contribution, the openness of the organization, involvement, understanding, and full ownership of the professional contribution of nursing.

THE HOPES OF THE PROFESSIONAL NURSES

When professional nurses become a part of an institution, they bring with them a set of characteristics that are unique to their own experience in practice. As noted in the previous section, the characteristics of a professional are unique when applied to the workplace. Their application of professional nursing practice demands a response from the workplace that is significantly different from vocational and technical workers and is altered by the fact that nurses are knowledge workers.

Professional nursing practice demands a set of relationships different from technical workers' if it is to maintain its standards. To assure the appropriate practice of nursing, the environment should allow for:

- collaboration
- individual judgment
- policy formulation and framework
- broad latitude for changes in practice
- wide variations in the application of practice principles
- control over individual practice
- influence over the outcomes of practice
- incorporative, integrative relationships with other health disciplines
- positioning in the organization that allows for free flow of activity, information, and decision making.

These and other characteristics such as autonomy, time to accomplish professional work, impact on organizational decision making, and control over decisions affecting the delivery of services apply specifically to the needs of nursing practice. With those previously mentioned, these all form the basic components of the professional nurses' role in the organization. In turn, these demand additional responses by the institution beyond those for other workers.

Institutional Characteristics

Institutions must have certain characteristics if nurses are to operate freely. To the extent that these are present, nurses will be able to function fully; when they are not, and to the degree that they are not, nursing is constrained. It therefore becomes the obligation of the health care facility to incorporate the following characteristics into its organizational system to assure full utilization of professional nurses' resources:

- The professional nurse must be influenced more by lateral than by hierarchical relationships. Communication, collaboration, and interaction must be the central value of nursing practice relationships.

- Authority must be invested in the professional work itself. Therefore, each professional nurse must sense, accept, and exercise specific individual authority for carrying out her practice in the context of her role.

- The design of the nurse's role, and her work, must be based on empirical or systematic scientific information in order to provide a baseline for professional activities. This scientific rationale should provide for decision making to replace superior-subordinate relationships and their inherent controls.

- The primary relationship in the organization is between the professional nurse and the client/patient she serves. All functions, structures, and systems should be directed to supporting and maintaining that relationship.

- The practitioner is expected to exercise autonomy, consistent with the professional ethics and acceptable standards of practice, in applying skills, abilities, and resources in achieving the goals and objectives of nursing care. Interaction, cooperation, and relationship with nursing peers is essential in formulating organizational policy, goals, and objectives that impact directly and indirectly on care. Therefore, the distinction between administrative and practice responsibilities in decision making becomes less distinct and separate with each (administrator and practitioner) directed toward applying practice theory, structuring appropriate organizational framework and form, and delivering nursing services.

The expectations of nurses in meeting the needs of patient care are different from and often in addition to the managing structures essential to managing workers in any system. These expectations of the practicing nurse include:

- The absence of absolute policy and rule: Because the professional nurse requires a certain level of autonomy in order to make appropriate clinical judgments, rules affecting those judgments must be flexible. Fixed and absolute rules and policy may interfere with, rather than facilitate, the practice of nursing.

- A reduction in the impact of hierarchical authority structures: Collaborative, communicative, interactional, and group process structures should provide the framework for the governance and practice of nursing in the institution.

Clearly defined and solidly vertical hierarchical structures demand practice accountability but do not provide or facilitate the appropriate organizational structure to support it.

- Professional nursing practice standards: At national, regional and institutional levels, these should provide the guidelines for the appropriate practice and evaluation of nursing. These should be based on the perceived needs and requirements of the client/patient.

- A mechanism for client/patient relationships: This must permit a free, open, and nonmanagement controlled relationship between the nurse and the patient. No action, process, or structure of the institution should interfere with the development and maintenance of that relationship.

- Distribution of managerial activities: These functions, especially those related to the provision of resources, should be equitably allocated to facilitate the fair delivery of nursing services to achieve care objectives. The organization's structure should assure that the appropriate provision of resources is a central function of management.

- Nonconformity and behavioral variability: The organizational structure should provide for a high degree of these elements. Since nursing practice requires a great deal of flexibility, the institutional structure must accommodate activity that meets patient/client needs most appropriately. Narrowly formalized structure and controls can limit the ability to respond meaningfully to such needs.

- Learning-based authority: The institution's philosophy, purpose, objectives, operational character, and relationships must be based on authority derived from scientific- and research-based learning. The authority structure in the organization that supports nursing must be founded in the practice itself. Therefore, the authority structures must derive from nursing practice in the institution rather than solely from institutional authority. The legitimacy of authority stems from accountability (from within the profession) to application, rather than from responsibility (external to the profession) to function. Authority, accountability, and practice therefore must be self-described. The institution thus places its trust in the professional nurse exercising her prescribed role in meeting the needs of the patient and the purposes of the organization.

- Problem evaluation: The nurse must be free to evaluate and assess problems resulting from nursing practice that have an impact on the outcome of patient care. This freedom requires that the nurse take an active role in self-assessment, peer assessment, and outcome evaluation. It is a clear statement that the professional nurse is accountable and must be given the support and freedom to undertake the peer-related activities directed to assuring that outcomes are the result of clearly defined nursing processes.

- Peer interaction: Peer relationship, collaboration, and decision making demand a mechanism for facilitating such interaction. This must not be limited simply to sharing clinical information but also should focus on responsibility for defining competence, reviewing performance criteria, evaluating peer performance, and participating in the privileging and terminating processes of nurses. The organizational framework and relationship should assure opportunities for the nurse to play a defined role in peer evaluation.

These elements indicate certain specific expectations of nurses in the exercise of their role. If they cannot do so consistent with their practice, their professional application of the nursing role is somewhat compromised. The fact that most institutions do not have many of these elements built into their governance system indicates the degree to which they are or are not truly professional organizations. However a group may describe itself, if it does not have as a part of its functional life behaviors consistent with that self-description, it cannot claim to operate under the auspices of that condition. Since nursing demands the kinds of relationships and structures in the organization that reflect its professional character, these elements must receive structural and behavioral support. (See Figure 2–4.)

Basic Beliefs

Certain basic beliefs involved in the role of nurses can be described. They provide a framework within which nurses implement the mandates of the profes-

Figure 2–4 Interactional Responsibility Model

Authority — Accountability

Institution — Professional

Policy Based
Delegated
Institutional
Responsible

Internally Generated
Self-Described
Social Approved
Knowledge-Based

Empowering
Measurable
Outcome Oriented

sion. It is on this philosophical basis that the institution places its trust in those it defines as responsible for carrying out its work. By offering nursing services, the institution clearly makes a statement about the need for such care and attests to its unique character. The hospital thus acknowledges that nursing is a special service that has a rational basis for the work it provides.

The basic beliefs in the organization that are essential if it is to support the practice of nursing and provide it with a managerial framework include:

- that people are self-concerned, interested, and committed to the work and services they can provide
- that individuals, given appropriate and meaningful information, become the best judges of their own interests and those of the institution they serve
- that group goals are achieved more readily through group activity rather than by independent, individual action
- that all individuals have diverse interests regarding costs and benefits of pursuing organizational goals; generating support for this diversity of interests will facilitate the institution's achievement of those goals
- that control and coordinating functions are equally important in the management and achievement of goals
- that equality exists among all individuals in the organization; this equality must be emphasized through the distribution of power and authority
- that individuals have the right and the responsibility to share and to delegate their individual powers to those who best represent their interests in the organization
- that a high level of specific knowledge and skill is required in order to make professional decisions
- that all systems exist only to fulfill goals and it is the responsibility of the system to continually refine those goals.

These statements are based on beliefs that form the character of the relationship between professional workers, in this case nurses, with the organization in which they serve.

Other Characteristics of the Organization

The institution also must have the following characteristics to fully utilize its resources and the professional contribution of its individual nurses:

- All members must fulfill their duties as described by their organization. If they cannot or do not, they are free to leave.

- All participants in the professional entity have a right to information that facilitates their work and that affects how their professional practice is delivered.
- All members have equal rights, equal access, and equal authority for decisions that affect the practice of each individual; this authority may be delegated and exercised within a representative constituency.
- All professionals in the organization have a right to privacy.
- The organization (nursing) must clearly describe and distinguish between its coordinative and control functions.
- Clarification of organizational functions must be based on a full understanding of the role of each of its participants.
- A contracting, contract-like, or accountability agreement exists between the health care institution and its participants.
- Components of the governance process will need specialized knowledge and skills in order to make specific decisions on behalf of the professionals.
- Salaries, benefits, working conditions, and levels of satisfaction are issues of concern for all practitioners; nurses then must play a role in their determination.
- Nurses may play more than one role in the institution, depending on the need, the position, and its accountability needs.
- Nurses must share with each other responsibilities and resources for implementing their role; no professional nurse may take for her own exclusive use any role or the resource of that role. Resources must be available to all who need them.
- Assessment, evaluation, and disciplinary processes are sanctioned and fully participated in by the professional nursing staff.[9]

These factors have a major influence on the kind of structure and organizational system that operates in governing professional nurses. It is clear that traditional approaches will need to change if the institution truly reflects and respects the professional character of nursing practice. Relationships, functions, governance structures, and the overall professional standards of nursing may require dramatic changes in the organization if it is to become truly participatory and integrative in nature.

The management process for integrating all of the elements of the professional association and for encouraging nurses' work is significantly different from traditional processes. While it requires unique skills and abilities, it need not be any more complex than for any hierarchical, rigidly structured, and perhaps bureaucratic system. The institution's responses, abilities, character of relationship, and values will have a tremendous impact on the success of management.

Relations with the Managed

The managed—in this case professional nurses—require a different kind of relationship with their managers. The managers will need a different kind of perception about themselves and their relations with their professional peers. Clearly described policies, processes, roles, and responsibilities as used in highly structured organizations will not serve a good purpose for nurse managers in the kind of institution that facilitates professional practice.

Equally important is the change in demands on nurses themselves. If the professional character of practice is to continue to grow, it must assume additional responsibilities. They must be as clear to the practitioners as they are to the nurse managers. Nurses no longer will be able to settle for the traditionally expected kinds of functional and vocational behaviors. The safety the nursing staff feels by relegating to the nurse manager the responsibility for handling conflict resolution and decision making that involves clinical practice will be missing from the environment that encourages professional behaviors. Practitioners will take over designing and implementing strategies and activities to resolve clinical problems, in regard to both relationships and patient outcomes. Indeed, in participating or open organizations, much more responsibility rests with practitioners than ever before. The organization will concentrate solely on developing strategies and mechanisms that will help practitioners function better in their role as clinical nurses. The institution builds on its belief that nurses will perform as prescribed by the regulations of professional practice.

Accountability is not an escape from the obligations that exist in the practice of nursing. If anything, it expands on them. This focus on developing the professional role of nurses has significantly more impact on them than it does on their managers. While it is obvious that the managers' role must be structured differently in order to support this concept, it is equally apparent that the role of nurses also must change in scope and in focus in order to assure the continuing growth of the profession and the application of practice at a level parallel with other professionals in the delivery of health care services.[10]

The medical profession has been struggling with these issues for decades, yet the responsibility and accountability for the practice of medicine rests clearly and solidly with individual physicians. All medical structures, systems, supports, and interaction are based on the freedom of the individual physician to practice medicine.

Relationships between and among physicians constitute a central value in the practice of medicine. All activities, resources, and systems are directed to assuring (1) the independence of individual physicians and (2) the clinical relationships.

While medicine's structural applications may not be appropriate for nursing, the medical profession's purposes and impetus for maintaining high levels of interaction could be of real value to nursing. Mechanisms that develop the relationships and practice bases of nursing care can be valuable not only to the profession but also to the organizations in which practitioners serve. Perhaps least discussed, but most important, they may serve the best interests of the patients who come to the institution looking for and expecting high levels of nursing care.

When confronted with the extent of transition and change recommended for creating a truly professional organization, the reader may engender thoughts of uncontrolled anarchy occurring in the nursing organization. Using traditional concepts of relationship and organizational integrity, such feelings can easily be understood. The only organizational models managers and practitioners have been exposed to have been those that represent the bureaucratic form of governance. Much new work has shown that such forms of governance may not only be inappropriate for the management of human beings but in many cases may even be detrimental to the human organism on both a personal and a sociological basis.[11]

Anarchy only occurs in a civilization, society, or organization when it has failed to govern as its members need, require, or expect.[12] To suggest that a clear and strong definition of control, rule, policy, law, etc. in and of themselves constitute a reason or basis upon which people act or live in a society, family, or workplace is to think in contradiction to current evidence.[13] Further, to suggest that such processes are essential, as currently constituted in most organizations, tends to denigrate the value of self-direction, self-control, and personal discipline. This author believes that there has been very little opportunity to actually determine what professional workers (in this case, nurses) are capable of doing on their own behalf—in the interests of the profession, to the benefit of the institution and, ultimately, to the benefit of the patient—when not constrained by institutionally defined rules, policies, and objectives. Conversely, it is to the discredit of nurses that they have failed as a body to behave in the manner of and consequently be treated as professionals. They have therefore missed the opportunity in most health care institutions to be autonomous, self-defining, key decisionmakers, board members, and a host of other positions and symbols that make a statement of social and professional significance.

The script that nurses are being asked to write here is to define different ways of relating, organizing, and governing themselves where the outcome is a more collaborative, interactive, relationship base established for nursing practice and governance. Nurses are being asked to form the kind of liaisons and interrelationships that recognize professional peer values and the ability of every nurse to participate in some way with her peers in a form of representational governance. Certainly this process models a more realistic organizational process than the one that most nurses confront.

The work that must be done, however, is nursing's work. Most of the changes and movement to group effectiveness outlined in this book depends upon nurses taking action. Nurse managers and practitioners together, within the context of the role of each, must work to bring the elements of this professional script and structure to reality. The institution has no reason to take such action on nurse's behalf. It can change from bureaucratic beliefs and structures, but not before it has a reason to.[14] Nurses, providing leadership in changing its own organizational design, may furnish that reason.

Personal Characteristics

Practicing nurses, in the context of their own profession's expectations, must begin to recognize certain characteristics in their role that they must implement as individuals. The following items should be at least the minimum for every practicing nurse as she conceives her role in preparing for professional practice into the 21st century:

1. She is fully accountable, as a professional, for all activities relating to the delivery of nursing care services for which she is responsible. This cannot be transferred to the institution or any other individual.
2. Her responsibility for professional nursing practice is more than the hands-on delivery of services. Much of the political, social, institutional factors having an impact on the delivery of nursing services has little to do with the patient care on which the nurse spends most of her time. It may be advisable to attach more significance than is evident historically to the professional, organizational, political, and social responsibilities of the profession.
3. The nurse's personal relationships with professional peers must reflect respect, trust, support, communication, and involvement above and beyond the current level in most nursing organizations. The values of professional practice must be expressed in terms of both the role and the relationships of each individual nurse.
4. The nurse must understand that there is diversity in practice. She should not expect that all others will practice consistent with her values, experiences, mandates, and processes. The individual can expect that all those using basic scientific principles will exercise practice in the context of their own experience for the benefit of the patients each one serves.
5. The nurse no longer can expect the institution to insulate and protect her from the realities and demands of defining, structuring, and offering care. As a professional, she not only must be willing, but is required, to play an active role in all organizational issues affecting the delivery of services.
6. The clinical nurse must accept responsibility for problem-solving activities involving her role. She no longer can transfer to the nurse manager all responsibility for conflict resolution, staffing, scheduling, assigning, and planning nursing care activities. At the very least, she shares that responsibility; at the very most, she assumes accountability for it.
7. The nurse must leave behind traditional vocational attitudes. "Blue collar" behaviors no longer will occur in nursing. These include a shift-by-shift

focus, evaluation of tasks only, avoiding professional involvement beyond the confines of her work role, valuing the LPN/LVN as a parallel nursing peer, acting in the context of the physician description of her role, and, finally, failing to assert the values of her role.

8. The nurse must recognize a continuing commitment to excellence and to competence in practice. Therefore, she must be committed to an organized, systematic program of continuing education and development that leads her to higher levels of professional practice. She has an obligation to support continuing academic development and growth to the fullest levels of potential she is capable of achieving in the context of her personal life plan.

9. The individual must look at the career aspects of her role, recognizing that it presents long-term demands with all of the influences, responsibilities, obligations, and challenges that they provide. As a career choice, nursing has the same weight or significance for professional growth, development, and service to the community as any other professional career choice. Such factors must be taken into consideration when making decisions regarding career, personal growth, spouse selection, and rearing children.

10. The baccalaureate in nursing is the basic element upon which the future of the profession must be evaluated. This is not to say that associate degree and diploma nursing education cannot fall within the context of professional practice. It does indicate a willingness by all levels of practice to accept definitive criteria for establishing a base line for the future growth of nursing.

Obviously the needs of professional nurses are significant and complex. Managing such practitioners will demand a specific set of skills and abilities unique to the role of nurse managers. The professional character of nursing demands managerial ability that will support individual practitioners in the exercise of patient care responsibility. If truly professional nursing practice is to be evidenced in the provision of services, nurse managers must develop skills and resources to those needs.

Along with the challenges of this approach to management will come the rewards of a truly professional environment. Participating in this kind of workplace promises the highest levels of satisfaction for both nurse managers and practicing nurses.

NOTES

1. Marshal Shashkin, "A Guide to Participative Management," *The 1984 Annual for Group Facilitators* (San Diego: University Associates, Inc., 1984), 227–41.

2. JoAnn Ashley, *Hospitals' Paternalism and the Role of the Nurse* (New York: Teachers College Press, 1977), 75–84.

3. JoAnn Ashley, *Hospitals, Paternalism, and the Role of the Nurse* (New York: Teachers College Press, 1977), 123–134.

4. G. Blane, "The Hospital as a Professional Bureacracy," *Trustee* 28, no. 10 (October 1975), 13–16.

5. Chris Argyris, *Interpersonal Competence and Organizational Effectiveness* (Homewood, Ill.: The Dorsey Press, 1962).

6. Douglas McGregor, *The Human Side of Enterprise* (New York: McGraw-Hill Book Company, 1960).

7. Ibid., McGregor, 56–158.

8. Frederick Herzburg, *Work and the Nature of Man* (New York: World Publishing Company, 1966).

9. L.L. Wade, "The Neoteric Model," *Human Organization* 10 26 (Spring/Summer 1967): 40–46.

10. P. Abell, "Hierarchy Versus Democratic Authority," *Work and Power* eds. T.R. Burns, L.E. Karlson, and V.H. Rus (Beverly Hills, Cal.: Sage Publications, Inc., 1979), 141–71.

11. William Pasmore, et. al., "Sociotechnical Systems: A North American Reflection on Empirical Studies of the Seventies," *Human Relations* (December, 1982): 35–38.

12. Thomas More, *Utopia* (Roslyn, N.Y.: Walter J. Black, Inc., 1947), 15–175.

13. Marvin R. Weisbord, "Participative Work Design: A Personal Odyssey," *Organizational Dynamics* (Spring 1985): 5–20.

14. Manfred Kets deVries & Danny Miller, *The Neurotic Organization,* San Francisco, California (1984): 1–45.

The Needs of the Manager

Objectives for Chapter Three

Outline some of the basic needs, both personal and professional, of nurse managers.

Discuss the self-assessment skills necessary to understand the managers' personal as well as professional needs.

Review concept changes nurse managers will need to undertake to change their style to the participatory approach.

Identify the functional activities nurse managers must incorporate into their management role.

Explore the constraints in the system and in the role that prevent managers from effectively undertaking participative activities.

Investigate some concept processes that affect the ability of nurse managers to meet the needs of their role successfully.

3

Judging from the complexity involved in practice nursing, it is evident that the role requirements of the manager are significant. It is true that the manager who takes the nursing profession into the 21st century is going to need a broad-ranging set of skills that will depend more on the development of human resources than almost any other one she will utilize.

Since nursing is primarily a people-intensive professional activity, the skills essential for human interaction to carry out its work are important to the manager's role. The manager preparing for the 21st century will spend a great deal of time learning how to work with groups and to improve the work of others. Some of the responsibility for defining the specifics of that work rests with professional nurses, but most of the responsibility for facilitating the interaction of professionals and developing the parameters for work will rest with the nurse manager.

The front-line nurse manager will be at the heart of the development of the new organization systems supporting the practicing nurse. This will be a challenging opportunity, however, where the nurse manager will find herself afloat, often with little support. Since she will provide the leadership and assure that the defined outcomes of nursing actually are achieved, she often will find herself in places where no one else has been. As a result, her courage in managing the human resource will have to be strengthened considerably.

To exercise the assertiveness necessary to undertake this role, the professional nurse manager will have to spend a great deal of time in understanding her own personal resources, skills, and abilities, as well as the constraints in her own job context. Self-assessment is an important beginning place to search out her purposes and opportunities in this role. Questions relating to her reasons for being a manager, for accepting the responsibilities and challenges, and for undertaking the obligations that the role will demand are important considerations requiring personal clarification.

The first and perhaps most important question to be answered is why she became a manager in the first place. Much of the results since will have some relation to her answers to this question.

THE MANAGER AS ESCAPEE

In the traditional hospital framework, there are few options available for practicing nurses to grow and to reach their professional peak. For example, the clinical opportunities are limited at best; even to this date, in most institutions, such opportunities are severely limited. Perhaps with special education, certification, and an advanced degree in a clinical specialty, individuals may have a variety of opportunities to advance, but even those are limited to the kinds and numbers of positions available in the institution.

This real problem of growth is one that has been a part of the nursing profession since the turn of the century. Hospitals seldom gave opportunities to do other than what they were assigned to do: offer care that was primarily supportive in nature and meet the needs of other individuals in the service environment. It was these other individuals—primarily physicians and administrators—who had the opportunity to grow in ways beyond those available to nurses.

What often happened as a result of these limitations was development of opportunities for excellent clinical practitioners to climb the management track. This permitted a broadening of responsibility, increased challenges, and opportunity concomitant with economic and personal rewards. The management track, therefore, has become the best and sometimes only option available to provide nurses with opportunities for growth and achievement.

Any impetus for growth in the delivery of nursing care has been limited by the lack of opportunities to practice nursing at levels commensurate with the individuals' skills and abilities. This has left feelings of frustration and a sense of lack of control and influence over their circumstances and lives. Often key decisions that have had an impact on practice have been made by those in administration in the hospital.

Professional nurses who would have preferred to grow in clinical practice and would have taken advantage of such opportunities had they existed, turned to the only alternative route for advancement—management. Clinical practitioners opting for the management role can be viewed as essentially "escaping" from the limitations of the staff nurse role. As a result, excellent nurses left clinical practice for a role for which they often were inadequately prepared—a reality that still exists in many, if not most, institutions today.

What was happening, or more accurately what was not happening, served to motivate good nurses to quit clinical care in an effort to meet their need and desire to influence their circumstances and control their own lives.

The satisfaction people get from work relates to their ability to assert themselves and to make a difference based on their skills and abilities. In the case of staff nurses, they lacked opportunities for self-identification, for making a difference in the work environment, and for growth in the work itself.

The management role did meet those needs, providing opportunities to share their opinions and views, to influence the workplace, to direct others in achieving their own objectives, to have control over the circumstances that affected the outcomes of work, and to relate professionally and equally with other disciplines, most notably physicians. Nurses as managers developed a level of respect in their new role, with others in the hospital acknowledging them as the leaders in a given area of practice and service.

Even so, the framework for this management role often was rigid, structured, and highly controlled. Its parameters for responsibility and accountability were specified in some detail. Organization rulings were handed down from one level of the hierarchy to another. It was simply a matter of complying and assuring those in charge that the orders had been carried out. Nurse managers preparing for the new role never had a sense of commitment from the hospital or an understanding of human relations management, its complexity, and the demands of change. Whatever was discovered in the new function was acquired either by orientation, by experience, or in short-term classes on specific areas of nurse management. The professional character of nursing and of its practitioners was not clearly identifiable and was not otherwise defined by the administrative bureaucracy. The skills essential for developing this professional character thus were not a basic part of the novice manager's development.

The process of accommodation, or learning the rules of the game and applying them, has become the predominant educational device for beginning nurse managers, especially those in the first line. While the scenario is changing and more graduate nurses are moving into management, most of the individuals in such roles are nurses with basic preparation and who reflect a personal affinity for leadership and responsibility.

Administration regards personal leadership characteristics as the primary indexes to nurses' ability to assume the role of manager. While that perspective may be of value, a propensity for leadership and the accompanying personal characteristics do not often a nurse manager make. Still, there are the ego satisfaction, the economic rewards, the position power, and the opportunity to influence and control. All of these are reinforcing and encouraging to the new managers. Whether or not they are skilled enough or able to exercise fully the responsibility essential for managing professional practitioners is subject to question. (See Figure 3–1.)

In Chapter 2, it was made clear that the skills and resources of managers of professional nurses will require specialized development and ability beyond the basic preparation of most nurse managers. Managers will have to undertake a

Figure 3–1 Nursing Accommodation/Adaptation Pathway

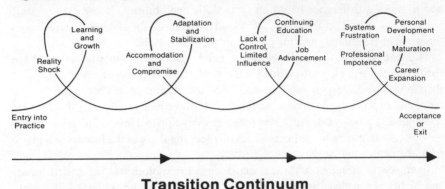

Transition Continuum

systematic assessment of their existing skills and abilities, where they stand currently, and what needs and resources they must develop. To do all this, they first must look within.

The self-assessment should include time spent in looking at personal needs, goals, and desires in the professional frame of reference. Some hard nonjudgmental questions must be asked as to why they are seeking or remaining in the role, the opportunities available, and the joys and satisfactions, the pains and discomforts of leadership. Taking time to reflect on those issues and to determine the impact of the new role in relation to the governance of nursing practice will provide a base line of information from which, if the novice managers (or manager candidates) are honest and nonjudging, they can begin to develop mechanisms for growth.

Those who already are nurse managers should, in their self-assessment, look at specified approaches to their role: whether they are controlling and directive, facilitating and developmental. To control and to direct means to provide the primary decision making for the activities of their unit; to be facilitating and encouraging is to provide opportunities for the staff to determine direction, process, and outcomes. To do that, the managers will need to ask themselves some basic but important questions. The answers will give them some idea of their approach and style in management, and whether that is consistent with the behaviors essential for managing professional individuals:

1. Do I supervise the nursing staff members closely in order to get them to do the work they are required to do?
2. Do I set the goals for the nursing staff members, then encourage them to fulfill those objectives?
3. Do I allow the nursing staff to participate in goal setting and in objective evaluation?

4. Do I establish the authority and controls on the nursing unit for which the nursing staff is responsible?

5. Do I do all of the staffing, planning, scheduling, and assignments for my staff?

6. Do I talk openly and daily with my subordinates regarding their needs, their ideas, their feelings?

7. Do I step in as soon as there are problems, issues, or concerns? Do I then take over and provide the leadership and direction for problem resolution?

8. Do I define for my staff members the requirements of their role, my expectations for them, the rules I have made to make sure that they understand clearly what I want them to do?

9. Do I have frequent meetings with the staff as a whole to discuss issues of mutual concern? Do I allow other staff members to lead meetings at times to provide opportunities to discuss issues different from the ones that concern me?

10. Do I discuss the alternatives with staff members, when a decision needs to be made, and provide them with an opportunity to assist me in the decision-making process?

11. Do I make decisions, and afterwards communicate them to the staff?

12. Am I the communication channel between the organization and the staff? Do I provide the staff with all of the information or are there other ways to facilitate the transfer of information for which the staff should be responsible?[1]

A careful review of the nurse managers' answers will give them some idea of whether they are motivated to participative or to directive management. Those who answer these questions honestly can get a sense as to which they are, just by reviewing their own responses.

At this point nurse managers must get a strong sense of the need for a different set of relationships they must establish with the professional nursing staff in order to meet the staff's goals and objectives. Utilizing the nursing staff provides a different basis from which decisions are made and establishes a different location in the control of the responsibility and the structure necessary to assure that nursing is practiced appropriately. In the context of the dozen questions above and consistent with the values of professional nurses, a new set of questions must be raised. Some of these relate to the managers' own belief systems regarding managing the human resource, others to new concepts needed to integrate her role with that of her professional peers as they are asked to assume more responsibility for their own practice. Nurses and professional peers might ask the manager:

1. What opportunities do you provide professional nurses to work as independently as possible? Do you believe that these will result in an increase in effectiveness?

2. Do you offer professional nurses more responsibility and the authority to implement it? Do you find that without the authority, they seldom utilize the opportunity?

3. Do the professional nurses on their own undertake new and challenging opportunities or do they find themselves locked into their role and rarely operate outside it?

4. Do your professional nurses seek opportunities to determine the nature of the work and their obligations in relation to it? Or do you define that for them?

5. Do you manage as the controlling agent of the organization, moderating its constraints and resources and maintaining behavior in the context of those controls? How does the staff react to you and to that process?

6. Does the professional staff really participate in decision making? Do you find that there is substantial harmony, unity, and interaction not only among your nursing staff members but between them and you?

7. Does your staff members' sense of responsibility indicate they are committed to the organization, to you personally, and to each other? Is there a sense of unanimity and clear support for one another?

8. Do you allow your nursing staff members to manage their own leave time, sick time, vacation, holiday-personal business? Do you believe that allowing them to do so would result in abuse or in more responsibility?

9. Do you allow your professional nurses to share in their own scheduling, their own assignments, assume responsibility for vacancies in the schedule, and to schedule themselves in any way that would make the assignments work to the benefit of patients and staff? Or do you do all of the scheduling?

10. Do you believe in participative decision making by allowing others to identify the issue, to negotiate the solutions, and to recommend or determine the best possible outcomes? Or do you solve the problems and share the results with your staff?

11. Do you believe that when professional nurses are given more responsibility and assume it that they will accept it? That they can be committed to it and will meet organizational goals and objective? Or do you believe that you must do this because they have neither the time nor the interest?

12. Do you have a high degree of flexiblity in the scheduling and allocation of work? Do you allow numerous schedule variabilities or do you have a set schedule, set time frame, set rule of scheduling that all must participate in? If staff members seek changes, must they ask permission from you?

13. Do you believe that professional nurses, when left on their own, will do the work required of them or must you be present? If you must, what does that say to you about them and about you?

14. Do you believe the professional nurses who are committed to the organizational goals and objectives still require your constant supervision and

interaction? Do you believe they are unable to act independently of your supervision and direction?

15. Do you believe your nursing staff members can make decisions without you? If they can't, why can't they?[2]

Certainly these are tough questions. They require a degree of insight and honesty that may not have been asked of the nurse manager before. They may be demanding even for the nursing administrator who is responsible for a number of first-line managers. The questions relate to the concepts and beliefs of governing the professional practice of nursing, even to basic beliefs about human activity.

Many of the traditional values that have become associated with the management of human resources are involved in the answers. Research has indicated that workers will accept responsibility and accountability and are willing to accomplish tasks.[3] The organization may not yet have developed the beliefs, systems, and practices that reflect this research. The two sets of questions constitute an effort to sort out how the nurse manager confronts the issues that lie at the heart of her role.

NEW NEEDS IN THE ROLE OF THE MANAGER

Those who manage nursing human resources need many different kinds of skills that are analytical, observant, and carefully planned. There must be integration of goals and effectiveness in relation both to the demands of the profession and to the needs of the institution. The extent to which individual nurses (or groups of them) perceive their goals as being consistent with those of the organization and link their levels of satisfaction with the institution's objectives will help determine the effectiveness of the manager.

The goals of nursing management obviously must be compatible with those of the institution. The institution's goal should be to provide an opportunity for the professional practice of nursing; when these have been met, the manager's objective is to act in congruence with these goals. Nurses must interact closely with the institutional goals, their own professional aims, and the needs of the patients they serve. Needless to say, there should be commonality between the needs of the institution and of the nurses. Such compatibility provides a set or framework within which nursing can be practiced. The role of the nurse manager is to integrate these elements in the delivery of nursing services.

In any institution, the professional nurse group performance should be formally prescribed by the group. The nurse manager will need to develop skills to assist the group in deciding its short-range and long-range goals and then, through the use of group process, help it identify ways in which it can meet its objectives. This accomplishes two things: (1) professional nurses participate in determining the criteria upon which their performance will be assessed and (2) their involvement in the process of setting goals increases their commitment to achieving them.[4]

A certain style of management, of managerial behaviors, fulfills the needs of the managed to achieve their goals. Managers most successful in this have certain personal characteristics and style that lends themselves well to helping nurses attain their objectives. This is an important point.

Nurse managers move from directing and controlling on behalf of the hospital to encouraging, developing, and interacting with peers using all the strategies that are supportive of such behaviors. These roles may require nurse managers who come from the traditional style of management to change a good deal of their activities. These will emphasize interactional and relational elements much more than previously. The following list of functional activities gives some indication of the activities that managers must emphasize to meet their own needs and those of the professional staff:

1. The nurse manager will need to spend more time in listening activities. These may relate to a broad range of items not necessarily specifically related to work processes. Listening may include concerns and issues that have an impact, but may not be related directly to, the workplace.
2. The nurse manager will need to identify mechanisms for establishing some personal relationship with individual nurses. That personal connection, the identification of one individual with another, may become a key component of the management and relational process on a nursing unit.
3. The nurse manager and nurse group should establish a forum for problem statements, complaints, issues of concern, and resolution process. The professional nurses should have an opportunity, openly and without judgment, to communicate these concerns and their ideas for future action.
4. The nurse manager must have regular agenda meetings with the nursing staff at least monthly (more often if possible) to discuss issues of specific concern to the workplace. These should be business meetings on the functional aspects of the delivery of nursing care services. They should provide for a free-flowing information exchange that helps both the staff and the manager.
5. The nurse manager should set a specific time each day for interaction in the workplace: making rounds, talking with employees and other nursing staff members, patient visitation, praising, commenting, and encouraging.
6. The nurse manager at all costs must be available to the professional staff for any issues, problems, or concerns that might arise. The manager's availability should be of such a priority that all other activity comes second. Availability, responsiveness, and immediacy are values that produce high levels of participation, commitment, and response from the nursing staff. (See Figure 3–2.)

Figure 3–2 Management 'Style' Model

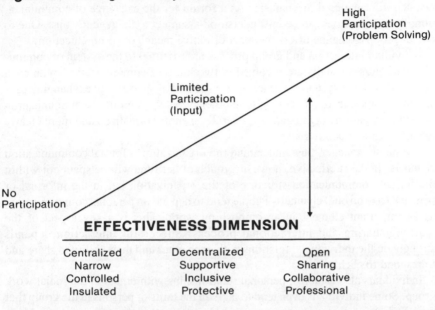

These basic characteristics demand a reorientation of the nurse manager's time. This will pay off in a number of ways in relation to her roles and responsibilities for managing not only the human resources but also the fiscal and material elements. When the human resource component is addressed successfully, the other issues of concern to nurses—finance, materials, relationships, and problem solving— almost always will be easier to address.[5]

The Need for Communication

Communication, too, is significant. Perhaps the biggest single job for the nurse manager will be to establish and maintain effective communications and relationships, a process that will take a great deal of her time. Effective communication is vital. It is the process by which management transmits its plans and directives. It also enables those who carry out the work to transmit problems, issues, and concerns. Communication makes it possible for all elements of the organization to integrate their responsibilities and tasks to meet patient needs.

The least-used type should be written communication. In a people-intensive organization, direct one-to-one communication is the most successful. This does not mean that written communication does not have a place; however, its place is to inform, to educate, to validate, and to support interactional communication that has occurred already. Written communication should be understood as a secondary step informational mechanism. As a forum for the exchange of communication, written material can be misunderstood—subject to the reader's bias. One to one or group exchange offers the most effective means of communication.

Individual interaction and group process are essential to the system of communication. Nurses usually are involved in two kinds of communication: with each other and with the system. Interaction is a method of sharing and exchanging data and information from one person to another or between groups. Communication with the system (the organization) generally is more formalized and more clearly identified in a structured way.

The nurse manager must understand the organization's formal communication channels. If she is effective, however, much of her time will be spent not within the formal communication structure of the organization but in the informal or personal (one on one) channels. People tend to depend on personal communication as an important element in accomplishing work. This is a key aspect of the teaching/sharing and interactional process. Successful interaction depends strongly on the individuals' relations with each other and their ability to share and to respond to each other.

Individuals also establish personal relationships with others in the social work group. Some individuals even tend to take on the traits of persons in the group that they find supportive and appropriate in the context of their own values. In an organizational situation, the infantile mutual dependency that most persons shed at maturity is replaced by a sense of communication, interaction, and the ability to establish independent relationships.

The ability to create such relational characteristics will serve the nurse manager well. The professional peers with whom she works can come to depend upon her as the coordinator and interactor. Individuals tend to identify with the characteristics of a role that best meets the needs of the situation. To the extent that the leader fulfills the perceived managerial and social responsibilities that others attach to the role, she can increase its meaning and effectiveness. The communication strategy she adopts to relate to her peers will determine her effectiveness and relationships in that role.

The Feedback Factor

Communication obviously is not a one-way process. Mechanisms for sending and receiving must be in place for communication interaction to be complete. Effective two-way communication occurs when receipt of a message has been acknowledged and that receipt made known to the sender. The interactional process then should somehow terminate, completing the communication loop and assuring a measure of understanding.

However, a third element enters—feedback, from either side or from both sides. Most communication difficulties occur in the feedback process. Feedback can be both direct and indirect. Direct feedback is clear: the receiving party reaffirms the agreements and understandings. But it also can be indirect and subtle. It can be expressed through body language such as gestures indicating agreement or disagreement, the shaking of a head, the leaning forward in excitement or acceptance or back in rejection. It can be recognized in a frown, angry features, a laugh, and a wide range of other body and facial expressions. Obviously, accurate direct feedback is achieved better face to face, but that is not the only method.[6]

Personal sensitivity to individual communication modes, personal expression, and styles is an important component of the role of manager. To be successful she must have some understanding of transactional processes and the ways in which people normally communicate their needs, as well as some of the other ways that are used. Understanding the communicator's viewpoint in terms of expression and individual needs is important.

The nurse manager must be able to understand, to the extent possible, the needs, desires, and expressive behaviors of individuals with whom she works. This should develop from her having established a relatively close personal relationship and interactional style with them. Understanding and reviewing transactional processes also is helpful.

The manager also must be able to identify internal barriers that individuals bring to the communication process. One of these is the tendency that everyone in society has developed to judge and to criticize. Individuals who examine the character and content of much of the interaction in their lives will find it filled with interpersonal judgments and criticisms: about others' presentations, behavior, dress, abilities, competencies, social position, responsibilities, effectiveness, communication, marital status, personal presentation, and many other factors.

It is, in fact, the very process of judging that most often interferes with effective communication. The tendency to judge is common on almost all levels of interchange and interaction. Because interaction and communication involve the whole person, many feelings, values, and emotions are called into play. The stronger one's feelings on an issue, the stronger the judging response and communication strategies related to the issue.

When an individual is emotionally involved and is related to the issue being discussed, that factor often affects communication itself. The perception of the issue, the mechanism for relaying it, and the receptiveness to others' responses to it all are colored by the individual's emotional involvement and judgment. The tendency to react internally and judge meaningful and value-laden statements with an emotional response is perhaps the largest single barrier to interpersonal relationships.[7]

Nonjudgmental Strategies

Managers thus should establish personal strategies that do not reflect judgment and criticism. As difficult as that may be, since it is so much a part of socialization, it is a vital element in the process of effective management and productive communication and interaction. Managers must develop an attitude of listening, with the goal of understanding the communicated message. This means understanding the other individual's point of view precisely in relationship to the topic or communication element involved. An earnest attempt at understanding others' communications can help managers understand their own response and facilitate the feedback essential for full communication.

Carl Rogers suggests that a person who gets in an argument with a friend or with a small group should stop for a moment and undertake an experiment using a single rule for interaction: each person can air her view after she first restates the ideas and feelings of the previous speaker as accurately as possible and to the other's satisfaction.[8]

This certainly would change the communication process. It would require the manager, before expressing her point of view, to understand and to articulate the other speaker's frame of reference; in other words, to understand the other person's thoughts and feelings well enough to summarize and communicate them satisfactorily back to that individual. The manager would discover quickly that that is a very difficult, but necessary, process because articulating another's point of view is a part of completing the feedback loop.

If Rogers's experiment were carried to its logical conclusion and this strategy were used in all forms of communication (with both individuals and groups), it would be interesting to evaluate the effectiveness this could develop in the nurse manager's communication style. Again, however, this process demands the ability to communicate without sitting in judgment and without prior criticism. When communication bias is dropped and people are free to understand, a whole range of variables, options, and possibilities exists. For nurse managers, this is an essential and meaningful skill to develop that, with time, will work to their best advantage.

Needless to say, such changes will take courage and skill on the part of nurse managers. Unfortunately, they may not receive much reinforcement. Much of the social interaction on nursing units contains elements of judging and criticizing, so it is difficult to establish a communication pattern that does not utilize strategies that have judging and criticizing as main elements.

The courage necessary to alter this process will be a measure of the leader's willingness to take a risk and attempt to open a new dialogue reflecting others' perceptions and needs. The courage also involves the attempt to disclose and understand others' perceptions without the evaluative judgments that run counter to effective interaction. The risk managers must face is the possibility that their perceptions (and actions) may be changed, perhaps to the extent of reaching a conclusion different from that originally intended. Indeed, managers may accept and incorporate a perception developed by the staff that alters their own attitudes, behaviors, and even personalities.

This risking for change and openness with staff can be a frightening prospect for the leader and one not historically considered a part of the managerial role. Traditionally, it was the leader who was to have the ideas, the information, and the insights necessary to make most effective decisions. In a professional environment such as nursing, all participants can participate equally in discussions of issues, problems, and processes. The solution may come from any of the participants. This will change the role of the leader as the authority, the decision maker, and the director. In this situation, the manager will work to lead the process in as open a forum as possible in order to arrive at the most effective solution for all involved.

MANAGER ROLE ANXIETIES

As discussed in the two previous sections, much of what occurs in communications depends on individuals' openness, willingness, and freedom to be accepting and to facilitate meaningful exchanges. Managers also have other areas of concern that can lead to fears and problems in responding fully to their role. Many of these needs are based on internally generated perceptions and responses to their own performance. Two anxieties that frequently are present but are not generally discussed in management texts involve these specific issues. Zaleznik has done much work on the inner conflict that individuals bring to the role of management.[9] He identifies the two primary conflicts as (1) status anxiety, which he defines as the internal dilemma experienced by those in key management positions and (2) competition anxiety—the feelings generated in the leader as she grows in her management role.

Status Anxiety

Status anxiety relates to the individual's achievement and success orientation and recognition at work. In the context of that recognition, the individual may realize suddenly that as manager, she now has a significantly different relationship with her associates. Her prior peer relationships have changed into a subordinate/ superior interaction, regardless of the manager's efforts to diminish that perception. As a result, professional peers appear cautious, distant, and constrained in the give-and-take exchanges that once were a part of the work relationship. It is at this point that managers develop status anxiety. They become torn between the responsibility and authority required of the job and the fundamental urge and need to be liked and wanted by the group.

A fundamental principle is operating here. When the manager has control and influence over the actions of others by virtue of her position, the relationship tends to change from one of friendly association to one of distance, perhaps respect, but not one that is filled initially with warmth, friendliness, and a sense of closeness. These perceptual difficulties are a challenge to be overcome.

Managers can overcome some of the difference by playing down the authority and playing up likeability by acting as the nice guy. This status stripping, in which the individual attempts to reduce the impact of status and authority, is a process frequently undertaken by new managers. The symptoms of this kind of reaction can be openness, an egalitarian or "I'm just like you" attitude, and a host of others seeking to make roles seem parallel, not boss vs. bossed.

In the short run, the manager becomes aware of another insidious aspect of her dilemma: trying to remove the distancing social elements does not always work because it affects the ability to be effective in the workplace. This diminishes the respect and acceptance of the manager as leader and coordinator, and the group tends to develop negative feelings. As a result, the manager traps herself by her own behavior in a situation that she may find difficult to escape because she has lost or reduced the respect and acceptance needed in her role by her efforts to be considered "one of the girls."

Status anxiety also is created by the other side of her role—her proximity to the senior executive levels and her need to establish relationships and trust with that group. In this position, she seeks to achieve and, to the extent possible, to be consistent with the expectations and motivations of her superiors. As a result, the nurse manager becomes caught in a "Catch-22" situation: her sense of obligation to fulfill the goals of the organization as perceived through senior management vs. her inability to communicate the role effectively to the professional staff because she sees herself as one of that group. The expectations in both roles become confused, and as a result, her effectiveness is diminished.

Here, she has two problems—personal frustration and role ineffectiveness. At question is her ability to function for the organization and for the professional staff.

The solution lies in understanding clearly the expectations and responsibilities of the dual role and meeting the needs of both constituencies she must recognize where her supports are and how she can develop her relationships to support her role as a manager and as a person. The manager will need to analyze the strengths and the constraints of her own personality, acknowledge where she is strong and where she needs development, and take steps to address the results. This will help her understand the role as she perceives it and as it is perceived by those she reports to and those who report to her.

One of the most important aspects of establishing acceptable expectations is communicating well with both superiors and with professional peers. Discussing and resolving the conflicts between her perceptions and those of others can do much to reduce or eliminate role and status conflicts. Here again, an honest and unjudging attempt to understand her role and relationships, and effectively communicating that to all who participate with her, can play a major part in meaningful growth and effectiveness as a manager.

Competition Anxiety

Internal conflict also is created by competition anxiety. Many of the characteristics of this anxiety relate to those involved in status anxiety. However, its source is quite different.

The role of nurse manager is demanding, new, and strange to the practitioner who assumes it. The rules that govern practice behavior do not always translate 100 percent to management behavior. As a result, the new manager has worries over succeeding and fear of failure. New managers often are short on the self-esteem that comes from years of experience and education in the role. Worries and fears gradually either grow or diminish, depending on the individual's ability and development.

The role can produce many dilemmas:

- There can be a lack of resolution about the individual's comfort with the role.
- There can be a feeling of helplessness in her ability to control the circumstances that influence the role.
- There can be strong feelings within the individual that the demands of the role are too great, that the obligations are not always fair, and that much of the needed personal satisfaction cannot be found in the position.
- There can be a lack of a full understanding of what the role involves, what it means, and how it will be identified in terms of expectations.

These internal anxieties and conflicts remain with the individual regardless of what direction the role takes and will continue to affect the manager's activities and abilities. They do not disappear unless dealt with.

These and other inner conflicts are important issues that often are a part of the manager's development. She must recognize that much of management involves relating with others, as noted earlier. If she is to relate effectively, communicate consistently and clearly, and participate fully in the goals and objectives of the institution and the profession, she must develop a high level of self-understanding. She must recognize factors that facilitate interaction and those that constrain her personal effectiveness. The ability to identify inner conflicts and to develop new strategies to manage them can help the nurse manager to have a better understanding of her needs as an individual and as a leader. This is as important as the ability to perform the technical tasks. Understanding her own response to her situation in management role is an important part of assessing her needs as an individual and her expression of herself as a manager.

Diversity of Motivations

Zaleznik identifies some guidelines that provide a rational basis that can assist the nurse manager in this self-assessment.[10] The nurse manager must acknowledge that she has a number of diverse motivations that influence her response and actions. She should recognize that everyone would like to believe that the individual's inner world contains only things that are socially positive and that relate to high-level drives and wishes. However, that is not true.

Everyone has both positive and negative motivations and feelings. Feelings of jealousy, competition, anger, hatred, inferiority, insecurity, and rebellion all are part of the emotional package in everyone. The manager's self-assessment must recognize that those characteristics are part of her makeup and must understand their influence in her decisions, actions, and responses. She must be aware of how she reacts in various situations and what is influencing such reactions; this can provide an opportunity to incorporate more flexibility and variability in her thinking and responding.

In order to apply these processes, the manager must be fully aware of their influence on her actions. A close understanding of self, a sense of being in touch with one's self, and the influence of all the internal variables provide a better opportunity to work toward effectiveness as an individual and as a manager. Such understanding is not an option for effective management—it is essential.

Strong Sense of Self

The nurse manager also must clearly identify and establish a firm sense of herself, a strong self-identity. She should take time to articulate for herself, in writing if necessary, how she perceives herself in relation to her own goals and objectives and to her world as a manager. The nurse manager should recognize when she cannot be all things to all people, including herself, but that she has various characteristics, strengths, weaknesses, successes, and failures that are part of the person she is. She must identify their potential in developing some sense of self. Identification of who she is as a person and who she is not can help her recognize the kind and quality of the relationship she has with herself and, ultimately, with others in management.

Establishing identity prevents the nurse manager from being influenced in a way that is inconsistent with her particular self-understanding and behavior pattern. It allows her not to be subject solely to the perceptions of others. While others' opinions should have some effect on her consideration of her sense of self, she should not build that self-concept solely upon the perceptions of others. This also gives her a strong point of reference for measuring her behavior and its outcomes and her effectiveness in the role.

One of the factors that can develop out of this firm sense of self is a basis of understanding of what is necessary to assist her in growing and making changes. This will help her function as an individual and as a manager. Having a firm sense of where one is can give the individual a strong start on the road to expanding awareness and effectiveness and providing opportunity for making changes.

Consistency and Continuity

The nurse manager must recognize that it is important to maintain consistency and continuity in her responses to herself and to her work situation. While situations may require some variations in response, there should be a basic consistency. The nurse manager must be flexible in how she handles both role and process and be consistent with her personability.

However, some basic elements of her behavior should be evident both to herself and to those with whom she works. Wide variations in behavior breed distrust and produce a lack of continuity in the workplace. Where there is not trust, there is no commitment; where there is no commitment, there is no effectiveness. Trust and commitment can be assured if others can rely on the manager to be fair, consistent, and dependable within the context of her personal style and relationship with those with whom she works.

Activities and Relationships

The nurse manager must exhibit care in selecting activities and relationships. One of the most important things she can do for herself is to recognize that she cannot be all things to all people and therefore should develop her trusts and her relationships carefully to reflect her own needs and, of course, those of fellow workers. She must guard against a willingness to be involved in everything in the workplace. She must be selective in what she undertakes or she will be overwhelmed.

This does not mean that she cannot develop communication strategies with all those with whom she works; however, she must be careful in establishing personal relationships so that they do not interfere with the achievement of goals of those in her area of accountability. The personal relationships may involve peers at the same level of professional responsibility.

A good guide to the effectiveness of her associations with others is her ability to say ''no'' without a loss of relationship or of self-esteem; if she cannot do that, she should reexamine the nature and quality of the relationship.

Effective Communications

Another area involves the absolute necessity of learning to communicate effectively. Much has been said here about communication, with emphasis on the communication relationship. It obviously is a major key to the effectiveness of this role. Continued attention and development to this particular skill will be mandatory if the nurse is to be a successful manager.

Life Patterns

A final area of concern is the necessity of the nurse manager to be able to identify and to live within a life pattern that works for her. Energy is not constant. All of life represents rhythmic patterns alternating between differing levels of energy response: daily work patterns, biological patterns, sleep patterns, and a host of others. These cycles are different in all individuals. Recognition of these cycles should be an integral part of the individual's assessment of self. Self-understanding is vital to the success of fully meeting the needs of both the organization and those who serve in it. Developing skills in recognizing self-generated processes that influence the manager's expression of her role will help clarify her perception of self and its application in the workplace.

ESSENTIAL SELF-SKILLS FOR THE MANAGER

Some factors that relate to the management of self are not often found in nursing management texts. Much of what is missing in managers and in the management role involve the individual's sense of self and the feeling of control over her own circumstances. If the nurse manager can influence and guide others in professional and personal growth and meet the goals of the organization, some issues related to her own self-perception must be clarified. Some of the following items may appear simplistic and rather basic to understanding the role of management. However, a lack of understanding of, and insight into, these characteristics often makes the difference between a successful and unsuccessful manager. Simplistic or not, they are basic tenets of the individual's mode of operation and necessary prerequisites to undertaking the role of manager.

Sole Responsibility for One's Own Life

When people are very small and in a dependent situation, and before they are able to make any meaningful decisions about their lives and their future, they are shaped and influenced by their environment. That early environment is a part of the matrix that molds and formulates the basic parameters within which people experience their lives.

As people grow, they are influenced more strongly by the key individuals they identify with—parents, teachers, other individuals, and friends. Family experiences may be healthy and productive, or they may not be. Relationships with others sometimes are positive and life generating; sometimes they are not. Many of those experiences, good or bad, influence the kinds of choices people will make as individuals and as leaders. They also will help identify the kinds of needs that individuals carry with them in exercising the leadership role.

As people begin to develop as individuals and, ultimately, as leaders, they must exert some influence over the matrix that has formed their personal adaptation to life. Openness and flexibility in self-assessment and insights constitute important components in developing strengths and in understanding roles and responsibilities.

People should not be limited by those early life influences that created the set of adult behaviors. People as individuals have the opportunity, if they are open and flexible, to make changes in those basic sets and to alter their life processes in such a way that they can benefit and grow. The important characteristic is the attitude brought to that experience. Attitude is vital in altering the basic perceptions needed to create or deal with new experiences.

In this context, the role of the nurse manager will demand a great deal of responsiveness and openness to new insights in order to provide a creative framework and opportunity for her professional nursing peers to grow also. This is a shared responsibility with the work group, with implications for the outcome of work. Insight into this process of self-development will provide further skills in helping others as individuals and in groups to develop and manage their own environment.

Understanding and Overcoming Fears

The nurse manager working closely with professional peers requires a high degree of courage and willingness to undertake the risks of growth and change. Many people have had experiences and exposure to fear-creating circumstances and carry those fears (of whatever degree) throughout their lives.

Fear obviously serves a purpose. It is a protection, it warns against danger, and it provides an opportunity for immediate response. Total fearlessness is total foolishness. Somebody who is totally fearless can expect a relatively short life. But much of fear is inappropriate and dangerous. It stands in the way of the individual's growth, change, and renewal. Fear can destroy love, it can create failure on the job, it can interfere with the ability to relate with others. Relationships with others sometimes reflect individuals' basic fearful experiences.

The nurse manager who wants to provide leadership and to interact closely with others must have basic security and trust. She must have courage in conquering fears that interfere with relationships and with risk taking. Emotionally healthy persons, when they have learned to cope with fear, can help others grow.

Many studies have shown that people who are cautious, operate out of fear, and are afraid to take the risks necessary to carry out even the basic components of their job, tend to be afraid of life itself.[11,12] Since life is essentially a struggle to grow and become whole, living in the context of one's fears prevents the individual from participating fully in the creative enterprises that cause growth and productive change. Persons who live in the context of those fears are not likely to be good leaders or to succeed in enhancing the organization.

Much of the energy and knowledge necessary to provide leadership as a nurse manager can be undercut by internal fears that may inhibit growth. The manager must understand personal fear and its influence on herself as an individual. She must develop strategies for overcoming the fears or for taking the risks that will advance her beyond those fears in developing herself and meeting her own needs.

As in anything important it is vital to get to know the source of fear. Fear is often not directly exhibited. It can be covered under a whole host of other emotions, feelings, and expressions: anger, depression, moodiness, passive-aggressive behavior, kindness, etc. Taking time to assess how the nurse manager is feeling in any given situation and getting to the roots of the feeling is a major aid in getting in touch with and dealing with emotional bases of fear. Sometimes it is individuals or situations that engender feelings of fear in the manager. These may relate to past situations or people who created fear feelings in the nurse when she was either young or in a very dependent position. Stepping out of the present situation and attempting to recall the original source of her fear feelings helps the manager get through and past them so they have less impact on her current and future feelings and behavior.

Fear limits. Overwhelming fear limits not only the individual but those she leads. Coming to terms with fears of inadequacy, role limitation, relationship, and self-identity provide the base line for the nurse manager in her behavior for both herself and the people with whom she works.

Humor and the Ability to Laugh

These two gifts are essential for getting through life and most especially for dealing with the role of nursing manager. A sense of humor actually reflects a sense of proportion. The individual who can express humor in relationship to herself and her role clearly maintains a fair and balanced view of that role. Obviously, this does not suggest that an individual always look at the world from the realm of the comic. Those types abound and are a threat to maturity and growth in the workplace. Rather, the desired individual is one who can see humor in her dilemmas and can recognize aspects of the role that are humorous.

People who are emotionally healthy and have a strong sense of proportion generally are cheerful. Those who are balanced and involved in their lives in ways that they want express this cheer in their relationships. They tend to be positive and oriented to things that facilitate creativity and positive change. Usually these individuals are highly realistic. They recognize that almost everything that goes on around them is not funny but they also do not permit those negative influences to dominate or overwhelm.

Ralph Waldo Emerson said health is a condition of wisdom and is demonstrated by the individual's cheerfulness. Kay Underhill wrote that a sense of humor is a sense of proportion. Samuel Butler once said that a sense of humor keen enough to show a man his own absurdities as well as those of others will keep a man from the commission of all sins, or nearly all, save those that are worth committing. Clearly, he was not troubled with humorlessness.

There also is something to be said for the health of laughter and of sharing. Laughter is an opportunity to break down barriers, to open doors, to share responsiveness with others, and to express the collective human condition. It is important to be able to look at things in light of the effect and impact they may have on the individual. A part of that involves the humorous processes and the absurdities that confront nurse managers in their jobs.

There is a time for everyone to laugh. There also is a time when laughter is not appropriate. The nurse manager knows how to balance the two. First and foremost, of course, she must participate seriously in meeting the goals and objectives of the profession and the organization, but there should be room for the full range of human responses, including humor. The nurse manager who can recognize these processes and laugh at herself, at situations, and at others can stimulate trust, commitment, and a sense of communion with those with whom she works.

Reaching Out and Touching

Among one of the more difficult things to overcome in society are the strategies people develop for distancing themselves from each other. The strategies seem to be almost culturally mandated. Certain formal relationships and some kinds of traditional introductory and greeting mechanisms actually provide superficial opportunities for isolating persons from each other. Those who breach those barriers successfully and reach a depth of sensitivity and relationship that is inspiring and supportive are individuals others look to with feelings of warmth, closeness, and humanness.

Individuals who can reach past those social barriers have done so as a part of their attempt to establish meaningful and human relationships with others. The fact that such individuals are rare is an indication of the degree to which society submerges this process. One of the characteristics in a nurse manager that others appreciate is her ability to reach beyond herself and to connect meaningfully with those others. One way in which this is done most successfully is in touching, reaching out, in a special way, physically and emotionally.

People are acculturated away from touching, believing that that should be reserved for significant intimacies. They all are human, however, and touching is one way of expressing closeness in relationships with each other. The ability to touch in a gentle and meaningful way represents to both those touching and those being touched the character of human bonding. This reaching out results in a sense of joining, of relationship—familiarity juxtaposed with human solidarity that helps to banish fear, isolation, and a sense of separation from each other. If these elements are among the manager's basic characteristics, many of the kinds of behaviors that result from people's isolation can be avoided and, when present, often can be overcome.

Every individual has a desire to be a part of her community. People need involvement, commitment, social affiliation. Traits that can help bridge the gap among individuals, including the use of touch, can break down some of the barriers that prevent them from working together, sharing, or interacting. Certainly, the workplace is one of the environments where this kind of relationship, aided by touching, is necessary to meet the needs of individuals as well as of the entire group. In nursing, especially, the willingness and ability to touch should be valued highly, not only in a therapeutic sense with patients but also among nurses committed to maximizing the patient's own internal resources for healing.

Taking Time Out to Get Away

Every individual in her effort to become whole and to understand life and relationships with others needs to spend some time alone. Aloneness is a time of silence and quiet, away from the normal routine and the individuals involved in the circumstances and relationships of one's life. In the professional environment, the need for growth, creativity, insight, involvement, and interaction are essential to the fulfillment of work. Because of the strong demands of such a working environment, and its human intensiveness, the nurse manager must expect to take time away. Time provided by the institution for them to be away could be one of its best investments in its management individuals. Self-renewal is needed by the individual (and the hospital) so she can reaffirm and renew herself and fight off the stagnation that inevitably comes from any daily routine.

The nurse manager also must recognize that she is responsible for meeting her own needs. She must set aside time to give herself the attention she needs. She will be effective for others in the workplace to the extent that she deals effectively with her own needs. The manager can reach out to others successfully when she has learned how to address her own needs as a person and as a manager.[13]

As people get older (it does not have to be very old), they tend to become fixed and staid in their ideas, thoughts, and actions. They are not as able to bend with the winds of change. They begin to oppose almost anything that is different and new, and when changes are essential they are slow to respond. They fail to act in a timely manner or to be active in undertaking changes.

Those in nursing frequently isolate themselves in their own institutions. This behavior is called the "this is how we do things here" syndrome. It is dangerous, because it indicates a practice that may be limited unnecessarily, even arbitrarily. Such practices lose perspective and may be inopportune or even inappropriate. Nurse managers need to be able to indicate in their own work a flexibility, creativity, freshness, and renewed sense of understanding and creativity.

Hints of stagnation and lack of self-renewal often can be found in the answers to these questions:

- How excited are we as individuals?
- How many times have we changed the character of our activity during the past year?
- How do we feel about the work we are doing?
- How much time have we taken for ourselves, just to discuss with ourselves our relationship with ourselves, our values, our family, and our work?
- How much of what we do is routine?
- How much time do we spend with the creative, with the insightful, with the generative, and with the new?

If nurse managers find themselves sitting comfortably in the context of the status quo and the system, perhaps it is time to rethink their roles, their positions, and, most importantly, themselves.

The Need for Thinking Well

Finally, one of the most important aspects of self-assessment and development is the way in which the nurse manager implements the thinking process and the time she takes for thinking. Obviously thinking must be a major component of the manager's role because that is the way new and creative responses to old and long-term problems and situations can be discovered and addressed. It also is a mechanism through which the nurse manager can begin to look to the future and to prepare for it before it reaches a crisis in the workplace. The way people think may influence the way they work.

It is difficult to believe that many of the great discoverers of history had no formal education or whose education seemingly was inadequate for the discoveries they made. Michael Faraday, the English physician noted for his work in electricity; James Clerk Maxwell, the Scottish physicist famed for his work in electricity and magnetism; Charles Darwin, Albert Einstein, Thomas Edison, and others had limited formal education in the areas in which they are considered geniuses. Their originality or selection of options clearly were not limited by their education. One of professionals' problems is that they become locked into the perceptions, values, and systems in which they are taught. The kind of thinking that takes advantage of other kinds of psychological and mental connections, often is "educated out" of them because the values and processes taught in a particular educational framework may not have included alternative values.

Nurse managers must develop the kind of thinking that does not operate within prescribed limits but goes beyond them. This can be described best as lateral thinking—moving laterally and unearthing new ideas from new (and old) sets of information. The creative thinker looks for new solutions by investigating new areas of study, rather than simply enlarging the established frame of reference. The best possible solution may come from outside that frame of reference and is applied creatively to the work or situation at issue.

Essential to developing lateral thinking skills is an immense curiosity for information and for processes that lie beyond the framework of one's own work. Being open and responsive to the ideas and thinking of others in the group can help this process. More importantly, however, the nurse manager should be willing and able to expose herself to information that may be outside her normal operating frame of reference. Availing herself of these kinds of opportunities will help develop one of the strongest assets the nursing manager can have.

FLEXIBILITY AND THE FUTURE

These and a host of other personal attributes are necessary in addressing the role of nurse manager. Much of what will occur will depend upon her relationship with herself, her perceptions, her ideas, her flexibility, and her creativity as an individual and as a nurse. Applied to her management position, these factors influence the quality and kind of relationships she establishes with her peers. They also will demonstrate the mechanisms she uses to resolve problems, seek solutions, and develop newer creative strategies.

With such preparation, the nurse manager is ready to confront her professional role and the environment in which she operates. If she cannot do this, she will have an extremely difficult time in addressing problems and concerns of her work group as well as of others with whom she works. Many of the failures in the management role and its problems in relationship to individuals and to professional nurses as a group relate to the nurse manager's inability to apply her skills. To be successful, she must be able to articulate her own needs, identify strategies to address her role, then develop the skills and abilities that translate that position to the work environment and to the other nursing professionals.

For the nurse manager of the future, the ability to understand herself and to incorporate self-assessment strategies into her role no longer will be optional. To the extent that she adapts these processes, she will benefit. The professional nurses with whom she works will benefit in their relationship to her. Finally, as in all nursing activity, those who are served—the patients—will benefit.

NOTES

1. Robert Ford, *The X-Y Scale* (New York: ATT Company, In-house Training Seminar, 1972).
2. Barron Harvey, "Increasing Employee Self-Control," *1980 Handbook for Group Facilitators* (San Diego: University Associates, Inc., 1980), 108–9.
3. William G. Ouchi, *Theory Z* (New York: Addison-Wesley Publishing Co., 1981), 137–164.
4. L.P. Coch and J.R.P. French, "Overcoming Resistance to Change," in *Group Dynamics Research & Theory*, eds. D. Cartwright and A. Zander (Evanston, Ill.: Row, Peterson, 1960).
5. Joseph Cargenis et al, "Difference Between Prounion and Procompany Employees," *Personnel Journal* 55, no. 9 (September 1976): 451–53.
6. Harry Levenson, *The Exceptional Executive* (Cambridge, Mass.: The Howard Press, 1971), 160–64.
7. Muriel James and Dorothy Jongewood, *Born to Win* (New York: Addison-Wesley Publishing Company, 1971).
8. Carl Rogers and F.J. Loethlisberger, "Barriers and Gateways to Communication," in *Executive Success: Making It In Management*, ed. Eliza Collins (New York: John Wiley & Sons, Inc., 1983), 42–48.
9. Abraham Zaleznik, "The Human Dilemma of Leadership," in *Executive Success: Making It In Management*, ed. Eliza Collins (New York: John Wiley & Sons, Inc., 1983), 214–25.
10. Ibid, 200–240.
11. Claude Steiner, *Scripts People Live* (New York: Grove Press, Inc., 1974).
12. Thomas Harris & Amy Harris, *Staying OK* (New York: Harper & Row Publishers, 1985), 71–133.
13. Earl Nightengale, *Insight* (Chicago: Nightengale Conant Company, 1984).

Creating a Professional Environment

Objectives for Chapter Four

Review the bureaucratic environment and its constraint on professional nursing practice.

Discuss the participatory approach and its compatibility with professional nursing values.

Outline the role of the nurse manager in helping to move the nursing organization from a bureaucratic to a participatory structure.

Identify the characteristics of the role and relationships that operate in a highly participative environment.

Consider the skills base of the role of the nurse manager in the workplace where participation is the management system.

Clarify some strategies for obtaining support from others in making changes that move to the participatory ''style'' of management.

Discuss the needs of the nursing staff and the best alternatives for meeting those needs using a participatory approach.

4

After the key concerns of developing the role of the manager and understanding that of the professional nurse in the institution, nurses must make a concerted effort to alter the structure of the nursing organization or unit so that the nursing workplace reflects the professional behaviors described earlier. Professional nurses cannot fulfill their functions if the workplace is designed in such a way that it interferes with their options and opportunities to participate fully with each other.

Nursing traditionally occurs in a highly bureaucratic environment, with certain basic rules and processes within which all components of the organization must function. The predominant processes relate to authority, responsibility, and the delineation of work and of outcomes. (Figure 4–1 outlines a centralized, bureaucratic institution.)

Within the bureaucracy, many conflicts arise that limit nursing practice. Bureaucracy demands a highly stratified system with a hierarchy of decisions that are made for the benefit and needs of the organization. It is in the context of this hierarchy of decisions that significant demands in nursing practice are in opposition to the structure of its own organization. Nursing needs a strong interactional and lateral structure if it is to function fully as a professional group. The bureaucracy, on the other hand, does not include the processes and practices that would permit a strengthening of lateral or parallel relationships and peer decision making by nurses.

BUREAUCRATIC AND OPERATIONAL CHANGES

Many bureaucratic changes in recent decades have decentralized organizations and assigned decision making to units at lower levels. This has spread the process

Figure 4–1 Centralized Organization

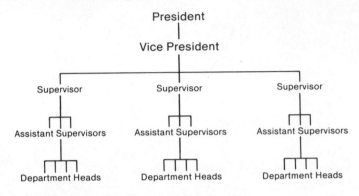

over a wider base but accountability, authority, and responsibility still are invested in individuals, designated by the organization as solely responsible for the decisions. This is most clearly shown by decentralized decision making structures. (See Figure 4–2.) That description of these individuals' roles and their placement in the organization differs fundamentally from the basic needs of the professional staff. This placement of individuals represents the institution's vertical structure, thus putting into place formal "up and down" communication and decision making. It differs significantly from the professional nurses' needs for lateral or horizontal communication strategies. Decentralizing management decision making reduces the vertical "layers" of management but does not essentially change the location of decision making. The nursing staff still does not become a partner in the management process that impacts on her clinical practice.

Figure 4–2 Decentralized Organization

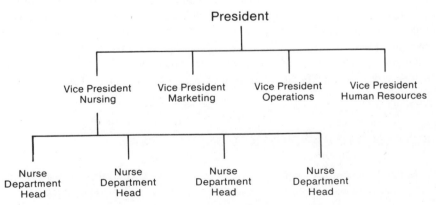

This is where the most difficulty arises in the organization. The professional need in nursing for collaboration, peer judgment, standards-based decision making, care flexibility, credentialing, and continuing education work in opposition to bureaucratic tendency toward highly structured policy, formal power mechanisms, authority-based decision making, and formalized organizational relationships. The bureaucratic organization favors form and order; professionals need less formality, more relationship, broader involvement in decisions and processes related to what they do.

The problem with consistency in process is emphasized by the differences in form. The bureaucratic structure uses the management system and its authority and control processes as the mechanism for initiating, maintaining, and assuring productive results. Professional nurses' responsibility is to assure that the basic tenets of practice are implemented properly. The profession is based on a scientific framework, guided by specific principles that delineate the self-established parameters of practice. Fitting those processes and requirements into the bureaucratic organizational framework has created a major operational conflict that often remains unresolved.

Most frequently, however, the bureaucracy takes precedence over the professional demands of nursing practice, reflecting how the institution values the interactions and relationships. As a result, since both the professional and bureaucratic structures cannot be equally predominant, one is subordinated to the other. In the case of nursing, its practice generally is subordinated to the bureaucratic administrative structure that controls nurses' activities in the institution.

This produces frequent conflict between nursing and the institution. The roles of the nurse manager and the hospital administrator often are too structured and directed to bridge that perceptual and operational gap. This produces major problems for the nurse manager caught between the way she is perceived by her staff peers and the organizational demands of the institution she represents.

This struggle places her in an awkward position. She is "first a nurse" and therefore has a professional mandate to assure that nursing practice is conducted appropriately in the institution. However, she is also a manager with a dual role of representing professional practice in a defined area yet operating within the process and trying to meet the expectations of the larger organization. While there have been many changes in organizational design in recent years, the basic structure remains essentially bureaucratic. Therefore, the role of the nurse manager is aligned essentially with bureaucratic imperatives.

The bureaucratic system seeks to provide environments that are stable and predictable. Max Weber in 1957 identified the following elements of a bureaucracy:

1. Its division of labor is based on functional specialization.
2. It has a well-defined hierarchy of authority.

3. It has a system of rules defining the rights and duties for each member of the organization.
4. It has a system of standard operating procedures for dealing with work situations.[1]

However, since then, significant changes have occurred both culturally and socially in the United States, altering the relationships, demands, needs, and technology of work and the format for governing it.

Because of the accelerating rate of change, much of work and environments in a highly technical age is unpredictable. Organizational stability through standard operating procedures and control concentrated in the organization's hierarchy no longer is sufficient to stimulate the creativity, energy, and drive that the modern elements of change require. The system of bureaucracy tends by its very structure and nature to respond slowly to those processes. Communication, information, and decision making need to be relatively fast, with immediate outcomes expected, but the bureaucratic framework in and of itself is slow, systematic, and highly structured and does not respond rapidly when it must act or adapt quickly. Often, the technology physicians require to maintain state of the art practice is available long before the hospital can obtain or utilize it. The need, demand, skill, desire, and finances may often be available before response or even anticipation can be determined.

In nursing practice, most of the decisions are made and actions taken in a relatively short time frame, and all facets of the practices and processes of the delivery of care are immediate. The variations among patients in the same illness category require different care responses, demonstrating the need for adaptability. The use of high technology and even more complex machines also influences how nurses practice. The stability of sameness, the uniformity of activity, and the structure of policy in a bureaucracy all are inadequate to meet the high variability essential to practice nursing appropriately today. Critical decisions must be made in extremely brief periods of time.

Change, adaptation, and restructuring in the organization also must be consistent with the needs of nursing practice in the modern health care environment. Nursing practice today is confronted with a magnitude and complexity of adjustment and change that goes beyond the ability of the traditional bureaucratic organization to cope with. The explosion of technical knowledge and its application to nursing practice also is well beyond the bureaucracy's ability to deal with it.

The inadequacy of bureaucracy to operate effectively with professionals should not be construed to mean that there has been no progress and that there is no fundamental value in bureaucratic structures. Where work demands a high level of structure and is routine and technically repetitious, and where close supervision of work must occur, the bureaucratic framework operates very effectively. In fact, in the case of product line production it may be the structure of preference. Where the work can be aligned to material production, where there is limited exposure and need for human interaction, intervention, and judgment, formalized processes can operate very effectively. Even here, however, the introduction of quality circles has indicated the need of the worker to be somehow invested in the work and relationships she enters into.[2]

The question is not whether bureaucracy will work. Regardless of its flaws, it does work. The major issues are: does it operate effectively? does it meet the real needs of the professional workplace? is there a more effective way to organize work and provide for the important relationships that professionals need to work to their maximum potential and make the contributions of which they are capable? Nurses have made it clear in a number of forums that it hasn't and doesn't work today.[3] Levels of dissatisfaction among nursing professionals at all levels of the nursing organization remain consistently high and very little in the traditional approach has been able to address this problem.

What nursing needs, therefore, is a different set of relationships and a structure to support those relationships. It must be unique and appropriate to the professional environment. The leader who provides this environment will be the nurse manager, who coordinates and integrates the process of nursing in the new framework.

There are a number of organizational systems that have been postulated for addressing a systems change to the current inadequate structures. These contain a high level of participatory elements and are directed specifically to managing and organizing the professional worker. These governance formats are worth further investigation by the reader.[4] It is not the intent of this book to pursue discussion of these systems. However, much of what is articulated in group process in this book is supported by such professional governance systems and the reader is encouraged to become familiar with these concepts.

THE NEW PARTICIPATORY STYLE

Nursing organizational dynamics depend on the ability of professionals to adapt to the variabilities of practice and to incorporate them into the organization. In a participatory organization, nurses regard their involvement in the process of delivery of care as equally as important as the outcome. An authority-based, hierarchical structure no longer is adequate to the needs of the participatory professional system.

The operating principles of a participatory organization have been developed by a number of writers since 1950.[5,6,7] Organizations of the future, especially those in which nursing practice will be a major component, will view the need for adaptability and broad-based decision making as an important element of their structure. The ultimate measure of these organizations' adaptability will be how they respond to the multitude of changes in the new environment. Bureaucratic organizations are controlled and highly structured; participatory organizations are flexible, open, and interact closely with the environment where people work. Communication strategies, with emphasis on feedback mechanisms, are a cornerstone for building these organizations.

The organization also must be responsive to the participants and the processes that seek to implement its goals. This will require recognition of the multitude of diverse values and motivations, the perspectives of the professional practitioners and their objectives, and the resources available for nursing practice.

In bureaucracy, most of this is determined in settings other than where nursing is practiced. Major decisions are made at the policy levels. In participatory organizations, policy and practice levels may not be different; in fact, those who practice nursing may also be responsible for establishing and maintaining the policies that support and guide that practice. The participatory organization encourages this process and develops mechanisms to support it; the bureaucratic organization is unable to do so fully.

One of the most important characteristics of a participatory system is the heavy demand for planning and involvement by all levels of the organization. The nurse manager changes from control agent and articulator of the hospital's direction on policy to one of facilitator and integrator. She manages the processes that occur at a staff level integrating them with those goals and purposes of the institution. In the bureaucratic organization, this usually would be done at the administrative level.

Essentially what occurs in highly participative environments is a change in the locus of control. Instead of developing a top-down structure, a participatory organization uses a bottom-up system. The bottom of the organization becomes its center. Rather than rigid hierarchical lines of control and responsibility, there are concentric patterns of facilitation of information, responsibility, and activity that flow freely through and within the organization rather than up and down the structure.

In the participatory organization, the nurse manager will find unity and coherence are valued. This entity is based on the relationships developed among individuals who participate in its construction. It promotes a sense of responsibility and awareness in individual positions and assigns them some accountability for fulfilling the organization's goals and objectives. This is consistent with the values of nursing practice insofar as individual accountability is a major component of the professional delineation of responsibilities.

Most of the components of the participatory organization are interdependent rather than rigidly hierarchical. This interdependency is recognized as part of the responsibility of each group in fulfilling the obligations of the organization. Internal responsiveness must assure that each of the elements has a collaborative relationship with the others and facilitates responsibility for fulfillment of the professional obligations of nursing.

The achievement of goals and objectives involves collaboration in their definition, design, structure, and implementation. This assumes that the nurse manager
is mature and evidences that maturity through her creativity, her attendance to her
own growth, her responsiveness to others, her acceptance of responsibility as a
nurse, and her full participation in the organization.

Need for Different Strategies

In examining her role in the context of creating a new organizational environment for professional practice, the nurse manager must recognize that this requires
strategies different from the traditional ones. She will have to consider several
factors in shifting strategies from bureaucratic to participatory processes.

The nurse manager must understand that there is a significant difference
between providing direction and working with a group that provides its own
direction. Since the group will assume some responsibility for decisions affecting
practice, the primary role of the leader (the nurse manager) will be to undertake
facilitating, rather than directing and authority, strategies. In so doing, she will
have to deal consistently with change strategies and processes.

Her emphasis will be on human relations rather than paper processes, creating
the climate for interaction and group dynamics. This will help in the transition
from an authoritarian to a participatory system. Since participation demands
human resource skills, they will be an essential trait of nurse managers. Integration
of knowledge and utilization of a wide variety of skills to accomplish work
objectives also will be necessary. Since knowledge is becoming infinitely more
valuable in the organizational structure, especially in nursing, the nurse manager
must know how to access knowledge base resources. She also should have access
to peer experts in other areas in the institution and use their resources and
information.

Honesty and trust will be essential to participation so the nurse manager will be
responsible for creating an environment in which they are the cornerstones. This
will involve essential components such as openness and responsiveness in information processes and strategies that facilitate group interaction and problem
solving. Honesty relates not only to the work itself but also to interactions and
issues dealing with the individuals in nursing.

The staff must participate actively in developing systems of shared setting of
goals and objectives and for their achievement. The nurse manager must establish
a program of individual and group goals. Her ability to develop the process of
setting and achieving goals will be a key characteristic of her role. Through this
process results can be evaluated.

In developing and using this skill, a number of tools are available to the nurse
manager that she should investigate as a part of determining the most appropriate
strategies she can implement, such as the Johari Window[8] and the Seashore[9]

expansion on use of the Johari Window for developing abilities to manage other people. Other valuable aids include Rotter's trust scale,[10] Deutsch's prisoner's dilemma matrix,[11] Jourard's Self-Disclosure Questionnaire,[12] and Mulford's intergroup assessment.[13] These and many others obtainable through any good library will enable the nurse manager to assess the organizational and relational constructs in her work group.

While the above tools are worth investigating and are included here to motivate the nurse manager to further investigate them, one of the best processes is to answer a series of goal-related questions:

- What is our present situation?
- Who here knows and cares about what we do?
- What are our current problems (perceived)?
- Where do we want to be?
- What are our current constraints?
- How will we get to where we want to be?
- What support and resources do we need?
- How will we know when we get where we are going?

The key in this process is to have an organized systematic plan for both determining your current status and the progress you want to make. This needs to be incorporated into all the staff-management processes that will be undertaken by the nursing unit. The questions are universal and can apply just as easily to practice as to management and organizational planning and goal-setting processes.

The Nurse Manager as Change Agent

An increasingly larger portion of the role of the nurse manager of the future will be devoted to helping and encouraging participants in making change. In today's high-tech era, change is constant for all participants in any work group. This is especially true for nurses, who are participating in a segment of society—health care—in which technology and innovation are second nature. Practicing nurses will be a part of that innovation and will play a major role in the implementation of new technologies in delivering patient care.

Newer technologies and processes will be at the heart of inherent organizational dynamics. The way organizations have operated traditionally will change radically to respond to the high-tech/high-touch needs that are evident as nursing moves toward the 21st century. The nurse manager must be able to integrate the human relations processes and the technological applications.

Since change will be a common characteristic of work, skills and insights in the management of the change process will become a basic element of the nurse manager's work. Practicing nurses always are dealing with the outcomes of change; in many cases in the future, they will be on the front lines of initiating change. The nurse manager must be able to pull together all of the resources, information, and systems necessary to ensure that the processes involved in change are carried out consistently and with strong organizational support.

This role of the nurse manager takes on broader implications than historically experienced. Many of the rewards found in the manager's role in the past have been attributable to the power, position, and opportunity to control events and situations. The decision making power and ability to influence the work of others helped make the role of manager a positive and personally rewarding experience. On the other hand it has also been most frustrating, especially for nurse managers. Frequently the nurse manager experiences a high degree of frustration because she feels more like a caretaker or parent than a manager. Nursing staff have become very dependent and in their dependency have expected more and more of the nurse manager. While this may fuel the ego needs of the manager, it does nothing to change the role of the practicing nurse or to improve her investment in her work and all that is associated with it: staffing, problem solving, attrition, overtime, and professional governance.

Professionals share in the governance process. Through a representative framework a professional practitioner expects to have played a role in all facets of decision making that has an impact on what she docs and how it gets done. Examples of this in other professions are the organized medical staff, bar associations, faculty governance, presbyterate governance, priests councils, etc. Governance, standards setting, quality assurance (QA), education, practice, peer relations, and social or association affiliations are all very much accepted as characteristics with which to judge professional behavior (see Figure 4–3).

A part of the assessment skills of the nurse manager must be devoted to determining how many of these professional characteristics actively operate in her nursing organization and on her own nursing unit. This assessment process must be objective and critical. It is clear that developing good assessment skills both in the context of the organization and with her peers is a basic and essential skill.

3 AREAS OF ASSESSMENT

There are three major areas of assessment the nurse manager must understand as a prerequisite to undertaking strategies to address the change process: self, other, and organization, including its systems.

Figure 4–3 Shared Governance Organization

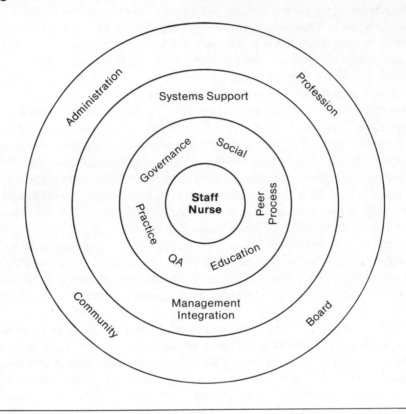

The Role of Self

In relationship to self, five major characteristics form the framework for her cognitive and operational processes:

1. style of management
2. readiness
3. management knowledge base
4. quality of relationships
5. personal power and ability to influence.

Style of Management

This obviously is an important consideration. In the 21st century nurse managers will need a different kind of style. While there is much debate as to whether there is one consistent style of management that works in all situations or whether management style should be adapted to each situation, there are some common characteristics useful to the nurse manager.

The range of styles appropriate to identifiable situations will be considerably narrowed in the future. This range will be narrowed for meaningful reasons. The reason for this is that participation obviously is the process of choice as professionals move into the 21st century. Styles that are supportive of participation will be important. If the nurse manager's role does not support the participatory processes, then that function obviously will fail to meet either the needs of the institution and of those responsible for nursing practice.

What styles are most successful? Those that meet the needs of group process and group interaction are important, particularly those that enhance the dynamics that this interaction demands. Unsuccessful styles will include those that are highly centralized, that focus solely on the role of the leader, and that emphasize directing, managing, and unilateral decision making. Indeed, these may be deleterious to the transition of the change process and in managing tomorrow's professionals.

The nurse manager must confront this conflict between styles if she is to be successful. Analyzing the elements of her personality and her character in relationship to others in the participatory framework will assist her in assessing the kinds of skills, abilities, and personal changes she will have to undertake. If she traditionally has assumed much of the responsibility of the work unit and of her professional peers, she may have to examine her own needs closely.

She must examine the needs the institution that has mandated her use of a directive style and whether that is the most appropriate mechanism to use. If her professional peers in nursing have become dependent upon her and expect her to operate on their behalf, making decisions that might rightfully belong to the group or to individual nurses, she may have to develop strategies to divest herself of those obligations. She will need to return those responsibilities to the practitioners as a part of her own obligation to her own role, accountabilities, and functions. Her ability to do this successfully, making clear the need and the process within which this transition will occur, will be a fundamental part of establishing her new role.

Personal issues she must clarify relate to functional items that have significant meaning in the participatory environment. Her ability, for example, to enter into meaningful dialogue with a wide variety of individuals is not an option, it is required. The nurse manager will have to communicate and make decisions with many individuals and groups who can contribute meaningfully to the provision of quality patient care.

Before undertaking these major steps of changing the work environment, the nurse manager must ask herself:

- What is my particular belief about the management role?
- How do I relate with other individuals in my family, with my spouse, and with people in the workplace?

- What do I believe about my relationship to nursing and to facilitating nursing practice?
- What do I believe about nurses' responsibility for issues that relate specifically to practice and to efforts that enhance practice?
- How much do I allow others to make a difference in regard to my learning processes and to influencing me in making changes in my management style?
- How do I integrate participant differences and facilitate the group process? Do I work well with groups? Do I participate fully in group endeavors? Am I a willing and energetic participant with others?
- Do I work alone? Do I feel better in working alone? Do I feel I have skills in working alone that I would not have working with or through others?
- Do I take direction well? Do I do what others ask me to do because they are my superiors or have more power than I do in the organization?
- Do I believe that professional practicing nurses are equal peers with me and therefore share an equal burden of responsibility?
- Can I let others in my work group play the predominant role and accept direction and guidance from them?

These and a host of related concerns are important considerations for the nurse manager, who must spend time in dealing with them. They can make a difference in whether she makes a successful transition from the traditional role to one that meets the demands of the new era.

Readiness for Growth and Change

Another important consideration is a sense of the readiness of the nurse manager to accept certain options and opportunities for growth and change. She must be able to assess her own readiness to make these changes if she is to provide leadership in the shift to consensus thinking and group problem solving.

The nurse manager first must be able to assess her own readiness, as an individual and as a manager, to move to a participatory environment and away from being director, controller, and boss. For some managers, this may require a long period of reflection and self-assessment, with some even making choices that will lead them out of the leadership role.

Whatever the outcome of this assessment process, it will lead her to make some important decisions. She may assume additional responsibilities in line with her changed role and that of the practicing nurses with whom she works. An assessment of the readiness for change also involves the nature of the relationships in the work area. The nurse manager must recognize that much of her success depends on the kind of relationships she has established. Certain preset expectations of her role have been provided by the staff. Certain behaviors have been accommodated by the manager. Certain conditions have existed in the environment, whether acceptable or not.

What happens when the leader begins to assess styles and readiness for the transition to participatory approaches? She begins to recognize that a whole new set of behaviors will have to be introduced, creating some dissonance in her relationships and in perceptions of her role in comparison with those of the nurses. These expectations must be addressed first by the manager and then by peers. The ability to begin this process and assess the appropriate timing for certain steps will be a key to a successful transition. The nurse manager must establish this for herself first, then work through the processes and transitional steps she has devised, leading others to accept new behaviors, new expectations, and new conditions of relationship.

Management Knowledge Base

All of this, of course, requires a major effort. Hospitals cannot select the nurse managers of the future solely from those who are most able to handle accelerating levels of clinical responsibility. Clinical responsibility, while an essential corollary to nursing management responsibility, does not provide a sufficient background of knowledge for managing nursing resources into the 21st century.

This new role demands some level of formal preparation, perhaps special academic training. It recognizes that there is a clear distinction between clinical and management processes, although there are elemental similarities. The strategies, activities, and energies in the management role have an entirely different focus. Management is not any more significant a role than is the clinical but it has a dramatic impact on the success of clinical practice. This distinction must be understood clearly.

The nurse manager must assess her skills and abilities and the degree to which she has accommodated the needs of her role. Managing professional workers demands a specific set of skills that contain elements of a management process to which she would not have been exposed as a clinical practitioner.

Special skills in specific processes other than those generally involved in the management process will be necessary for the nurse manager of the future. Some exposure to these skills, at least at a basic level (with potential for advanced exposure) will be essential. The following processes can provide her with a relatively broad basis of preparation:

1. motivation
2. delegation
3. change process elements
4. conflict management
5. stress management

6. group process
7. integrative problem solving
8. collective goal setting
9. planning methodologies
10. contracting skills.

These are a representative sample of processes involved in managing the transition to participation. Obviously, the nurse manager has been exposed to many of the more traditional skills but they must be readdressed in assuring success for the future.

Quality of Relationships

Along with these concerns comes the issue of the kinds and nature of the relationships the nurse manager establishes with the people with whom she must interact. Her professional peers must be able to perceive her in a context different from that traditionally accepted by institution-based nurses. The perception that the nurse manager should be responsible for taking care of all the issues related to the work group is perhaps inaccurate. This concept has been perpetuated by regarding the role of the nurse manager in the context of its caretaker elements. She traditionally has been looked upon as the central leader of the nursing organization and thus, in that function, responsible for both nursing practice and its management design.

This perception has been difficult to square with professional practice. What has emerged generally has been a dependent role for the practicing nurse and a superordinate role for the nurse manager. This strictly superior/subordinate relationship is not characteristic of professional peers nor is it generally successful in a truly professional environment.

The relationship between practitioner and manager must change in a participatory environment, requiring different kinds of perceptions, expectations, and behaviors by both. The professional nurse may need to be responsible for elements different from those she traditionally has assumed are part of her "turf." The nurse manager on the other hand also may have to give up some of her traditional activities. Changing such perceptions of role expectations will be an initial step in clearing the way for meaningful participatory strategies in the work unit. The nature and construct of the roles of the professional nurse and the nurse manager, and their relationship, must be a part of the dialogue between the two in establishing the new environment.

Initially, of course, no move to participatory management can be undertaken without some implementing individual or locus of action. The individual traditionally best prepared for this is the nurse manager. In the traditional hierarchal organization she is invested with the power and the authority to implement processes to meet the organization's goals. She thus should be the first to take steps in starting the transition. The professional nursing staff generally will not want to undertake the activities essential to the transition—indeed, it may not even know what will be involved. While it is the expectation in nursing that participatory systems will emerge, those who have been functioning in the traditional hierarchical framework may have neither the insights nor the abilities to cope with that transition. Therefore, the individual most responsible for initiating these changes will be the nurse manager.

Personal Power

In beginning to make these changes, the nurse manager will have to identify in her own role her kinds of power bases and personal influences. When she has begun the changes she herself must make in adapting to participation, she moves on to make necessary changes with the work group. She will have to make most of the initial efforts as the formal designated leader of the group. That clearly places the responsibility on the nurse manager. This can create some difficulties with staff perception of the nurse manager espousing participation but acting directive. She should be comfortable, however, in utilizing traditional power and authority in the first steps.

Depending upon her placement in the organization and her relationships with those to whom she reports, at the outset she may find a lack of support for her and what she is trying to accomplish. She may feel relatively isolated and unable to involve a number of significant resources without other management support. The movement toward participatory strategies should (indeed, must) be a corporate or institutional activity and should stimulate the organization to move toward higher levels of participation. However, this is not always possible, often depending upon the organization's situation. To win support, the nurse manager may have to face, perhaps even confront, those who provide organizational leadership and whose traditional kinds of roles and behaviors have become entrenched in the hierarchical environment.

STRATEGIES FOR CHANGE AND COMMITMENT

The nurse manager caught in the conflict between the needs she perceives for her work unit and the operational characteristics of the environment will have to use politically sensitive strategies with those at the top in initiating change before dealing directly with the practicing nurses. Obviously, clarifying her power base and her peer and superior relationships will be an important first step. Some of the following steps may be helpful in developing political acumen in and approaching her superiors before starting the change to participatory strategies. The nurse manager should:

1. Obtain significant and supportive literature on participatory strategies for professional workers; one good strategy might be to have superiors read this book, and others like it. (See also chapter notes.)
2. Discuss the need for change, opening up for consideration the needs of the professional nurses and the desire of practicing peers to participate more fully in nursing decisions.
3. Provide a clear and understandable framework within which to undertake change, showing how it is systematic and beneficial.
4. Give evidence of how change to participation is consistent with the organization's goals and offers an opportunity for the institution to obtain the most from its resources.
5. Discuss participation's potential impact on cost effectiveness, better nursing practices, higher levels of quality, and other issues.
6. Involve the superior in the planning and discussion of a transition to participation—in the formative stages of assessment, discussion, and review related to the appropriateness of the move.
7. Show how current strategies are limiting, prevent making the kinds of changes desire, and reduce opportunities for utilizing the nursing resource to its fullest potential.
8. Give evidence where possible that participation has resulted in success and that involvement of the nursing staff has made a difference in the process of delivering services to patients.

These and other strategies may help get the transition under way. Clarifying these roles and responsibilities assists the nurse manager in dealing with issues, concerns, or conflicts regarding participation with those with whom she works. If she can induce her superiors to participate fully in the processes that lead to full staff participation, they can be expected to make additional resources available to her.

The nurse manager next must analyze the role of the other individuals with whom she works. Clearly, her success in a participatory framework will be highly dependent on the nature of the relationships she has established with others, and vice versa. She must get some sense of where the others stand in relation to goal setting. The following six basic components in relationship to fulfilling the nursing commitment must be emphasized:

1. commitment
2. involvement
3. information
4. independence
5. understanding
6. organization.

Commitment

The professional nursing staff members' degree of commitment to the organization in regard to the roles provided for them is an important consideration in assessing their relationship with the nurse manager and the institution.

If their prevailing attitude is to put in the regular eight hours of work and then go home, that gives a clear indication of their relationship to the institution. If on the other hand they are more cooperative, less time-focused, have more opportunity for involvement, and accept additional responsibility, those factors are evidence of their commitment and involvement.

Levels of commitment should be measured primarily by the degree of involvement and the quality of interaction the professional staff members demonstrate in their relationship with the institution.

Involvement

If the environment and the relationships in a nursing work unit are positive, encouraging, and responsive and there is not only a professional role obligation but also an expectation of staff participation, levels of involvement should be higher. However, where there is dependency and a subordinate relationship both with the nurse manager and the institution, there may be limited involvement and communication between the professional staff and the institution.

Information

The level of information available to nurses is either a help or a constraint in the staff relationship to work and to the institution. Productivity depends upon the availability of adequate and meaningful information necessary to perform work. Some questions the nurse manager must ask in relation to information and professional staff members are:

1. Do they have the information they need?
2. Is the free flow of information a part of the information-generating process of the institution?
3. Can the individual professional nurse be heard and will there be organizational response to what she says?
4. Is there an opportunity for staff members to provide input for decisions by presenting a variety of viewpoints that may influence those decisions?
5. Is the feedback loop of the organization's information system adequate and does it provide the information nursing staff members seek?

The ability to manage and communicate appropriate information is a key characteristic of the nurse manager. The management of information in the future will become even more central to the success of the organization. Since high technology makes information available at a faster rate and a higher level, the ability to respond, to manage, to communicate and to make judgments based on that information will be an important skill not only for the manager but also for nursing staff members. This will help them make judgments about the quality and meaningfulness of that information, then take action based upon the feedback they receive.

Independence

Nursing staff members must get some sense or feel for the independence that being professionals generates. It is inappropriate and meaningless to identify as a professional any individual who does not demonstrate some of the characteristics of that role and show them in her work. One of the key characteristics of the individual nurse is the ability to feel independent of some and, in relation to others, interdependent. When this is missing, the dissonance between reality and perception causes the nurse automatically to discount her own belief about the professional role. To the extent that the individual nurse has a sense of both her independence and her interdependence, she will begin to evidence her belief through her behavior. The nurse manager will have an interacting and working relationship with the professional who has a sense of her professional character that is different from the nurse who does not.

Understanding

One of the most important relationships in the workplace is that based on understanding. This is not just understanding as to the expectations of one's role and the values and processes of the workplace; rather, it is an understanding of nurses' role in meeting goals and the way in which every participant in the organization plays a part in meeting collective objectives. Keeping the organization's goals and objectives at the management level limits nurses' ability to carry them out.

Often the goals and objectives may be developed at the wrong place in the organization. Aside from trustee policy goals, objectives should be initiated in the workplace itself. In the case of nursing objectives, since the practitioners are close to the realities of patient care, they should play the largest initial role. If the professional staff has participated fully, the expectations and processes for meeting objectives will be well understood.

The relationship among the objectives, the work, and the participants is determined by the degree of interaction of these components. The closer the relationship, the more the involvement. The more ownership provided, the more opportunity for productivity and completion of the objectives. The more the objectives have been formulated elsewhere, the less demand for understanding and involvement, the less commitment and opportunity for achieving desired results.

Understanding these relationships will provide a better opportunity for achievement of whatever goals are set. The role of the nurse manager centers strongly on the need for obtaining and maintaining high levels of understanding.

The Nursing Organization

The final consideration in this series looking at the prerequisites for change is the nursing organization itself. The people there cannot operate in isolation; the organization has obligations to provide opportunities for them so they can represent its best interests, perform its work, and commit themselves fully to their own responsibilities. Earlier, the need for professionals to be involved and to sense their commitment to their work was analyzed; there also is a need for the organization to provide a framework in which that professional commitment can be implemented.

PROFESSIONAL PRACTICE FRAMEWORK

The framework for professional practice obviously is different from that required for vocational work. Because the hospital environment demands a unique set of variables and relationships, certain kinds of preexisting conditions and processes must be available. Five key issues are involved:

1. freedom
2. support
3. clear expectations
4. appropriate resources
5. open organizational climate.

Freedom

As noted earlier, the professional nurse must be able to practice in the context of open information, interdependence, and understanding. The commitment and involvement that result provide her an opportunity to fully exercise the obligations of her role. This relates to the freedom necessary in the organization to permit its participants to function effectively.

This freedom has not always been apparent or even addressed consistently and universally in most institutions. Bureaucratic organizations allow only limited freedom; however, in a professional organization where lateral relationships and interactional elements are more important, a different kind of freedom must exist.

The practitioners must sense the freedom that comes with their expectation for full participation. This creates expectations for commitment by both the management and the professionals. Management's role in this context is to provide and maintain an environment that assures a sense of freedom to communicate. The organization has an obligation to provide certain strategies to assure that freedom will not be violated by arbitrary and rigorous controls that interfere with nurses' ability to interact with the institution, its staff members, and the patients they serve.

An environment that is free is one that does not permit retribution. It does not have fear of sharing information and viewpoints. It uses consensus decision-making strategies. It involves all individuals to their highest level of competence in their role in the institution and in decisions that affect them. It limits emphasis on status and stresses role identification. It understands the basic human needs for a sense of belonging, sharing, and interacting.

The institution that supports the professional practice of nursing has these characteristics as a basic component of the organizational system. They are basic components in the work environment that stimulate creativity and professional expressions. Arbitrariness, sectionalism, and authoritarianism are resisted. An open organization is less structured, less definitive, and less formal in its structural relationships. Accountability, role, communication, interaction, and consensus decision-making strategies all are characteristics of the open structure.

Support

This kind of an environment needs a sense of support and of identification of the professional nurse with her peers and with the leaders of the organization. Because most work groups are interdependent and socially communal in nature, they reflect the interactional needs of their members and the encouragement that comes from organizational support of strategies, systems, and structures that enhance relationships. These factors are important to workers' security.

Obviously, there is a higher level of need for security, trust, responsiveness, and care in an open organization than in a closed one. Open organizations are based on beliefs in the basic value, commitment, and involvement of all those in the work group. Closed organizations do not believe that individuals want to participate, are capable of involvement, are committed, or are concerned with the institution's needs. Because of the difference in focus and the variety of behaviors, including a wide latitude for input and involvement, the open organization has a stronger need for the communication and support of the professional leadership group.

Expectations

The expectations of the work environment must clearly reflect the kinds of characteristics that an open, highly participatory organization would have, especially when considered in the professional nursing context. Professional nurses must be able to relate to each other as peers from a base that is research oriented and utilizes the knowledge and science bases of their practice as the foundation for making decisions. Nursing process strategies and decision-making systems are integrated into the behavioral expectations of the professional environment. In the workplace, as shown by its structure and its leadership track, the nurses' behaviors reflect the expectations of the environment.

If the professional nurse is not willing to participate fully, to take responsibility for decision making, to define problems, to seek solutions, to take responsibility for her own practice, to be able to join in peer relationships, interactional communication, and patient care decisions, then she is refusing to reflect the basic needs of the organization of which she is a part. Expectation must be founded in these factors. If the environment supports and provides opportunities for professional practice, then the obligation of the nurse is to truly practice and fully participate. The institution should expect every nurse will fully implement all aspects of practice and its attendant behaviors.

When the nurses are operating as professionals and the environment is supportive of the independence and structure necessary to ensure involvement of nurses, then a change in expectations should be evidenced. The internally generated motivation that is a part of human growth and development when allowed freedom to develop will result in a stronger degree of commitment by nursing staff (see Figure 4–4).

Resources

None of the work of nursing can be done unless the appropriate resources are provided. Since the work in nursing is primarily care of patients, the resources for that process should be assured. The organizational structure, through its systematic approach to providing resources, should include processes that indicate such supports are indeed available.

The practicing nurse must play a role in determining whether the resource support is or is not adequate. However, she does not do this alone. The systems available to management should provide sufficient data to indicate whether the organization's supports are appropriate or need review and perhaps supplementing or changing. The systems that are developed to assess, utilize, and alter resources

Figure 4–4 Professional Role Characteristics

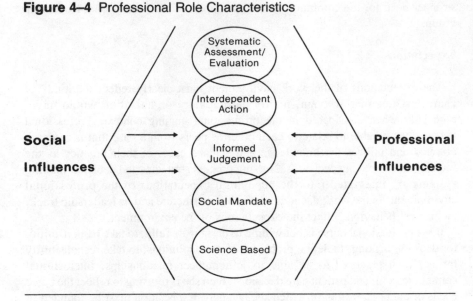

must be totally responsive to the individuals who use them. Therefore, they must involve the decision-making processes that the practicing nurse uses in her delivery of patient care. The opportunity for her to do so must be built into the process the organization provides to make systems assessments, implement programs, and evaluate their outcomes.

Climate

Finally, there must be a sense of security that the systems, freedoms, opportunities, and obligations will not be removed or changed arbitrarily without the involvement of the individuals upon whom they have the greatest impact. In a professional structure, the nurse should participate and play a role in defining rules, regulations, processes, practices, and behaviors. If the nurse has been so involved, then obviously her role must be supported in any change that might ensue.

When changes are made, they should be rational, meaningful, and well understood by those upon whom they will have the greatest impact. Since here again the professional nurse will be involved, the communication strategies and structures that will facilitate implementation of the changes will be highly dependent upon her participation. Once a professional environment has been structured, the systems and processes that maintain it and provide opportunities for alterations and adjustments must be related closely to the overall expectations of all those who operate within it. Consistency in approach and stable management of the environment will be essential to maintaining trust and to assuring that it achieves its objectives. That continuing framework of trust will be key to the open organization's continued success.[14]

It should be understood that thorough assessment and examination of individual roles and the institution's commitment are prerequisites to the management of change toward a more professional context. It is true that the demands of a professional organization and the method of operating in it are different from the traditional ones. In traditional, hierarchical structures, a careful examination of these components is an important factor in changing to more participatory systems. Full discussion at a number of levels in the organization will have to be undertaken before utilizing strategies to facilitate professional nurses' interaction and involvement with peers, the institution, and the patients they serve.

THE NURSE MANAGER'S NEW ROLE IN CHANGE

In a participatory organization, in stimulating growth and change, management undertakes a different process from that in traditional bureaucratic organizational structures, as noted earlier. Much more encouraging, interacting, and group processes are involved in the participatory environment. The ability of the nurse manager to lead in areas that enhance the roles of all participants will be important, so developing the skills and abilities to do so will be a clear prerequisite to its success.

The key difference between the manager's traditional and new roles relates primarily to style of operation and the basis of influence, rather than the function of director. The manager must be able to lead and support developmental mechanisms to introduce change into the structure and processes of the organization. With her peers she also must be able to maintain balance between the stability provided by the institution's structure and the temporary instability of the transition.

The nurse manager as change agent must be able to diagnose her environment, conditions, situations, and influences that work to support or to interfere with her role. She also must be able to recognize the need for and use additional resources inside and outside her sphere of influence.

It is important that the nurse manager recognize that in a participatory organization she initiates change from her position of power and authority, using her role as a leader of the work group, helping it achieve its goals. There often are performance conflicts in each of these elements, especially in relation to change. She then should reflect more her role of providing leadership in the change than in changing her own role.

The nurse manager must have a fairly broad and thorough knowledge of how to implement change, including the use of additional resources, other persons familiar with components of the process.[15] As change agent she may need to reflect a set of behaviors different from those traditionally identified with the nurse manager role:

1. She will need to be the link between the organization's goals and objectives and the participants who will carry them out.
2. She will be a resource to those involved in the decision-making process.
3. She will define and outline the planning processes essential to complete the work of the organization.
4. She will be a stimulus to information gathering and to assessment of the varying components of change.
5. She will be a continuing catalyst and energizer for maintaining the change momentum.
6. She will assess the varying changes in the demand and flow of components of the process.
7. She will be sensitive to the impact of change events on individuals and on the work group as a whole.
8. She will be a communication link between the work group and the other individuals involved in the change process.
9. She will be a conflict identifier, mediator, and resolution facilitator.
10. She will be a stimulator of discussion, identifying new and creative ways to move the process forward.
11. She will be a facilitator of problem-solving strategies when difficulties arise in advancing the changes.

EFFECT OF TRADITIONAL PROCESSES

The nurse manager similarly must recognize that certain traditional kinds of behaviors do not work well in a participatory workplace. Although those behaviors are identified in what can be called rational processes, they do not necessarily produce the kinds of outcomes anticipated initially. Bureaucratic behaviors also tend to put a lower value on the human and interactive characteristics essential to enhancing the humanistic aspects of the workplace that will be necessary in high-tech environments of the future.

A major concern in creating a participatory environment thus involves the traditional processes that are solely product oriented. The nurse manager, in developing such humanistic systems in a health service organization, focuses on consumer values, needs, and wants and the processes associated with obtaining them. The use of objective processes divorced from the human element does not necessarily produce the best results in terms of meeting consumer needs. Since satisfaction, health, and wellness are subjective as well as objective elements, it is necessary to address the parts of the process that support the subjective factors. Dependence upon rational approaches, using only objective systems and scientific approaches to solving problems and making change, may not be consistent with the real needs of the environment.

One of the problems that develops in highly analytical, objective processes is an almost obsessive focus on costs and related factors as a sole measure of value. This tends to reduce emphasis on both quality and values. Workers become more interested in the product and its cost than in their work and its viability. When outcome is compromised and viability is endangered, emphasis on cost and cost-saving strategies will tend to undermine the parallel necessity for emphasis on satisfaction, renewal, and changing opportunities in the service environment.

Nursing is essentially a service-oriented profession, so its services, satisfaction, and results are as valuable as, if not more valuable than, the initial costs of providing them. Some balance between these factors must be struck. Compromises in quality and value can be as detrimental to the institution as compromises in cost.

A focus on the more objective measurements such as cost makes evident a weakness of the analytical approach. Traditionally, the rational, bureaucratic problem-solving model maintains a very short-term focus. Management concentrates on current concerns, often pulling problems out of the context of related long-term issues. Quantitative processes tend to focus on immediate issues of concern in health care: the patients and their needs. Nursing also has been affected by quantitative approaches to problem solving and as a result has been "overly objective" in measuring its heavily consumer-oriented service. Dependence on management engineered staffing systems which cannot adjust to intensity and acuity variances, and productivity measurement processes that are time fixed rather than outcome based are two such examples.

The profession thus has victimized itself and, in the long run, the patients it serves. While objective and rational processes are a necessary corollary to qualitative and value processes, such heavy dependence on them creates a disequilibrium in service-outcome relationships and can result in the nursing service's failing to meet its objectives.

Too much emphasis on analytical processes in a participatory environment can lead to a focus on objective and lifeless values that may alienate the nurse manager from concern with the central human values in delivering care. The institution traditionally has emphasized fiscal, material, support, and human resources using objective measurement systems. As a result, work often becomes the reflection of those rational measures, and institution and staff members begin to evaluate performance and outcomes against those objective terms.

However, those particular devices or systems may not in fact accurately or appropriately measure the achievement of goals or missions in human terms. Hospitals must identify more qualitative, human dynamic methods of measurement if they are to assure that the human characteristics of their service that their consumers value share priority with objective measurements.

The point of all this is that the nurse manager in the change process must value not only objective measurement devices but also methodologies that reflect individual insight, relationship, and experience. Experience and relationship are viable measurements of achievement in a human-intensive industry. Not establishing strong values and evaluation mechanisms based on those factors may deprive the nurse and the institution of much of what human service achieves.

Caution and Risk Taking

A lack of experiential, insightful, and relational skills can push the nurse manager even further toward extreme caution and alienation from the risk taking essential to developing a successful human-intensive organization. Creativity, thoughtfulness, and the ability to plan over the long term, to implement, and to access human resources requires trust in one's insights, one's relationships, and in itself is an act of faith and commitment. Risk taking often requires a belief and a commitment in a thought or process that lies outside the realm of traditional management processes. The ability to articulate those processes in a highly variable framework may provide more support for meaningful change than any step-by-step, systematic, logical process may ever produce.

It must be emphasized again that the nurse manager is confronting a new kind of environment in the 21st century, where relationships must be enhanced to the same degree that technology is. While technology uses rational processes, they must be offset by the human intuitive, inductive, and relational concepts essential to stimulate the cooperation and communication that results in better relationships and sound work output. Since rational processes reflect the formality of the traditional bureaucratic system, nonrational, developmental human processes demonstrate a high level of informality. Analyzing, planning, specifying, directing, and controlling reflect the kind of tightly governed, closely held interests produced by the traditional organizational model.

As noted, interaction, testing, attempting, failing, evaluating, relating, learning, communicating, adapting, and modifying all are characteristics of the work environment of the future. In assessing her role in relationship to that future, the nurse manager also must recognize that she must always reflect the creative, organized environment that meets the professional needs of the nurse and the patients to whom she directs her practice.[16]

Creating an open and participative work environment that enhances the professional character of nursing is a challenge with a new set of variables. The old roles, regulations, policies, and procedures that drove the traditional bureaucratic organization no longer will work in the highly technical and human-intensive system of the future. Bureaucracy and participation are dichotomous processes and cannot operate together successfully. Therefore, saying that one can modify the traditional in order to facilitate the professional is rounding the corners off reality. They are incompatible processes.

The manager of the future will have to reflect in her role and in the character of her performance a different set of values, beliefs, and practices that will result in different kinds of relationships, interactions, processes, and, ultimately, outcomes. It will call for the nurse manager to be able to establish new kinds of thinking and performance. It will demand that she be creative in her approach to situations and concerns that arise. She will have to value her role in an entirely different context. Emphasis on status and placement in the organization will have to give way to bringing together diverse functions, to consensus-seeking opportunities for problem resolution, and to crafting creative strategies for program development and organizational success.

As indicated, this effort will require of the nurse manager a great deal of reflection and self-analysis in terms of herself, her role, and its application on the job. Out of that self-assessment will come the need to evaluate the organization, its commitments, its impact, its relationships, and its support of human-intensive strategies and processes. From that she will have to evaluate her peers and assist in their appraisal of themselves and effectiveness, their mode of operating and relating, the impact of their commitment and involvement in the institution, and the relationships that they have established with each other and to the organization as a whole.

Functioning as Change Agent

In the context of all of these factors, the nurse manager will have to act as change agent in moving the organization forward, utilizing human-intensive skills to mobilize the resources available to her and her professional nursing peers. All of this effort will serve to define, implement, and evaluate the strategies and processes that will meet the health care needs of the future. She will utilize new kinds of interactions and new frameworks for cooperating and for involving others, including other disciplines and other health care professions. The ability to bring diverse resources together for consensus seeking and problem solving will be key elements in her growing and developing role.

This leader's primary obligation will be to work with and to manage groups and to develop an organizational and environmental framework in the work setting that enhances the interaction and activities of groups. Much of her time will be devoted to managing group process, seeking individuals' support for group work, aiding the integration of diverse work groups, and bringing together a complexity of information, processes, solutions, and creativity into a meaningful whole.

None of this is to suggest that she does not need organized, systematic, and logical processes. All organizations must have some means of clearly articulating achievement of objectives through the development of a highly structured goals evaluation process. While the process is important, the means of operating it is even more vital. Integrative and participatory strategies tie the work of individuals with that of the group and, in that process, contribute to the goals and objectives of the institution and their projected results.

Certainly, there must be good relationships. These must be consistent with the needs of the institution and in the context of the nurse's role. Every participant should have a clearly prescribed responsibility and role in fulfilling her portion of the organization's goals. The nurse manager's role is to bring together each one of those elements and to assure that each nurse contributes to the fullest extent possible.

A key to the success of a participatory environment is the pulling together of many disparate and often separate functional groups and functions into a uniform, systematic process. Using participatory strategies in new ways is fraught with risk. The nurse manager's role will have to incorporate analysis and assessment of the processes, elements, and functions involving each person, element, and component in the process.

The ability to understand and use the realities and the constraints of the organization will be of major importance. No organization has unlimited resources, economic or human, so the nurse manager must understand those limitations and possibilities and define work within those parameters. Professional staff members place trust in the nurse manager in the belief she will help them make the kinds of decisions that are consistent with the needs of their practice and of the institution. The nurse manager, having provided the appropriate supports and information, can join the professional staff in activities that can have a positive impact on the institution and on its patients.

THE REAL WORLD AND THE TIME FACTOR

The nurse manager must always keep an eye on reality. The environment in which she functions will reflect the kinds of practices and processes she sees. Either they operate consistently with the professionals' values or they don't. Balancing the possibilities against the realities is important. Reality, however, is always subject to one's perception. It should not be limiting, it should be challenging and should offer a basis on which the nurse manager assesses her progress in the transition in the work environment.

There always will be constraints in the real world. There always will be opportunities, too, that the nurse will have to create out of her own urge to grow. She often will have to provide this leadership without much support from either those she reports to or those with whom she works. Insights that she recognizes as important may not be shared by others. As a result, she may have to do much persuading and informing those around her in making many of the transitions she will undertake. The ability to do this and to persevere in the struggle to make change will be a part of the human dynamics associated with the effort to move toward a fully participative environment.

Expecting that everyone will be accepting of the role of the nurse manager in the new context described here may be naive at worst and a dream at best. All nurse managers will have to begin where they are, which will constitute the baseline for determining progress and the rate at which it is achieving results.

What is most important is that the nurse recognize she is not a victim of time. Because this is a fast-paced society where time is short and everybody wants everything done yesterday, people can become caught up and victimized by the limitations of time.

There is plenty of time—there always has been. The institution in which the nurse manager works probably has been there long before she assumed her role and is likely to exist long after she is gone. It is important to keep the concept of time in a realistic perspective. Time is a valuable and important tool in making change. One is always wiser to utilize all the time available than to hurry time along and make change and initiate growth toward highly participatory strategies before there has been sufficient preparation and transition.

Important elements of undertaking meaningful change and achieving higher levels of participation and involvement involve taking the time essential to make basic decisions regarding one's own role, to make a detailed self-assessment, to assess the work environment as to its readiness and viability for movement toward participation, then slowly and carefully implementing the strategies and processes essential to arriving at higher level participatory systems.[17]

There will be many opportunities for success—and for failure. The new manager must be able to realize that failure is as much a concomitant of progress and growth as is success. Often, failure provides more opportunities for change and for meaningful transition than does success. One thing failure does provide is a clear sense of what does not work. Having tried things that do not work, the new manager has a stronger base of information about things that will work.

The only failure that is unacceptable is the failure to learn and to take that learning to the next step of growth. In developing a creative, open, professional, organizational environment, nurse managers will have many opportunities to learn and to grow.

NOTES

1. Max Weber, *The Theory of Social and Economic Organization,* trans. T. Parsons (Glencoe, Ill.: The Free Press, 1957).

2. Rosabeth Moss Kanter. *The Changemasters: Innovation for Productivity in the American Corporation* (New York: Simon & Schuster, 1983).

3. National Commission on Nursing, *Summary Report on Nursing* (Chicago, 1983).

4. Tim Porter-O'Grady and Sharon Finnigan, *Shared Governance for Nursing: A Creative Approach to Professional Accountability* (Rockville, M.D.: Aspen Systems Corporation, 1984).

5. Jean Piaget, *The Psychology of Intelligence* (New York: Harcourt, Brace and Company, 1950).

6. F.E. Kath and J.E. Rosensweig, "General Systems Theory Applications for Organization and Management," *Academy of Management Journal* 15 (December 1972): 447–65.

7. P.R. Lawrence and J.W. Lorsch, "Differentiation and Integration in Complex Organizations," *Administrative Science Quarterly* 1, no. 12 (1967): 1–47.

8. Joseph Luft, "The Johari Window," *National Training Laboratory Institute for Applied Behavioral Science,* Chicago, 1969.

9. Charles Seashore, *Seashore Levels of Group Functioning* (Washington: Charles M. Seashore Consulting Inc., 1977).

10. J.B. Rotter, "A New Scale for Measurement of Interpersonal Trust," *Journal of Personality,* 3, 37 (1973): 651–55.

11. M. Deutsch, "Trustworthiness and F Scale," *Journal of Normal and Social Psychology* (March, 1961): 138–40.

12. S. Jourard, *The Transparent Self, Self-Disclosure and Well Being* (New York: D. Van Nostrand Co. Inc., 1964).

13. W.R. Mulford, "Line of Four: An Intergroup Competition," *1979 Handbook for Group Facilitators* (San Diego: University Associates, Inc., 1979), 21–27.

14. Oscar Mink, James Shultz, and Barbara Mink, *Open Organizations* (Austin: Learning Concepts Inc., 1979), 77–87.

15. Warren Bennis, Kenneth Benne, Robert Chin, & Kenneth Corey, *The Planning of Change* (New York: Holt, Rinehart, and Winston, Inc., 1976), 117–125, 137–147, 178–188, 231–245, 283–297.

16. Thomas J. Peters and Robert H. Waterman, Jr., *In Search of Excellence* (New York: Harper & Row Publishers, Inc., 1982): 44–52.

17. F.R. Manfred, K. DeVries, and D. Miller, *The Neurotic Organization* (San Francisco: Jossey-Bass Inc., Publishers, 1984), 54–71.

Establishing Staff Accountability— Management Supports Practice

Chapter 5

Establishing Staff
Accountability—
Management Supports
Practice

Objectives for Chapter Five

Identify two characteristics of organizational design that support the framework for professional nursing practice.

Outline one mechanism for developing the conceptual and operational base upon which professional nursing practice must be based.

Identify the use of critical objectives in setting the operating direction for the practice of nursing in the institution.

Identify the role of the staff in establishing accountability and developing a basis for practice autonomy.

Introduce the issue of credentialing and establish a conceptual base for developing a professional credentialing mechanism in an institution.

Explore the issue of competence and performance evaluation and suggest mechanisms for addressing these issues in a participatory organization.

5

The nurse manager of the future obviously will be unable to act in the capacity of professional facilitator without the basic components of her organization in place and operating effectively. As discussed earlier, the future nursing organization will emphasize accountability and the professional role of the nurse in exercising her responsibilities and functions.

By this point in the process, the organization must be structured in such a way that the nurse actually can demonstrate that accountability. Therefore, the processes that support nursing in decision making and in clinical work also must be in place. In the practice of nursing, as in any profession, there must be such supportive elements.

The professional nurse must begin to assume responsibility in areas that traditionally were the purview of management. Management and practice are not as clearly distinct from each other in nursing. Management supports nursing by providing opportunities for assuming broadening responsibilities. This can be described as a process of shared governance or self-governance.

ROLE OF NURSING MANAGEMENT TEAM

One of the first conceptual bridges that must be constructed by the nursing management team in the institution is recognition that the role of the nurse manager moves from one that controls, directs, and supervises, and decides outcomes to one that facilitates, coordinates, integrates, and supports decisions. (See Figure 5–1.) When the manager assumes the latter role, the other obligations for decision making, for structuring goals and objectives, and for follow-through and assessment of accomplishments move to another place in the organization—to the professional nurses through a formal staff governance process.

Figure 5–1 Role Change of Nurse Managers

Traditional (20th Century)		Contemporary (21st Century)
Control	⟶	Facilitate
Direct	⟶	Coordinate
Supervise	⟶	Integrate
Decide	⟶	Support

Each institution will have to look at its own situation in developing a shared or self-governance strategy in providing the framework that creates the best fit between the organization's needs and those of the nursing staff. The management team will take the lead in initiating these processes and in discussing the risks and possibilities in moving to the new system. Regardless of the governance system adopted, certain components of the organization must always be involved in delivering nursing services.

The work of nursing and its supporting framework must be described clearly so that everyone in the organization has a full understanding of the system. Without this understanding, the nursing professionals may have difficulties in fulfilling the obligations of their new role in the governance structure. Governance in this case means much more than the rules, regulations, and processes that support the work to be done; it designates a broad range of activities that everyone in the organization is responsible for in fulfilling the obligations of their role and the needs of the organization and of the patients they serve.

The key areas that must be addressed in reformulating an organizational design to support the new framework involve some specific fields:

1. philosophy, purpose, and critical objectives
2. standards of practice
3. measurement of performance
4. role criteria: credentialing and privileging
5. monitoring of competence
6. governance participation.

These constitute some of the fundamental organizational components that must be in place before any effort toward redirecting the new mode of practice can begin. Without having addressed these six areas, the organization may be at a serious disadvantage in trying to move to a participatory framework and in measuring that participation in terms of criteria designed to achieve specific outcomes.

THE FOCUS ON OUTCOMES

No organization, regardless of its structure, can proceed unless there is a way in which outcomes can be the focus of its work. One of the greatest problems in the history of nursing is its inability to validate its practice in direct relation to measurable outcomes. Research may be available to indicate appropriate therapeutic methodologies in nursing but it may not be evident in the service area in which these clinical processes have been incorporated into practice. Thus, it is difficult for the profession to say with confidence that process A, B, C, and D when carried out by nurses will achieve result E. This creates a significant difficulty in validating what nursing practice really is and achieves.

Outcome orientation is absolutely essential in the professional organization of the future. The ability to look at process in the context of potential outcomes and to focus on such results as a part of goal setting and achievement will be essential to the success of nursing practice in any future setting. This success will depend also on the ability of individual nurses to participate fully and to measure their own performance against predetermined criteria. Without taking this objective view of nursing practice—in effect standing back to put it into a context in which it can be measured—nurses will have difficulty surviving in that future era.

The outcome achievement process begins before any actual activity with the establishment or a definition or description as a basis for measuring its progress. Without this, there is no benchmark against which to validate the processes. To do that, the organization must begin the examination at a very fundamental level. Leadership must assure that congruence occurs at a very conceptual level, beginning with the basic definition of the service that is offered. This requires reexamining nursing's framework and belief system. Everything flows from this basic definition of belief: goals, standards, quality of care, learning, and, ultimately, nursing practice. If those basic tenets or beliefs are not viable, and cannot be articulated clearly, then the subsequent activity upon which they are based is questionable. (See Figure 5–2.)

PHILOSOPHY, PURPOSE, AND OBJECTIVES

The philosophies of many nursing institutions, and their elements, are non-specific and general. To be practicable, however, the philosophy of an institution, especially in its description of its nursing practice, must be somewhat concrete and contain significant statements upon which that practice can be built. Since a statement of philosophy is essentially an articulation of the beliefs of the organization and its members, it must reflect concrete elements upon which those who review the philosophy can attach some credence. If the statements are rhetorical, high-blown, nonmeasurable, and have little relation to actual nursing, it is difficult to understand practice based on such nebulus and unclear definitions.

Figure 5–2 Hierarchy of Process Components in the Nursing Care System

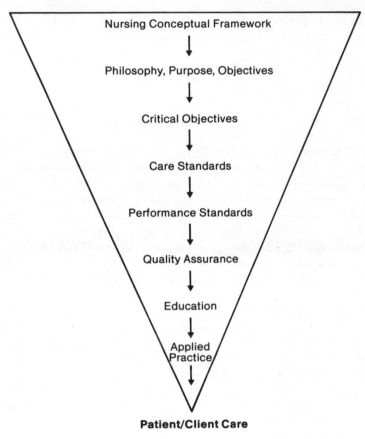

Nursing Conceptual Framework

↓

Philosophy, Purpose, Objectives

↓

Critical Objectives

↓

Care Standards

↓

Performance Standards

↓

Quality Assurance

↓

Education

↓

Applied Practice

↓

Patient/Client Care

Whatever the statement of practice belief, it should be concise, clear, understandable, and even pointed. Generic statements such as belief in God, belief in the dignity of man, and belief in the right of all to health care make little or no sense to the practitioner and the consumer of health care if they cannot be interpreted in terms that reflect the living experiences and values of the individual who comes to receive nursing services. It may be more important to include in the philosophy a statement of respect for life. But the philosophy needs to go beyond fundamental belief statements. Belief statements that are too broad make no commitment as to the nursing profession's obligation to seek to provide the health status that is consistent with the needs of every human being.

The development of a philosophy is a collective enterprise. It deals with issues that concern the group and upon which it must make decisions. Staff members must be involved in developing the philosophy since it will reflect their position on their role in the delivery of health care. The philosophy is useful only if it gives some direction and meaning to the work. If a nurse in reviewing the philosophy cannot get a sense of the work of the organization and the elements upon which it is based, she may have difficulty understanding the value of her particular service in meeting patients' needs.

The philosophy also should reflect many of the defined beliefs of the nursing profession. An institution that develops its own nursing philosophy that does not represent commitments of the nursing profession at the national level may unknowingly operate against the best interests of the nursing profession there. An institutional philosophy that is at variance with the generally accepted mandates of the profession at large can create dissonance among the practitioners and those who view nursing from the outside. One of the major issues in the history of nursing is this emphasis on institutional individualization of philosophies. Individual institutions rarely reflect the predominant professional values of nursing at the national and regional level. The new philosophy therefore should, at a minimum, demonstrate the integration of the professional and institutional needs in the application of nursing.

Need for a Conceptual Framework

One of the key elements often missing from a philosophy is the conceptual framework within which nursing professionals practice in the institution. This framework should provide a scientific basis upon which to measure practice and its outcomes. Without establishing the relationship between theory and practice or using a theoretical framework that is consistent with the institution's values, nursing has no basis upon which to validate its practice activities. Without this kind of scientific validation or beginning point, it is difficult to establish a logical and systematic way in which nursing practice can be viewed, then measured. When a conceptual base is missing, institutions frequently apply numerous modalities to delivering nursing services like team and primary nursing, none of which clearly have shown any more or less real significance in providing care that achieves some defined and meaningful impact on patient outcomes.

One major issue related to this problem is the need to value nursing services, to cost them, and to determine their impact on patient outcomes and on the cost of the care. It is difficult to develop a unit of measure for nursing practice based on a systematic, practice-based approach if the institution has no such clear delineation.

While detailed analysis of this issue is beyond the scope of this book, developing a theoretical framework under which nursing practice will operate is essential in establishing validated, measurable systems for defining, applying, and evaluating services. Because theory may not provide a nursing practice framework, in many ways institutional practice may be divorced from validated theory. This may have contributed to the significant difficulties in constructing a perception in nursing that it is scientifically based on sound logic and applied principles that are dependable and to which a high level of confidence can be assigned.

The problem of developing a theoretical framework for nursing practice comes out of a long history of anti-intellectualism in nursing practice. Christman identified this problem many years ago, when there was a general theme of anti-intellectualism in the basic education of nurses.[1] He indicated that it lay deep in the roots of the profession in its urge to create a high level of applied practice and technically skilled women. Also, the historical separation of "women's work" from academic and intellectual pursuits had some impact here. However, since the mid-1960s, while nursing practice has developed a stronger scientific basis that has become the framework for education, that base has not yet been strongly evident in the practice of applied nursing education, especially at the undergraduate level. Transition of theory into practice comes slowly. Since most general practitioners of professional nursing are undergraduates, the theoretical and scientific basis for practice is not yet fully present in their individual value systems and thus in the exercise of practice in most nursing service settings. Indeed, the service settings frequently are all but devoid of serious investment in any issues that relate to the academic, scholarly, or scientific basis for nursing practice.

Since many institutions do not have a mechanism for valuing nursing, and thus generally do not incorporate those values into the practice framework, it is no surprise that professional practitioners do not demonstrate any value for the scientific basis for pursuing practice there. The professional valuing of intellectual and academic applications in the service system must be an integral part of the environment itself if the practitioner is to be able to apply it as a part of the value of her own nursing.

The statement of philosophy therefore should define clearly the conceptual framework for nursing practice. This plus acceptance of a scientific basis for practice will provide a cornerstone of nursing activity in the organization. In this context, nursing leaders can begin to implement a logical, consistent, and systematic method of practice. (See Figure 5–1.)

The Need for Direction

The institution next must establish its direction and its purposes in meeting the needs of its patients. (Purpose is the statement of the institution's responsibility to the service it provides.) Since most nursing organizations have a multitude of clinical services, they should be factored into the institution's purposes. While each of these services may have its own set of purposes, the organization as a whole must address how they all fit into the overall purpose of nursing practice there. This purpose statement should cross specialty service lines.

Here again, purpose statements should not be diffuse or nebulous. They must be clearly directive and succinct and express meaningfully the work that is to be undertaken to meet the institution's needs in providing services to its patients. These purposes must be brief, easy to understand, and phrased in a way that can be used as an element of the measurement process in determining whether outcomes are achieved. Purposes that are long, involved, detailed, and nondirective are of little use to the institution, offer no real sense of direction, and are difficult to use as management and practice tools for measuring performance.

Professional Standards

The purposes also should reflect many of the general aims of nursing. They should demonstrate that the purposes for the institutional practice of nursing are consistent with those for the profession as a whole. The profession's written standards, such as the American Nurses' Association Social Policy Statement, should give the institution a general framework for its specified purposes. Among other things, these purposes create consistency in practice that provides not only credibility but also conformity with a national set of values. This framework refocuses the organization from looking at itself as an isolated entity to looking at the institution as the place where nursing is practiced. The new viewpoint is that professional nurses offer a specified service to the institution rather than that the facility owns its own framework for nursing. Here, ownership is different. Rather than the institution owning the service, the professional staff owns it and commits its services, standards, practices, and relationships to the institution. Outlining purposes within that conceptual context creates a radically different relationship and philosophical approach to the delivery of nursing services in any institution.

The most difficult part of developing this framework is defining the critical objectives for the division of nursing. Objectives usually are viewed as significant, specific, goal-directed activities that provide a point of reference and measurement for the completion or evaluation of specific functions. While there is a great deal of truth to this perception, it does not tell the full story in terms of the organization's mandates in providing services.

The critical objectives of the nursing division should be those that under all circumstances and in all situations must be met if the appropriate delivery of nursing services is to be achieved. If these objectives are not achieved, the work of nursing is not complete and may signal that it may be compromised. The critical objectives, then, are simply the specific objectives that relate to the general practice of nursing in the context of the institution and that must always be met if practice is to be effective. (See Appendix A.)

It might be asked: Why should these critical objectives be identified as a part of the organization's direction? What has occurred in the past is a real dissonance between what management expects of practice and what staff nurses actually provide? Staff nurses offer service under one image of their role and responsibility and the nurse manager perceives those elements differently. She usually values nursing practice in terms of her role in implementing the institution's mandates and desires. As a result, these two frameworks can produce dissonance that can lead to significantly different processes and outcomes.

All who are involved in meeting nursing needs must have a clear understanding of what their roles, principles, and objectives are. These objectives must focus specifically on the issues that give direction, support, and value to nursing practice and, as noted earlier, provide a framework for measuring accomplishments—or failures.

Clearly, nursing organizations must move more closely to frameworks and operating processes for nursing practice by national nursing professional organizations. This provides a consistent basis upon which nursing activity can be measured. The method of measurement should be accepted by the individual practitioner and should be based on criteria established by national nursing bodies. Activities relating to the nurse/patient relationship might include the primary nursing role, the need for nursing assessment of all patients, the process of planning and undertaking nursing care and activities associated with it, budgeting, utilization of human resources, and support resources. Each institution, of course, also will have its own standards, processes, and roles. There is a direct relationship between how the nursing service delivers patient care and how the policy/operational framework prescribes that such work be performed. In other words, nursing organizations get what they expect. If they provide for narrowly prescribed, task-based, directive, and functional work, that is exactly what will be provided. If the nursing organization provides for independence, autonomy, standards accountability, investment by their nursing staff, that too can be obtained!

PRACTICE, AUTONOMY, AND ACCOUNTABILITY

A major focus of the professional nursing staff obviously is the services provided and the standards upon which practice is based. As discussed, well-defined measurable nursing standards are imperative. They constitute the umbrella under which nurses practice. The individual most responsible for practice and for development of standards is the practicing nurse. In the participatory structure of the future, the responsibility for practice standards must shift from the management of the institution to the clinical nurse. So, too, must the framework designed to support practice. It is important to note that nurses will not express or invest personal accountability (versus institutional responsibility) unless they have some role or responsibility in formulating practice standards and processes. Again, the issue of ownership is important here. The individual professional nurse is responsible by law and by mandate for the way she practices. That responsibility cannot be enhanced if she does not have some participation in defining its parameters. Most professionals undertake a representative process in defining the parameters of their practice: in medicine, law, engineering, finance, etc. Nurses, too, if they are to behave as professionals must, at the clinical level, have representation and full participation in the provisions and parameters of nursing practice.

If nurse managers are the sole providers of standards, they have the responsibility to enforce them; however, if staff practitioners develop them, then they are responsible for defining, monitoring, and enforcing them. The organization that emphasizes the manager's role in standards development and control is different from the one that is structured to define and to support the individual nurses' role in such functions. The whole issue relates to the value and meaning each nurse attaches to her accountability for quality of practice.

Attitudes regarding nursing practice originate in the nursing education and academic process. Nurses are taught that a certain body of knowledge is essential to practicing safely and appropriately. When they have received the full measure of that knowledge as provided through the educational framework, they are prepared to be licensed and to assume responsibility for delivering the services based on that information base. If that were wholly true, the impetus for delivering nursing services would come from the practitioner—the individual most responsible for the service by law and by role.

However, what traditionally has occurred in health care is that the nursing management team has provided the authority, responsibility, and mandate for the nature and quality of professional nursing that will be practiced there. As a result, the management team has taken from the nurse her obligation and mandate for defining practical services. That framework assigns to the nurse manager the responsibility for assuring that nursing services are provided. As a result, ownership and control of nursing lies with the institution even though fulfillment of the work remains with the practicing nurse.

This dichotomous condition generates a dissonance in role and responsibility that cannot be bridged through the use of management strategies. It is only when ownership is placed with practicing nurses that they can experience full accountability. While responsibility is delegated to individuals by the agency or institution, accountability derives from the role of the individual offering a professional service. This is the basic distinction between professionals and other workers. This conflict between responsibility (management) and accountability (the professional nurse) has created discord in the workplace over the last century. As higher levels of preparation and expectation emerge, a more professional body of nurses will see the need to shift from the management track to the clinical track the authority, autonomy, and accountability for exercising the roles that are consistent with effective practice.

Change in the Organization's Construct

This change in ownership also requires a change in the construct of the organization so that nursing individuals collectively can define and advance accountability in practice. The staff responsibility demands collaborative strategies for defining standards of practice that can be applied in the clinical setting for the benefit of patients and of the institution. Specialty services also can benefit from the development of standards that apply particularly to them, and the professional nurse is responsible for participating fully in that process, with the organization allowing them the time necessary to do so.

In other words, the institution must apply as much significance to the role of defining nursing practice and its standards as it does to delivering nursing care. It must assign as much value and benefit to time that nurses spend in defining, monitoring, and evaluating care as it does to their delivering services. All other professional groups have "space" for evaluation of care as a part of their fundamental role, and that time is incorporated into the quality assurance values of their work.

Indeed, the medical staff is expected to monitor and evaluate the quality of medical care at a much higher level of accountability and precision than do nurses in the delivery of care. Again, the responsibility in the evaluation of medical care is the physicians', but in the evaluation of nursing care it generally is the institution's. However, when the practicing nurse plays the major role in defining, monitoring, and evaluating care, then she should have the obligation for assuring high levels of practice. The appropriate mechanics of nursing ownership of care in the institution must be in place to provide for this accountability. A number of shared governance models are available to address just such issues.[3]

Exercising Responsibility

The individual practicing nurse must exercise her responsibility in the organization in a precise and clearly defined way. Her responsibility is to carry out the actions essential in meeting her accountability for practice and in exercising the autonomy necessary to support professional nursing in the institution. This involves specific functional responsibilities such as these:

- The professional nurse should have some responsibility in determining and defining her job description, the position it represents, and the way it operates in the organization. She also should play a significant part in defining the roles and functions of all levels of nursing caregivers.

- The participating professional nurse should be responsible for incorporating and interpreting appropriate care standards in the context of the specialty she represents. The staff nurse must participate in defining and implementing the accountabilities in the organization to assure that the standards of practice from national, regional, and local nursing professional organizations are applied.

- The practicing nurse's role should include participating in the development of policies, rules, and regulations that govern the activities of peers. Each nurse is responsible for assuring that there is continuity and consistency in the practice framework as well as in its elements. She is not responsible simply for the "doing" of nursing practice.

- The professional nurse should participate in all group processes directed toward identifying, defending, clarifying, and evaluating the practice processes, and issues that arise from them (including conflicts), in the clinical environment.

- The academic, intellectual, scientific, and research based activities that are essential to any profession must be incorporated into the role of every nurse. Each nurse must view her role in the context of its greater responsibility to society to assure the appropriateness of care.

- The practicing nurse should represent to (and defend to) all other forums in the institution or practice environment the issues that are of concern to nurses. These include conflicts and problems that exist between and among the disciplines having an impact on the delivery of care.

In a participatory environment, the practicing nurse thus has broader responsibilities than those traditionally assigned to her role. The new professional obligations demand responses significantly different from those of traditional employee-based types. The "vocational" behaviors of the traditional employee environment no longer will be viable or meaningful.

All this will have a major impact on the role of the manager in tomorrow's environment. The manager who traditionally assumed responsibilities for all the functional elements of nursing practice in the organization no longer will take upon herself the obligation of fulfilling all these processes. While she now supports the nursing practice processes already in place in the institution, in the future she will do that as a supporting individual, not as a primary provider, and as facilitator and integrator. The mandate for action in the future will come from the staff. The responsibility to assure that the staff implements those mandates may be a part of the manager's role. In such cases, the manager will act as the staff members' agent, representing their interests in defining and evaluating, as well as correcting, the processes of delivering nursing care services.

Figure 5–3 Resource Management Role

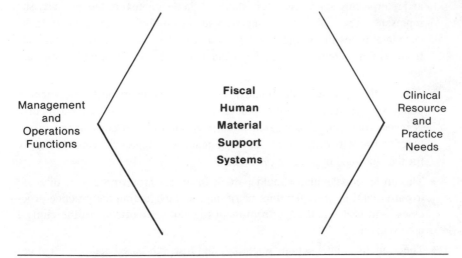

This is a major transition in role for the manager because she will assume a quite different position in the organization. This new role will be no less significant but it will demand a different kind of response and behavior and skills than in the past. These will include staff support and coordination of all fiscal, human, material, and support systems (see Figure 5–3). She will require specific skills in human resource management, group process, objective setting, and change management. She will bear the responsibility for integrating and coordinating the activities for which the staff is primarily accountable to assure that the functional aspects of nursing practice continue to meet the need for them. (See Figure 5–3.)

CRITERIA, CREDENTIALING, AND PRIVILEGING

If the nurse manager is to be successful, certain basic characteristics in the role of the professional nurse in her relationship with the institution must be understood at the outset. If the nurse manager is to direct the nursing process and the primary responsibility for the practice remains with the staff nurse, the latter must be fully aware of the specifics of her obligation and responsibilities.

It is at this point that the credentialing and privileging process of the organization has an impact on the practitioner in the delivery of nursing care services. In a credentialing and privileging structure, each nurse has certain obligations, of which the first is accountability. The professional organization through its staff establishes behaviors and processes and each individual practitioner agrees to uphold those criteria. These provide the baseline for expectations of her future performance.

At the outset, the credentialing process should clearly describe the responsibilities and functions of the individual practitioner. In the participatory practice that is emerging, she will have a broader base of responsibility, described through the credentialing mechanism, than under the traditional system. In traditional hiring processes, the job description usually provides a laundry list of criteria for the professional nurse's role. In tomorrow's institution, where true professional accountability provides the base line for activity, the nurse's responsibility is described through accountability statements.

Position charters with standards and expectations generally are more useful than job descriptions (see Appendix B). The position charter may describe the outcome criteria and the standards that evidence the achievement of those outcomes, rather than their functional elements. Focusing on function limits the delineation of accountability. Focusing on accountability broadens the nursing staff's ability and opportunity to respond more appropriately to the needs of the clinical environment.

However, it also strengthens an additional objective: that the performance of the professional nurse be uniquely her own. Her work will be measured in the context of clearly described behavioral expectations that are beyond mere functional application: Upholding standards of practice, clarifying practitioners' roles and responsibilities, peer evaluations, responsibility for taking corrective action, individual responsibility to incorporate quality assurance practices in the role.

The credentialing mechanism is a peer-based process and involves all practitioners in one way or another. It describes a different frame of reference for expectations of the individual professional nurse. Through it, she begins to broaden her frame of reference in viewing her role to include her peers. She no longer can remain focused solely on the functional elements of her role—hands-on nursing is only one part of practice. Her new role includes the responsibility for assuring that the professional practice of nursing as defined by the staff is consistent with the criteria. Role accountability therefore is generated both internally and externally through her responsibility to her peers.

The credentialing and privileging process should include characteristics defining the responsibility of members of the professional staff in reviewing the credentials of their peers and that all nurses behave consistent with the needs and the mandates of the nursing organization. The credentialing mechanism should allow for a variety of specialty nursing practice areas.

The following items should be included in the credentialing and privileging process:

1. a definition of membership on the nursing staff
2. a definition and description of the professional nursing staff
3. the conditions and durations of appointment to the professional nursing staff
4. membership on the nursing staff for those not employed by the institution but sometimes operating there

5. temporary nursing staff privileges for per diem staff
6. provisional nursing staff privileges for new members
7. an organized process for credentials review that focuses on the staff's responsibility and looks at the following items:
    a. appropriate licenses and other paper credentials
    b. successful interviewing and communication skills with peers and management
    c. acceptable experience for the position sought by candidates
    d. performance expectations related to education, quality assurance, research, practice, standards development and maintenance, and peer relations.
8. responsibilities of the credentialing officer and nursing staff credentials committee.

The criteria for the credentialing process are vital links to the organization because they form the basis for seeking to assure the quality and competence of the nursing staff; those factors will influence the processes and outcomes by which nursing care is measured. If the screening process in credentialing and privileging is effective, the quality of professionalism begins to improve.

The role of the nurse manager is to assure that the system is maintained by playing an active part in credentialing and privileging. The degree of her commitment will affect the quality of the nursing staff.

If competence is enhanced through an effective credentialing and privileging process, the implications for the institution and professional practice of nursing are clear. The institution, for its part, can expect a higher level of performance and of individual professional accountability in its nursing practitioners.

MEASURING PERFORMANCE AND COMPETENCE

Much has been written about performance appraisal systems and their use for assuring appropriate levels of performance in nursing. In the shared or self-governing organization of the future, where the staff takes precedence in ownership of the rules, regulations, and behaviors, there also is a transition in the placement and use of appraisal and evaluation mechanisms. Nurses will provide an evaluation process that looks at accountability rather than mere functional components.

Performance evaluation is derived from a system of position chartering that reflects the allocation of each nurse's accountabilities. Applied to the collective staff, this process seeks to assure that the delivery of nursing practice is consistent, uniform, and measurable. Any individual variations from practice standards can be worked out through the peer process. In specialty practices, variances from the norm would be addressed in the functional components of that practice, consistent with its overall criteria. (See Appendix B.)

Performance measurement methods should always focus on accountability rather than on function. Factors such as the following are as important to nursing as is hands-on care:

- responsibility for education (when not mandated by law)
- accountability for quality assurance activities as an obligation of practice
- analysis of the responsibility to others through a peer review process
- responsibility for reviewing and interviewing prospective applicants for privileges to the nursing staff
- other kinds of activities related to the professional character of nursing.

In the emerging era, the evaluation mechanism will look at individuals' participation in the activities that are internal to the profession as well as those related to the patient. That focus on components as they relate to the profession rather than only to practice will have a meaningful impact on practice itself.

If the character of practice is to be enhanced by the staff nurse, the new era's professional processes and principles must be incorporated into the expectations for her role. To the extent that this is accomplished, management can begin to travel the long road back to sharing with the professional staff some of the accountability that has accrued to the nurse manager through long years of staff default.

The new position performance appraisal, representing professional accountability rather than functional tasks, will be a different kind of document—one the nurse actually can use. The locus of control in terms of evaluation process also will change. In this new framework, it will become the obligation of the nurse to undertake her own evaluation process and to assure that each of its components as they apply to her own practice is logical and consistent. This, of course, diminishes or removes the emphasis on the nurse manager's responsibility for evaluations. In the future organization, the nurse staff member will be responsible for assuring:

- that she has addressed, and can validate objectively, all of the criteria identified in the performance appraisal
- that the peer appraisal processes eseential to support her view of her own practice and her contribution to the professional responsibilities of nursing are in place and functioning
- that she has instituted prescribed quality assurance activities to assure that she is meeting her responsibilities for the appropriateness and review of care she provides

- that she has assumed responsibility for her own competence and self-development and has taken the requisite hours and kinds of nursing education appropriate to her role, including educational activities she has provided for her peers
- that she is capable of accepting the responsibility for her own evaluation process in a professional manner, assuring that all of the elements are in place to obtain recredentialing.

All this makes it clear, again, that even in the evaluation phase the primary locus of control and accountability rests with the professional nurse. The performance evaluation essential to recredentialing is the obligation of the individual seeking to be recredentialed. The psychological and behavioral alterations in the role create a new set of obligations for the nurse and again heighten the opportunity for accountability in practice.

When the institution no longer assumes responsibility on behalf of the nurse for managing the performance criteria, then she must act to assure that it occurs. If the nurse does not, is not capable of doing so, and cannot follow up with the requisite behaviors, then she clearly is not prepared to assume the responsibilities that are a part of her professional mandate.

If nurses are to practice at a professional level and behave and be perceived as behaving at that level, then they must meet the criteria. The expectations and the performance behavior must be evident to all who participate, either directly or indirectly, in care processes. It is in this way that external and internal perceptions regarding the nurse in the practice environment will begin their transition to the new method of operation.

SELF-GOVERNANCE AND THE NURSE MANAGER

This chapter has focused on the development of the staff role in establishing clinical ownership and an increasing level of accountability. This holds no less an implication for the governance of the institution than it does for the actual application of professional practice. Governance, in this case, relates to the umbrella framework over all nursing activities. Governance traditionally has been a fundamental responsibility of the nurse manager to operate in the best interests of the institution and the profession. This role has been reserved traditionally as part of the nursing administrator's role, with her peers and subordinates. In a professional organization that expectation also changes. Governance of a profession really belongs to its membership, which should accept the responsibility for self-governance activities.

Simply stated, in a shared or self-governing organization, the staff has an organized, systematic way of governing itself in activities that apply to the practice and processes of all nurses there. Shared governance provides opportunities for nurses to participate in decision-making and policy formulating processes that occur at the board of trustees' level as well as in decisions that affect individual practice. Nurses play as much of a role at other levels of the institution as they do in delivering direct nursing care.

The responsibility for governance under this system rests with the professional practitioner. Not only is the opportunity provided for her to participate fully in decision-making processes but the obligaton for her to do so accrues specifically to her role. Therefore, she no longer is insulated from the realities of decision making at the corporate, division, and unit levels and is fully involved in those processes, including dealing with the stressors and constraints that affect all practice in the institution.

Shared governance represents professional interests because it expresses itself through the accountability of the professional nurse participants. It demands (not requests) involvement and therefore is an integral part of the obligation of every nurse.

The roles and responsibilities that are emerging in shared governance systems must in some way address the skills and abilities of the professional practitioner and apply them to governance activities. Professional nurses are not universally familiar with decision-making processes in a managerial context. However, the same factors that are involved in those obligations also are contained in the processes essential to the management process. Education and on-the-job development will enable individuals to acquire a decision-making ability for organizational decisions equal to their involvement in clinical decision making.

Therefore, the argument that the nurse practitioner is not capable of making those kinds of decisions is specious if she is defined in a professional context. That context makes clear that she is capable of making the kinds of decisions that professionals have incorporated into their role in clinical practice. If the professional nurse is not operating within her assigned clinical framework, then it can be said that she is not capable of making decisions that affect the organization and the structuring of her work and the workplace.

The important point here is to distinguish whether current practice in any way does or does not resemble a professional characterization of nursing. If it does not, questions must be raised as to what needs to be done to develop those processes. If it does, questions must be asked as to what prevents the performance expectations from moving toward an open governance framework that permits the staff to be fully involved and responsible for the governance activities concomitant with their role.

Participatory Governance Characteristics

As mentioned earlier, it is not the scope of this text to discuss the elements of shared governance. It is important, however, to emphasize specific characteristics that must exist in a highly participatory organization. These should include at least the following:

- a clear description of professional nurses' role in the review, revision, and approval of staff rules, regulations, policies, and practices for which they share accountability
- participation in decision making at the highest corporate levels that have an impact on nursing practice
- a mechanism for consensus seeking and for voting on issues of concern to the staff as a whole
- full participation in the development of goals and objectives for nursing practice and involvement in the institution's long-term and short-term planning process affecting the delivery of clinical services
- discussion and delineation of the responsibility of nursing in the institution, including the development of standards upon which practice will be evaluated
- a mechanism for holding the corporate nursing staff accountable for the standards, policies, rules, regulations, and behaviors identified and expected of each of its members
- a commitment to continuing competency and continuing education at the highest possible levels and staff participation in determining the parameters of education in the context of the institution's resources
- the ability to influence, make recommendations, or discuss issues related to salaries, wages, benefits, working conditions, and other elements that have an impact on professional satisfaction and patient care outcomes
- a formal nursing forum that includes a systematic relationship with the administrative bodies of the organization that provide opportunities for the professional nurse to participate in decisions affecting her practice and her relations with the institution
- the ability to make changes in the organization consistent with the emerging character of the profession, the needs of the nurse, and the patients she serves.

Creative activities will be necessary in most organizations to assure that these characteristics are included in the nursing environment. If the nurse is to be held accountable for various elements or actions, the organization must provide a governance framework that permits her to do so in a formal and effective manner. Shared or self-governing strategies in the organization requires establishment of some way in which that accountability can be expressed and met consistent with the greater demands of the institution. A formal structure that permits a high level of staff participation is a key to an effective governance system.

In the new era, the nurse manager will have a significantly altered role, as noted. She must link the pieces of the organization together and through those linkages provide the glue that maintains the functional integrity of the nursing profession and the institution. The nurse manager in this kind of environment has a responsibility:

- to assure that all of the elements of the organization operate smoothly
- to provide an opportunity for decisions to be incorporated into the organizational structure
- to act as a peer and to incorporate peer relational strategies into her management role
- to link the professional nursing service with other services in the institution
- to provide the bridge for problem solving and for establishing creative ways in which issues can be addressed
- to monitor and observe the flow of activity and of the various components of the professional organization
- to determine where there are breaks in the feedback mechanism and where communication fails
- to ascertain where the system does not operate as effectively as it could to support professional practice and decide what can be done to rectify the situation
- to help the staff identify where there are areas of concern, where current processes can be improved and where changes in the structure may need to be provided
- to alert nursing staff members to the processes they might undertake to resolve problems or to address issues and help them develop their skills and abilities for doing so.

All of these factors provide a different focus on the function of the nurse manager and offer the professional staff more opportunity for leadership development as the manager makes her transition.

Resource Management

Perhaps the most important function in her new role is resource management. This becomes the functional focus of her role to assure that appropriate resources are available to the staff to accomplish its work. The assurance of fiscal, human, and material backing, as well as problem-solving resources, is central to the nurse manager's support to the staff to facilitate its decision-making processes. Her role, instead of becoming less significant in the organization, in some ways becomes more important. She becomes a resource individual. She is vital in developing and supporting the nursing staff. She represents the best interests of nursing from the management perspective and as such acts as the staff's agent to assure the most appropriate uses of process and function to meet the needs of nursing and, ultimately, of the patients served.

In the new role, specific accountabilities and functions both similar to and different from the traditional become evident:

- She acquires a growing responsibility for fiscal resources, assuring the allocation of monies for budgetary, operational, capital, and contingency financing of the nursing organization.
- She develops a clear understanding of the economic implications of the marketplace and the service environment and their impact on the professional practice of nursing, interpreting them to the staff to assist their decision making.
- She focuses on problem solving with other administrative heads for issues that affect clinical practice, clearing away those that interfere with nurses' ability to make decisions.
- She develops a closer relationship with the staff as a peer, implementing the decisions of the nursing organization and assuring that they are made known throughout the division.
- She assures that sufficient human resources are available to do the work of nursing, assisting the professional staff on schedules and assignments.
- She provides peer leadership by developing the decision-making and leadership capacities of the nursing staff to assure higher levels of independence and quality.
- She represents the nursing staff in problems involving resources to the other forums of the organization where those issues have some impact and may be resolved.
- She undertakes the responsibility for assuring the smooth functioning and communication of problems and resolutions that affect the meaningful delivery of patient care services.

These and other responsibilities will characterize the nurse manager's role in the new and different environment. As the representative of the nursing staff for problems affecting its ability to do its work, she becomes more closely allied with its members, representing their interests, incorporating her problem-solving strategies with theirs, and communicating their decisions throughout the organization. She moves laterally and vertically to assure appropriate movement and flow of problems, decisions, and resolutions throughout her unit of management and through the institution as a whole.

These elements demonstrate why human relations, communication, and interactional skills will be essential to the success of the nurse manager in her new role. She will want to help develop those skills not only in herself but in her nursing peers. She will want to provide leadership in developing the strengths of practicing nurses beyond simply the application of their skills at the bedside, broadening them to include their application to decision making, to the governance of the profession in the institution, and to nursing's relationships within itself and with the institution.

NOTES

1. Luther Christman, "Educational Standards Versus Professional Performance" in *A Luther Christman Anthology,* ed. Jerome Lysaught (Wakefield, Mass.: Nursing Digest, Inc., 1978), 37–44.

2. American Nurses Association, *Nursing: A Social Policy Statement* (Kansas City, Mo.: ANA, 1980).

3. Tim Porter-O'Grady and Sharon Finnigan, *Shared Governance for Nursing* (Rockville, Md.: Aspen Systems Corporation, 1984).

Working with Groups: The Secret of Success

Chapter 6

Objectives for Chapter Six

Review the construction and work roles of groups in the work environment.

Identify key group-building activities that are essential prerequisites for professional group work.

Outline the necessary group skills that must be evidenced in the role of the nurse manager or group leader.

Understand the basic needs of group members as individuals and participants in the nursing group and the workplace.

Explore the nurse manager's trust-building activities before undertaking any group work.

Outline the processes associated with group work, their component parts, and the roles of group members.

Discuss the problems inherent in group action and suggest responses in dealing with them.

6

The ability to work with professional nursing groups will be a key skill for the nurse manager in handling human resources in the new, participatory environment. This will include an understanding of group dynamics and group process, the ability to manage related circumstances, events, and activities to assure effective interactions and relationships between and among group members.

The dynamics of interpersonal interaction and relationships, as well as the communication skills outlined in previous chapters, provide a blueprint for developing group skills and managing groups in relation to the opportunities they offer for effective decision making. Problem solving and goal seeking are critical to the fulfillment of the work obligations in delivering patient care services. The nurse manager of the future also will need to assist a broad cross-section of professional caregivers, both within and outside of nursing, in assuring appropriate delivery of care.

COMPOSITION OF THE GROUP

Deciding on the composition of the group is an important first step. The group usually is a collection of individuals who must work interdependently in order to obtain and meet individual professional and organizational objectives. For groups to be effective, especially in the professional context, they must have:

1. a strong reason for working together
2. a strong basis for interdependence—a need for each other's experiences, ability, commitment, and expertise
3. a commitment by each member that the outcome of working together will be more effective and meaningful than those obtained by working independently

4. a specified accountability for functioning in the larger organization and achieving both organizational and group goals.[1]

The members of each group must have a purpose that provides it with an identity. The group itself, and each member, should have a specified function that is defined and is integrated into the role of each member and of the group. The group members must be aware of the need for interdependence and interaction and must be committed to facilitating those elements to the fullest extent possible. Several factors are necessary for the group to work effectively, based on assumptions related to the members' skills, abilities, and roles:

- Everyone must have an appropriate commitment, understanding, and some competence in the group that directs itself to the achievement of a group goal.
- Every member should know what she as an individual wants to do to achieve the objectives of the group.
- Each individual should recognize that the prime focus of the group is on the members' ability to interact and to provide meaningful service in meeting goals and in achieving desired outcomes.
- Each member should want to belong to the group and to achieve the prescribed results.
- The group's potential for effectiveness is restrained only by the limitations each individual member sets on her own potential for participating.
- Each individual must be committed not only to the goals of the group but also of its work. In that context, she must be willing to lend all of her skills, abilities, and competence to the group.
- The work itself must be meaningful, valuable, valid, and, if possible, exciting.

Providing leadership for group process obviously is a challenging role for the nurse manager. Previous chapters identified the need for establishing a participatory framework for the leader and the group. This overlay to group process will provide the kind of environment that can facilitate group construction, out of which will come successful goal initiation, interaction, and outcomes. (See Figure 6–1.)

There are a multitude of groups that are used to accomplish work. These groups can range anywhere from small work groups of no more than two or three people to corporate or division wide groups of up to fifteen members. While the mechanics and logistics of managing these work groups are in some ways different, the processes that influence their construction and operation are virtually the same. Whatever the size or construction of the group, be it a board of trustees, executive

Figure 6–1 Group Construction Process

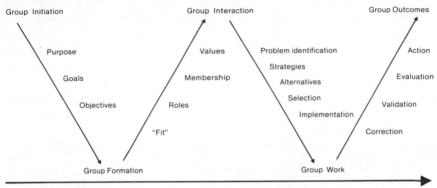

Group Process / Direction

group, professional group, or work team, many of the principles of human interaction and group process apply to their functioning.

The ideas, principles, and processes outlined in this book apply to any work group structures. While the focus is on developing professional work groups and teams, any kind of group operates and functions in the same basic framework. Governance work groups are not dealt with extensively in this book because they demand a depth that lies outside of the scope of this text.

Most of the kind of work groups that will be utilized in nursing are those that focus on functional activities related to nursing practice or to the needs of the nurse. Groups that focus on determining standards of care, quality assurance, patient safety problems, departmental and unit level problem solving, peer processes, performance evaluation, nursing education, leadership issues, new programs, staffing concerns, systems issues, developing nursing goals and objectives, etc., fall well within the scope of activities appropriate for use in the group process. Within these activities the nurse manager has the greatest opportunity to provide leadership in coordinating and structuring the group process in her areas of accountability.

Often there is discussion in leadership circles regarding the effectiveness of using work groups for decision making and planning as well as for governance activities. Ineffectiveness and time extension in problem solving are often cited as examples of why groups should not be utilized. Also, there is the worry that critical or immediate decisionmaking needs will be sacrificed to the group process. These concerns are often valid in the current management systems.

The purpose for the use of groups is to be able to put the most appropriate and best resources together to determine the best response or outcome to a defined issue. Where there is the necessary support from the administrative individual and the appropriate mechanics are in place, the collective action of a well constructed and directed group will always be superior to the mandates of any one individual. In key decisionmaking regarding the assignment of responsibility for specified functions in any one individual, the group can provide a clear basis for the individual's authority and even obtain a group adherence to that authority. This is a far superior process for assigning of accountability and obtaining compliance since those affected by both have played a major role in both determining the rules and articulating the method in which that accountability will be assured. To change either the principle or the process would require the same thoroughness and depth that went into constructing the original rules or guidelines. Since commitment is obtained at the outset and verified through the group's process, arbitrary and obscure behavior on the part of the leader assigned to carry out the group's decision will be minimized.

To be sure, group process and decisionmaking does not work with the critical decision. There is in the health care environment specified processes for the critical or immediate situation, and all health professionals recognize this. In disasters and emergency situations, even in the bureaucracy, all usual rules are suspended and the decisionmaking network is completely decentralized to establish authority in the individuals directly responsible for addressing the critical situation. Here again, however, these processes have been structured by those (again, a group) who are most knowledgeable about the situations with which they will have to deal. Broadening this process to operational decisionmaking does not essentially alter the need for or effectiveness of group process. In fact there is high probability that operational crises can be limited by the effectiveness of group involvement and group commitment. Effective time involvement, in this case, may even be shortened by the reduction of time in correcting errors or inefficiencies in the operating systems where individuals may have limited understanding or little personal investment.

Participatory leadership is the one best way to manage group process and development, particularly in helping groups undertake actions that provide value and meaning in terms of output and outcome. Autocracy and nonparticipatory leadership styles usually are not as effective because the ownership of decisions does not transfer fully from the leader to the group. The group therefore assumes, at best, an advisory role and, at worst, an elemental functionary process that may or may not be of any value in achieving the organization's goals.

The most important characteristic is the particular leadership style of the nurse manager in providing direction to and integration of the group's process and its output. That style will be an important component of the success of the group's dynamics, its ability to interact, and ultimately its outcome.

The nature of group work depends upon the degree of effectiveness of the interaction between and among its members.[2] Concepts of contact, role, and values all will have some impact. The ability to understand how each member of the group relates to the others, the roles each undertakes, and the values each brings to that group can indicate to the panel its potential for success as well as the constraints and barriers to interaction.

Certain kinds of characteristics in individuals must be identified and, to a certain extent, be present before any group can develop effectiveness. The members must believe they can establish an equal and collaborative relationship, working toward achieving mutually desirable goals or objectives and based on mutual trust and respect between and among the members of the group and their leader.

Conditions Involved in Building Group

Certain kinds of conditions must be present that provide some direction for building any group:

1. There must be a positive regard and respect among the members. Each must accept the others, recognizing their strengths and resources, deficiencies and limitations.
2. The members must avoid having hidden agendas. These are difficult to deal with and interfere with the group's intent, its interactional success, and its ability to achieve its goals. Everyone must visualize the others as equals, as real, and as communicating individuals. It must be recognized that each individual brings to the group a different focus, a different set of skills and insights, and a different experience of life. The group must respect those differences.
3. The members must have empathy—an ability to respect, to understand, and to perceive the feelings behind ideas, thoughts, attitudes, and issues that individuals bring to the group. People are social creatures. Within that context are many issues and concerns that have a personal impact on people's thoughts, emotions, feelings, and personal perceptions of self. The possible impact of decisions, of discussions, and of ideas on the relationships established must be understood by each participant and must be handled well by the chair or other person who is providing some direction for the group.
4. Members must be willing to understand and accept a level of self-disclosure. Effective group process allows the personal insights, feelings, and ideas of each member to be expressed in a nonjudgmental, noncritical environment. To the extent that any member feels afraid or reticent to express ideas, the effectiveness of the group process, especially, in terms of its outcome, will be diminished.

Group process is a human-dynamic and human-dependent function. In the nursing environment, human values and relations are vital to its success. Characteristics that allow the humanness in the group, as identified by individual members' thoughts, feelings, values, and mode of communicating must be allowed expression and respect. Systems that limit disclosure and close the doors on expression can only undermine the effectiveness of the group and its processes.

There must be a concreteness, a clear purpose, and an understanding of the group's function and its activities. Specific issues, well described and clearly outlined, with purposes understood and accepted, must be a part of the construct. A vague or abstract focus for the group and its work will seriously harm any sense of the participants' cohesion or meaning. The members must be clear on what its work is, its meaning, its expected outcomes, and its impact on the ultimate goals of the organization. Involvement in the process must be of value to the participants; if it is not, their interest, commitment, and undertaking will dissipate and prove noneffective over the long term.

Individuals who experience difficulties in interpersonal communication may have a problem in forming the kind of relationships essential to group effectiveness. The ability to establish such relationships is important. This makes members' introduction and orientation process to the group necessary. An important first step is entry into the group's socialization process. The group's relationship becomes in and of itself a continuing task and the nurse manager must continue to encourage and develop the relational aspects in order to provide a strong basis for trust and to continue to maintain the confidence of the individual in herself, in her group peer members and in the purposes and work of the group. This interrelationship among members can threaten the group's self-esteem and methodology if it is not monitored constantly by the nurse manager.

A sensitivity to the human dynamics of the group and its mechanism for responding to its interactional processes must be constantly before the group leader. This allows her to identify or change the work or process as needed. To assure an appropriate framework for group trust, the group leader's skills must be directed toward seeking openness and authentic interaction. The nurse manager or group leader must have some of the following core skills:

- the ability to structure the group and communicate its purpose effectively
- the ability to use interactional exercises and to program the group's functional aspects effectively
- the ability to help individuals deal with the here and now interactions and processes
- the ability to link ideas, thoughts, and characteristics
- the ability to confront issues and ideas directly and incorporate them into the goals of the organization
- the ability to block ideas, thoughts, processes, and directions that divert the group from its common purposes

- the talent to encourage and focus on the group's assets and to give positive feedback when appropriate
- the ability to facilitate group participation by identifying, confronting, and utilizing members' nonverbal clues
- the ability to facilitate the delivery of "I" messages and "I" thoughts (The members taking their own responsibility for contributions.)
- the ability to paraphrase and clarify statements, ideas, and thoughts to enhance the group's understanding
- the ability to offer direct feedback and to give it freely and honestly
- the ability to gather the data and discuss them together and to formulate tentative hypotheses for consideration
- the ability to establish a task base focus and to get personal, direct commitment from members to perform some functional work to fulfill the group's goals
- the ability to summarize the thoughts, ideas, and work of the group into a coherent whole and to present it in a systematic and orderly way to the panel.

Developing those skills provides the nurse manager with opportunities for leadership in a way the group can depend upon. The leader pulls together all of the activities, functions, and responsibilities of the group into a meaningful whole and builds on the trusts and interactional processes so that the purposes and objectives finally do achieve defined and clear outcomes.

This process can exert meaningful influences in managing the organization. The group itself can foster the growth of its members, enhance relations among peers, and help achieve the organization's objectives. It can create the conditions and methodology for success.

5 AREAS OF GROWTH

Five major areas of growth must occur in the orientation phase of the group process: the ability to develop skills in self-assessment, self-disclosure, feedback, risk taking, and validation of and by group members. Each of these processes contributes to the success of the interaction and of the relationships established in the group. The goal is to unleash through an orientation the processes that will assist individuals and the group to work together in making wise choices based on these factors.

The individual nurse's ability to spend time looking at her own skills and supports is important. The individual of the future, to be successful in group processes, must be able to look within and to assess, without criticism or judgment, elements that lend support to, and those that detract from, the group. She must be able to get beyond the areas of self-deception and personal distortion in order to see herself in the context of the group in a supporting and encouraging framework. The ability to recognize both constraints and resources will help her identify areas where contributions and changes can be made.[3]

Self-Assessment

The first criterion is to ask basic questions about the individual's own persona:

- Who am I?
- What am I doing?
- Where am I going now with my life?
- What difference do I make?

These questions about self are ones that every professional will have confronted sometime in her life. The answers will have an impact on her ability to relate to other individuals in the group. They give some idea of one's mechanisms of behavior personally and in relating to others. Answers can come from others' perspective of the nurse's behavior in interaction with them or from demonstrating willingness to respond or not to respond.

To see herself more clearly, the nurse must identify how other group members react to these questions and understand that their answers may be different from hers. Acceptance is a vital component of self-assessment—accepting not only one's own personal discoveries but also those of others.

Self-Disclosure

In addition to self-assessment, it also is important to have attained a certain level of self-disclosure. Everyone has a different level of ability to disclose things that are pertinent and appropriate to group and individual interaction. Individuals' experiences of life and relationships in the past have an impact on their ability to relate effectively to the group. Here again each nurse will have a different level of ability to relate her inner self to the group.

Talking about one's own views with relative security may be an important component of the interactional process. The nurse's ability to interpret what is seen as a part of the group's role in the light of her own experience is important in bringing personal meaning to group process. People tend to mediate much of what is discussed in the group process in terms of their own experience. As a result, it is important to nurses that the experiential component they apply to the group process be incorporated into their own responses. They must be able to disclose those experiences and thoughts with confidence and trust, recognizing that they are valuable insights necessary for the group.[4]

Self-disclosure is truly the individual's investment in the group. It is a basic constituent of trust and is perhaps the best evidence that trusting relationships have been established. Trust must be established within the group before this investment will be realized by any of its members. Trust is an important component of developing group relationships. A great deal of time in the orientation phase must be directed to developing that component. Trust is not something that occurs automatically as a result of a group's getting together to meet objectives and goals. It involves the kind and quality of relationships entered into, and specifically the feelings of confidence generated. Development of relationships will be an important part of the group leader's or nurse manager's role. Too often groups are called together, especially in nursing, without appropriate preparation.

Feedback

Another major component of the group process is feedback and feedback mechanisms—the nurse's ability to tell others how interactions, processes, and behaviors have an impact on herself. She must understand how the group process and its work responsibilities affect her willingness and ability to contribute.[5] In group situations, members get a sense of each other's feelings on the issues involved. Those feelings have an impact on individuals' thinking and interaction. Feedback should be made available to all participants in the group. This way, each member is aware of the sense and feelings of others.

Feedback is an important tool because it can result in either an expanding or a narrowing of one's choices and can allow one to choose between alternatives provided, or even shut off the willingness to participate at all. Feedback needs to be managed carefully. When any individual solicits sensitive information regarding process, individuals, behaviors, or outcomes, she must do so with caution and care.

Risk Taking

The group process involves the following risks: taking a stand, making unpopular decisions, grappling with tough issues, and representing one's peers. Many changes occur when group process is used as the major decision-making model in an organization. Authority is transferred from autocracy to individuals (or a group), creating an entirely new milieu. Responsibility for decision making is shared by the nurse manager and is spread over a broader base involving more individuals. Obviously, with that kind of involvement, these individuals begin to take the risks normally assumed by the leaders who previously made decisions alone.

As a result, the group, and its members individually, must understand the nature of risk taking and learn to deal with it comfortably. This will involve the ability to take risks beyond the basic levels traditionally expected of workers in the bureaucratic framework. In the participatory model, the risk in using group process is entrusting to the group the decisions previously made solely by the manager. She then must develop new ways of behaving, of interacting, and of making decisions that use all of the staff and institutional resources available to her and provide an opportunity for those with whom she works to make the kinds of decisions of which they are capable.

Here again the nurse manager as leader is vital to successful change and growth in the unit. Regardless of how involved the nursing staff has become in decisions and processes that affect their own practice, the nurse manager will be the identified leader who ensures that the rules, policies, standards, and practices that have been collectively determined are carried out. Invested in her position is the responsibility, with all the necessary authority, for assuring that the participatory system operates effectively. The location of the source of that authority has shifted to include the professional organization that now shares accountability with the institution. In addition to her usual obligations for daily staffing, problem solving, resource provision, counselling, and providing leadership for the nursing group, she becomes the bridge between staff and institution and works to assure congruence between the needs and goals of the institution and the nursing staff.

Here again trust is important. Trusting relationships and opportunities for interacting can provide a strong support system for reaching out and expressing views, problem solving, and discussing all issues and ideas.[6] This involves the nurse manager and staff setting the parameters for relationships, describing how roles will be implemented in the group, assigning responsibilities to each member, and opening up the group to act free of judgment and criticism.

All these are prerequisites to the risk-taking actions of any individual member. When the experience of success, validation, and support results in a feeling of safety in each member of the group, then a willingness to undertake changes in behavior, in thought, in process, and ideas for problem solving will be generated. The individual's comfort in being able to express herself, receive feedback, and attempt new ideas and behaviors all help to reinforce her in becoming more active in the group process. These changes also allow the group to seek the kinds of appropriate and meaningful solutions to issues that the members own and that fall within the context of its objectives.

Validation

In developing the trust relationship it is important to assure that the leader provides appropriate validation or confirmation of group work. The nurse manager must give feedback that is supportive and authenticating and that allows individuals to feel good about their responses and their interaction with the group.

Consensual support through supportive messages and confirmation of ideas is essential to maintain the group's momentum and energy. This does not mean that validation must be inaccurate, incorrect, inappropriate, or superficial; rather, it must be meaningful. Individuals recognize when they are being truly appreciated and rewarded. What is important in validation is to assure that when ideas are useful, as they often are, the individual is recognized and responded to it in a positive and sustaining way.

MAINTAINING GROUP DYNAMICS

If appropriate supports are to be applied to the group process, specific conditions and circumstances must exist. The ability to give and receive effective feedback and validation, information, and support is a cornerstone of the group's effectiveness and ability to grow. The following conditions must be met to ensure that the appropriate dynamics in the group are maintained and generate activity over an extended period:

1. The members must be ready for group interaction, work, and feedback. The leadership elected or selected by the group must be capable of integrating the member roles and functions.
2. The relationships and feedback must be descriptive. Interpretation and subsequent feedback to the group must be left to each individual.
3. Response, openness, and feedback must be undertaken at a time when specific behavior is identified in the group and when it occurs, not later.
4. The subject and the information at issue must be appropriate and meaningful to the individuals in the group.
5. Information and behavior, as well as relationships, are directed to and are fully capable of influencing change.
6. No individual should feel overloaded by the responsibilities, information, role, or dynamics of the group.
7. Group support and trust should be helpful and designed primarily to support the human needs of the work group. The group's goals and objectives always should be secondary.
8. The members of the group should be open, responsive, and willing to share and participate to the fullest extent to meet the requirements of the work group.
9. All feedback and relationships should be nonevaluative and nonjudgmental, should not preach, moralize, admonish, or demand, and should be free of criticism.

Providing leadership for the group process is challenging and can be difficult. The group leader, usually the nurse manager, must have been exposed to many of the issues discussed earlier. Before dealing with them in the group, she has to have resolved her personal relational issues that will have an impact on her ability to act as group leader. The nurse manager obviously is the natural individual to provide leadership for group work. Since, by virtue of her position, she already holds leadership responsibilities, applying them in the group process is merely an extension of her role. Here again, however, the nurse manager must have come to grips with significant issues regarding her personal management style, her ability to relate to others, and self-assessment of her relationship to those who work with her and with her peers.

To provide effective leadership, the nurse manager must be able to pull together a multitude of resources, especially human resources. She must assure that the multiplicity of personalities, resources, insights, and abilities blend together in a meaningful way to provide the group with direction, purpose, and outcome. She must have developed a high level of personal trust with the individuals with whom she works. Trust is as important in applied work as it is in group dynamics.

The elements essential to trust often are not clearly visible in the traditional nursing bureaucratic framework. Since, as noted earlier, the bureaucracy tends to operate with some degree of wariness, the principles the nurse manager uses with the nursing staff must come out of a different context from those historically provided in the bureaucratic framework. She must identify ways in which trust can be developed, especially with professional nurses. The demands and needs of professionals are different from those of vocational workers. The professional nurse demands a different set of interactions and behaviors. For that reason, the nurse manager must develop strategies in management style that address the issue of trust. She must build relationships that establish a common basis for understanding, for trust, and ultimately for nursing practice.

Characteristics for Developing Trust

Following are some key characteristics the nurse manager must evidence if she is to create and maintain an environment of trust in group process activities:

1. The nurse manager must have dealt with her own relationships and self-perception regarding her level of confidence and ability to relate, understand, and empathize with the needs of others.
2. The nurse manager must be committed to the belief that all individuals are worthy of respect and have a fundamental purpose and meaning in life that pervades all of their activity.
3. The nurse manager as a professional nurse must recognize that she is working and relating with peers and that as the leader she can provide

inspiration, direction, assistance, and support. She must always remember that the accountability for nursing practice rests with her peers.

4. The nurse manager must believe that all individuals have a responsibility to undertake activities that have meaning and purpose and that when these values are applied to the work environment they will enhance it, improve it, and offer it new and creative values.

5. The nurse manager must involve all appropriate individuals in making decisions that have a direct impact on their roles, responsibilities, and personal accountabilities.

6. The nurse manager must be sensitive to, and able to acknowledge, the contributions of groups and individuals in meeting the needs and the objectives of the work. This ability to acknowledge must be communicated comfortably to the participants.

7. The nurse manager must be able to build two-way loyalty and commitment with her professional peers. It is important that professionals delivering health care services assure mutual commitment and compatibility in meeting the goals and objectives of the group and of the organization.

8. The nurse manager and her peers must be able to accept the observations and views of other individuals and groups regarding the roles, responsibility, and work of the professional nursing work group. Openness to others' insights provides an opportunity for growth, for problem defining, and for seeking solutions.

8. The nurse manager must always be able to articulate the reasons for undertaking specific forms of action and for approaching problems, issues, and concerns openly and with no hidden agendas. The ability to be honest and direct and to allow her nursing peers the opportunity to respond appropriately is a cornerstone for building a basic level of trust.

9. The nurse manager must willingly allow others to participate fully in decisions that affect them. They should jointly review facts that have a bearing on decisions and the others should be encouraged to suggest alternatives.

Health care is moving into an era in the management of professionals in which they will seek continually to expand their responsibilities and their involvement in key decision making. With the groundwork for trusting established, trust now can grow. This helps make group process decisions truly effective. The group's power and responsibility will be better invested and more clearly defined when there is a sense of open interaction and an ability to communicate effectively. Successful interpretation will be based on a sense of security and trust among all members. At this point in the group's development, the functional components of the group work—participation, goal setting, interaction, and group process—have been addressed and incorporated as a constituent of all group activities (Figure 6–2).

Figure 6–2 Group Interaction Process

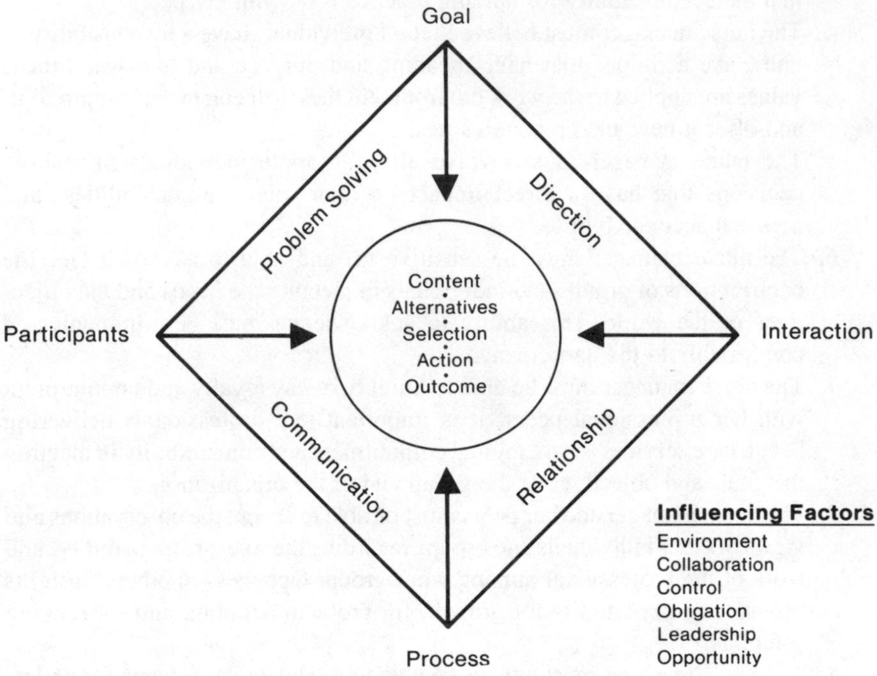

Influencing Factors
Environment
Collaboration
Control
Obligation
Leadership
Opportunity

Participation and Responsibilities

Each member of the nursing unit for which the manager assumes some responsibility has a stake in its activities and in participating in them as fully as possible. In the new era of participatory nursing, this will be mandatory, not optional. The ability to communicate, to interact, to relate, to problem solve, to discuss issues, to raise alternatives, and to seek solutions as a collective will be essential to the success of individual members of the group.

Each member must take the time to assess her skills and abilities in undertaking responsibilities in fulfillment of her individual role. The job descriptions or position charters of the future that relate to the roles of individual members will have as key components of their design those items that speak specifically to the nurse's ability to relate as a member of her work group. She will make decisions and undertake activities that have an impact on the nursing process and its outcomes and ultimately meet the goals and objectives of the work group.

The individual nurse's responsibility to provide input and to integrate her role with the organization will be an expectation in the future workplace. This will be especially true for professionals. Professional nurses in the new era will be unable to operate successfully with a 9-to-5 mentality (or, in nursing parlance, 7-3/3-11/11-7). The individual practicing nurse in the future will have to recognize that her role will be central to the success of meeting the organization's objectives. She must go beyond hands-on work itself and commit her person, insights, abilities, and skills that relate to delivering nursing care.

As discussed in previous chapters, the professional role of the nurse will demand additional kinds of responses that are important to the work environment. These will be lateral rather than vertical or hierarchical in character and will require interaction, deliberation, and group process. Nurses will share in the responsibility for meeting the goals and objectives of the nursing staff on a given work unit and in solving problems of concern to the staff as a whole. Issues traditionally allocated to the nurse manager now will become fundamental parts of the role of the collective of practicing professional nurses of the future. Traditional issues such as staffing, financial management, divisional and departmental problem solving, interdepartmental relations, and seeking alternatives for operational constraints all will be incorporated to a broader extent into the role of each practicing nurse.

Standards of behavior and response can be developed upon which the department or unit can operate by utilizing state of the art data generating systems that address patient acuity, available staff, nursing care costs, cost/benefits, budget characteristics, nursing service characteristics. When given sufficient information and expert resources, the appropriate group representing the full range of nursing roles from manager, clinical specialist, specialty nurse, staffing coordinator, personnel resource, business specialist, etc., can formulate the framework for action including the standards and practices that will form the response base for the matter at issue. Through the collaborative processes in group management and representing the staff and the institution, the best problem solving strategies and resources are thereby brought to bear on the problem. The outcome of this process then provides the basis upon which all members of the nursing organization, department or unit (depending upon who is affected) will respond and function. It now becomes the role of the nurse manager or other assigned nursing leader to manage nursing behavior and action within the context of the accepted standard.

A new economic environment is emerging that will provide both opportunity and constraint for the future. Institutions will have to use every resource, especially practicing nurses, to its maximum efficiency. It must be recognized that allocation of responsibilities, roles, and functions will have to be structured in a way that utilizes all the skills and abilities of each provider. The professional nurse of the future, to be a cost-effective value to the institution, will have to use all of her skills and abilities to maximize the benefit of her role and responsibilities.

The nurse traditionally has had a broad range of variability in applying skills to delivery of patient care services. The clinical problem-solving talent that she applies to her role in the future will have many of the same characteristics as in traditional managerial and operational problem solving. The mechanics are essentially the same. Broadening her scope of reference and her basis for responsible action will be a benchmark of her ability to survive and to contribute to health care in the future.

DEVELOPMENT OF A WORK GROUP

In developing a work group, the nurse leader must have a clear understanding of its construct so it can undertake meaningful work. She first must determine its purpose, its meaning, and its value. This is considerably different from developing the group's goals and objectives. She must evaluate those who will participate in the group work.

The nurse manager must understand the potential dynamics of the group before formulating its processes. She also must understand how the group as a working unit operates in applying nursing care on a particular unit. She must anticipate its strengths and potential flaws so she can address them in initiating the transition toward group decision making.

The nurse manager must be aware that each individual will present her own unique set of behaviors, practices, and expressive patterns that have evolved in her work experience and how these will affect the others with whom she works. The manager must understand that the group demands a great deal of interaction, collaboration, and support from each of its members. To obtain that, she must address potential concerns and problems between and among individuals and, if possible, resolve them.[7]

Individuals take a large risk in making a personal investment in a group yet this is vitally important to their operating as a successful work unit. The nurse manager must address and resolve this concern. This is an important part of the nurse manager's moving to unit-based group work.

Collaborative relationships based on mutual trust (as indicated) incorporating the democratic processes associated with group decision making are a major value of the participants. The assumption underlying a group is that people can and will function effectively in work settings if they can be taught to collaborate with each other in decision making and if they also can learn to treat one another with trust, openness, acceptance, understanding, and respect. This process also assumes that such concepts as MacGregor's Theory Y[8] and Argyris's Interpersonal Competence[9] are representative of the human relations and interactional theory applied to managerial decision making.

Role of the Nurse Manager

The nurse manager plays a considerable part in staff development.[10] She must allow potential group members opportunities to express their needs and wants as well as to describe their feelings related to growth. She must realize that she has an obligation to assist each nurse in developing her abilities and creativity and to accept and exercise the kinds of responsibility that comes with professional decision making. The motivation to do this comes out of the individual's urge to do the best she can in offering her services to others. The assumption is that individuals work effectively when they are provided with every opportunity to achieve, to create, to learn, to accept responsibility, and to move toward achieving self-actualization.

It would be foolish to assume that everyone in the workplace is at the same high level of self-achievement. Individuals have different levels of maturity. These personal variables make the workplace relatively complex and each of the individuals operating within that complexity presents a unique set of needs that increases the difficulty of establishing truly humanistic-oriented management processes. The differences in the ability of individuals to perform at consistently high levels is demonstrated by symptoms such as competition, conflict, struggle for power, need for identity, need for assurance, and a search for positive reinforcement.

All of these play a role in the complex human environment of the organization with which the nurse manager must cope. This can result in a frustrating and often discouraging process limiting the individuals' ability to achieve, to grow, and to relate effectively with each other. Often, they fear that collaborative and group processes will degenerate into win/lose strategies, so each individual is more interested in personal ego satisfaction than in meeting group needs.

All of these concerns are legitimate and exist in any organization. People adapt to change and to group demands at differing rates and with differing degrees of success. The important point is that honesty, openness, and an environment that permits variation and difference yet also confronts unacceptable or intervening differences directly and openly does provide the strongest opportunity for success in group management. The ability of the nurse leader to take a developmental approach is important. She must provide growth opportunities to the staff for identifying constraints and resources in exercising skills in group process. Staff members must be oriented to the purposes, meaning, value, and structure of the group before it is established in order to avert or diminish some of the more difficult situations the nurse manager might face.

Power and Peer Coercion

One of the most difficult issues the nurse manager may face is the nurses' continual problem in dealing realistically and effectively with power and individual peer coercion. Increasingly, it is evident that these are highly significant issues in nursing, affecting change and influencing stability in the organization. Power and coercion too often seem to be the mechanisms of choice among nurses undertaking activity that provides some meaning and value for the organization. Perhaps it is because nurses as peers and collaborators are at a rather early developmental state, not yet comfortable with the multilateral steps and stages of growth and development.

Whatever the reason, there is a strong indication that nursing practice is strongly fixed at an immature level associated with a need to use power and to provide direction using coercive tactics. The nurse manager must understand the impact of the processes that result from the use of such power strategies and coercive activities.

The nurse manager must have a realistic view of her role as group leader. She must understand that there often is an urge in group process that stimulates competitiveness, exploitation, coercion, control, experiential comparison, etc. These factors are countered by such other strongly motivated drives as openness, collaboration, productivity, responsibility, and accountability. However, these latter often are hidden and operate at a higher developmental level. The goal of the nurse manager is to begin to tap these higher level skills, regardless of how juvenile they may appear early in their expression.

The organization, perhaps unwittingly, also lends some support to the continuing childlike perceptions of interactions that nursing staff members have in their relationships, especially in undertaking the processes of change. In the traditional organization, coercion, competitiveness, and exploitation are amply evident and seem to be basic elements of the usual operating postures of managers in that environment. As nursing moves to open environments in the 21st century, it must recognize the essential failure and limitation of these strategies and seek to reach beyond them in order to involve individuals in achieving higher level outcomes.

The wise nurse leader must deal with these limitations, accept the fact that they are there, and help her staff members reach beyond them in ways that can provide broader meaning and more universally applicable outcomes. Needless to say, she will have to do a great deal of preparatory work for the alterations and transitions necessary to make a group work effectively. The nurse manager must be committed to undertaking the one-to-one interactions essential to identifying the basic levels of trust, understanding the individuals with whom she works, and locating their appropriate relational characteristics in the context of the work group as a whole.

This process will give the nurse manager a feel for how the work group will function, the time frames in which it will evolve, and the characteristics it will evidence as she provides leadership for it. It also will help her know where to begin the process of transition: (1) at what level of interaction to begin which developmental process, (2) which groups or individuals will require more of her time, and (3) what focus and levels of complexity in decision making will be appropriate as a starting point. When she has done this, she will begin to understand some of the basic dynamics that will be operative as she begins to define with the participants the direction of the work group and provide a framework for its activities. Needless to say, this development process is not brief. Depending on the level of group and individual maturity, this process could take anywhere from a few months to several years. In any case, the nurse manager must be committed to a long-term effort.

The nurse manager must incorporate into her information base an awareness of the politics involved in making a significant change in the decision-making and governance structure in her organization. Group process decisions will have a different set of political and social frameworks as peer and collaborative decision-making replaces authoritarian and unilateral control and management systems.

Stresses of Transition

The transition to a new system obviously will be stressful. The new nurse manager will face major uncertainties in adapting to collaborative practice and decision making and learning political and social norms. She must understand that many of the informal aspects of the organization may have more influence over her success in making the transition than any of the formal structures may. Political process is sometimes, even often, informal. Constraints in the formal organization limiting certain kinds of political activity frequently do not exist on the informal level.

The formal organization gives a strong sense of direction and of cohesion in their power structure; that is not so with their politics. Politics relates to the expression of power, either as perceived from the point of view of the individual having the power or as seen by others. There is no stronger example of the influences and risks of power than in situations that involve reorganization, personnel changes, budget allocations, and corporate decision making. All of these have an impact on the nurse manager's efforts to provide for collaborative and peer-based decision making.

These risks cannot be underestimated. She must be aware of the implications of making such changes and, as in all political organizations, she must be able to assess the support and opposition expressed by other key individuals before she makes any moves. Addressing the opportunity to engage in upward political influence is an important step in making a transition in any work.

Another problem for the nurse manager in making changes is the scarcity of people willing to put themselves on the line in the organization. People are social creatures who seek support from each other. If the nursing department by itself is undertaking new directions and new activities that will benefit the entire organization, many of the risks inherent in being socially isolated will have an impact on the nurse manager implementing the change. Her ability to undertake risk, to identify supports, and to seek opportunities to express personal values will require careful preparation.

In a traditional organizational structure on the way to making change, the nurse manager must recognize that her supports will be minimal at first. However, nothing breeds support like success. If satisfaction levels move higher, turnover lower, decision making improves, quality and productivity increase, these outcomes all will have an impact on those holding power and those sharing it.

The success of such outcomes can provide a stronger base for further building. Again, the nurse manager first must take a risk and must decide whether she is willing and able to undergo the resultant pressures. When she can develop her own political strengths in the organization, she can be assured that her support is available as she goes through the many traumas and strains associated with this major transition in governance and human relationships.

COORDINATION OF THE GROUP PROCESS

Once the bases of preparation have been addressed and the group processes actually begin, coordinating the group will demand a whole new set of skills essential to the panel's effectiveness and workability. The coordinator or facilitator will have to be able to manage and integrate the group process effectively. The skills essential for this process are concise, yet vital:

- The group facilitator must be able to identify her role clearly and to lead the members to perceive it correctly. It is important to note that the facilitator is not responsible for the full work of the group but rather assures that the task is carried out by its members.
- The group facilitator must keep the group fully focused on the issues at hand. Fully focused also means that the group must have a strong reality orientation (commitment to the truth) and operate within a present context, rather than from historical or future perspectives.
- The facilitator must identify the flow, processes, roles, and functions operating in the group and keep them on target.

The facilitator must have a clear understanding of the constructs of the group and the characteristics necessary for its successful operation. The role of the group can be divided into essentially five components or functional requirements.

1. Finding Problems and Seeking Solutions

- proposing solutions to problems; suggesting new ideas; applying new definitions to problems and undertaking new approaches to old ones; and looking at new organization, materials, goals, and objectives

- seeking appropriate and meaningful information; looking for clarification, suggestions, and ideas; requesting additional information; and looking for facts, research, process, and outcomes
- seeking opinions from members of the group, looking for ideas and thoughts about its work, implementing ideas and suggestions in relation to roles where members interact
- offering meaningful information to others; offering work, facts, discoveries, assumptions, conclusions, experiences, group decisions, problem identification, and any other such issues that relate to the work of the group
- sharing beliefs, ideas, opinions, suggestions, processes, and probable conclusions on several ideas; assigning work responsibilities for areas of accountability; and suggesting new facts, new processes, or outcomes
- clarifying, developing new examples, seeking meaning, developing meaningful conclusions, evaluating, projecting, applying, and expanding ideas and work
- integrating; showing the interaction among various suggestions, alternatives, and variables; incorporating and integrating ideas, suggestions, outcomes, and research; tying together group, subgroup, and committee activities; integrating functional processes, finance, and productivity
- concluding; drawing basic conclusions from data available; suggesting actions based on suggestions, alternatives, outcomes, assessment, evaluation of process and outcome, determination of effectiveness, quality assurance, and validation of goals and objectives.

2. Strengthening and Maintaining Group Activities

- supporting; developing close collaborative and interactional relationships; expressing understanding, tolerance, trust, praise, encouragement, agreeing, nonjudgmental attitude, openness, and warmth
- facilitating; allowing every member of the group to participate; drawing out ideas from reticence, opening up individuals; incorporating all individuals' work, suggestions, thoughts, and ideas; providing the opportunity for everyone to be heard
- developing standards; providing a framework for evaluating; for making choices and for decision making; for undertaking actions; and for determining appropriate routines and values based on established standards for operating in the group
- supporting group consensus decisions; accepting the group, its processes, its values, and its outcomes; participating by hearing, supporting, valuing ideas, agreeing with, and obtaining further support

- articulating feelings; understanding the emotional sense of the group of individuals; voicing concerns and defining feelings; describing reactions and looking for individual responses.

3. Task and Maintenance Roles

- providing measurements allowing group decisions to be compared, evaluated, and judged; assessing accomplishments against objectives
- diagnosing, determining difficulties, and defining problems; articulating process to undertake steps for resolution; looking at blocks; determining progress; assessing the need to change course
- offering internal support; looking for group opinions, views, values, and thoughts in relationship to role, responsibility, and decision making; assessing support for outcomes; testing ideas; looking for consensus
- mediating, resolving conflicts, conciliating, creating harmony and accepting diversity, resolving issues, obtaining support views, seeking compromise, establishing negotiation parameters
- lifting stress; addressing negative feelings, issues, and concerns; creating a break in process; lightening the environment; socializing; broadening the issues; supporting others in the pain of change; identifying key positives and providing encouragement and individual support.

4. Identifying Nonintegrating Behavior

- handling aggression; coping with individuals who criticize and blame, are hostile, seek to identify their own needs over and above those of the group; dealing with egos; raising status; restraining those who monopolize discussion and conversations
- running interference; handling those who block progress; undertaking direction of the group; restraining those who harangue or run off on a tangent; redirecting those who put personal experience above the group's needs; coping with those who discuss issues unrelated to the group's task or are argumentative, rejectionary, inconsiderate, self-centered.
- coping with the narcissism of those who use the group as a reflection of self and become solely involved in personal responses to and in the group, restraining those seeking to use the group as an extension of self-described needs, diverting those seeking to force the group to deal with their individual feelings and needs while attempting to keep the group from focusing on its needs

- restraining those who attempt bettering—trying to have the best idea, superior thoughts, and strongest viewpoints; deflating members bent on becoming shining stars, interested in the group's perception of themselves and its acceptance of their ideas
- eliminating lobbying, such as attempts to focus the group on issues of concern to the individual, work discussions around to supporting individual suggestions and ideas; curbing those who put forward personal considerations without regard to the group and who introduce and seek support for philosophies outside the group's interest or work
- turning serious those who insist on humor, making light of serious situations, joking, imitating, disrupting, clowning, not addressing issues with seriousness
- drawing out those who exhibit passive behavior by withdrawing, not responding, not participating, doodling, whispering, doing other work, thinking of other subjects; not involving the group or being involved with it.

5. Leading to Improve Group Members' Roles

- seeking to meet the goals of the group and maintaining the direction of the process consistent with its objectives
- becoming more sensitive to the individual needs of group members and applying that sensitivity to meeting its goals
- becoming involved in self-development and education regarding her own responsiveness to the group and its needs and the skills essential to leading it
- sensing changes in the group and the need for altered direction
- sensing when the group needs to be stimulated as well as when it needs to be recessed
- being sensitive to and identifying issues that interfere with the group's process and those that can bring the group back into context
- knowing the stage of development and interaction in which the group is moving and assessing the panel's effectiveness from the perspective of the stage of development at which it is operating.

The nurse manager must learn to resolve and deal with the conflicts inherent in any group process. Decision making always engenders different perspectives and viewpoints, thought processes, and alternative solutions. In that context, the manager has a number of alternatives, such as consensus seeking and expert input and evaluation, that must be discussed and pursued carefully in order to arrive at the most appropriate decision.[11]

ON REACHING A CONSENSUS

Reaching a consensus is one of the most difficult steps in the group process. However, it also is a major goal of problem-solving discussions. Before the group can reach a consensus, every member must feel as though she has been heard. Members must have participated as fully as possible in the discussions that help lead to the consensus. The very concept of discussion, in fact, always assumes that viewpoints differ and that there is legitimacy to each.

While the group should hear these viewpoints, its goal is to achieve some direction and outcome from those interactions. Sound decisions, which are the goal of problem-solving discussions, depend on the ability of the group leader to create an atmosphere and an environment that is open, responsive, and conducive to allowing individuals to express viewpoints, opinions, and thoughts related to alternative solutions.

The group process always should encourage activities that lead to problem solving and solution seeking. In that process, most discussions produce conflicts and differing points of view that are necessary components of the decision-making process. If the conflicts inherent in discussion are discouraged, chances are that the quality of group communication and decisions will be compromised.

Decision making usually starts with uncertainty. To alleviate such a condition, the group must collect information that can help it solve the problem. The use of meaningful information, and communicating it to members, can help guide group discussions and decision making. Failure in effective communication at any phase of the group process can spell failure in achieving objectives. (See Figure 6–3.)

One of the first steps is to agree on the issues involved. This provides a framework for subsequent discussions. This is not always a simple process. Significant steps and processes must be followed and certain kinds of information must be acquired. This also may produce conflict. Trying to reconcile varying viewpoints simply to pinpoint the specific issue can, in and of itself, engender conflict. However, it is only when the ideas are diverse that the nurse manager can be assured that the solutions will be creative and meaningful. Also, it is only in this framework that the problem can be understood in its broadest context.

Figure 6–3 Communication Breakdown Characteristics

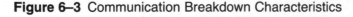

Input ⟶	Throughput ⟶	Output
● No goals	● Limited Interaction	● No cohesive direction
● Inadequate Information	● Insufficient Discussion	● Limited Participant Involvement
● Poor Participation	● Misdirected Process	● No Ownership of Outcome
● No Role Orientation	● Poor Problemsolving	● Unclear Action Plan
● Unclear Expectations	● Ineffective Strategy	● No Evaluation Mechanism
	● Poor Group "Fit"	

The nurse manager must elicit from the group members a wide range of alternatives related to both the issues and the strategies for solving them. Here again, conflict is inherent. Many alternatives may have significant benefits but premature commitment to any one without full discussion may limit its effectiveness. Therefore, the group's ability to seek, as objectively as possible, alternatives to problems and solutions will be essential in achieving its objectives. Alternative ideas are needed, but they almost always produce conflict. Members must learn to accept this reality.

Conflict: Good and Bad

Conflict itself is not all bad—it can stimulate creativity in solving problems. Under effective direction, ideas are expressed and countered, information is aired, and values are articulated. All of these come together to form a basis for creating the beneficial conflict that makes problem solving a dynamic process. It should be clear that conflict must not be avoided in discussion; rather, it must be used appropriately and developed and managed by the group leader in such a way that it leads to meaningful solutions.

Conflict can be dangerous when discussion becomes too vigorous because that can terminate the group processes and involve individuals' emotional responses in such a way that it may block effective discussion and decision making. Therefore, the group leader will have to implement creative strategies to prevent the conflict from degenerating into emotional and personal terms. Disruptive conflicts occur when the participants do not (or do not want to) understand the nature of the conflict in objective terms and begin to internalize it in a competitive manner. They then become closely and personally connected to the issues. That produces a win/lose situation in which one individual must win and another must lose. Since this occurs in most situations anyway, the leader's task here is to soften the blow for the loser (but not at the winner's expense, so it is a delicate task) and present the decision in nonconflagrationary terms. That will go far toward smoothing any ruffled feathers.

By contrast, positive conflict develops when the members understand that the objective is appropriate and will be selected from a number of alternatives. In the consideration of the alternatives, certain conflicts will arise that will generate disagreements, discussions, and eventual refinement of the solution. Integration is the key word in constructive conflict. If the conflict integrates the group and the problem-solving process and leads to higher, more refined levels of decision making, then it is positive and meaningful. When it degenerates into personal issues and creates win/lose situations, it is destructive and pointless.

The group leader must determine whether the conflict is an integral part of the problem-solving process and whether it can lead the group to resolving issues. When mismanaged, conflict can be destructive. When managed appropriately, it can improve the quality of the group's work and the effectiveness of its decision making. The nurse manager must be aware of the value of conflict and manage it effectively, maintaining its objective nature and avoiding members' personal intrusions in order to achieve the goals and objectives.

The Disruptive Individual

One concern in group management arises when a destructive individual participates. Some individuals may not be fully committed to the group's activity and can be a highly disruptive force. These individuals can create conflicts, seriously interrupt the problem-solving process, and cause trouble for the group leader. There are many kinds of disruptive behaviors that can occur in meetings and these must be addressed by the group leader in one way or another. These include:

Speechmaking	Chronic Complaining
Repetition	Withdrawing
Interrupting	Separating
Sidetracking	Subverting
Emotionalizing Issues	Personalizing Issues
Aggressive Behavior	Accusations
Sarcastic Language	Threats

These and a host of like behaviors can subvert the group and impede the leader in directing it and keeping it on course. Every leader must anticipate some such conduct in every group. Not everybody in the group is at the same level of maturity. Not everybody has achieved the same degree of comfort in the group. Based on these realities, the leader must recognize when immature behaviors begin to interfere with the group's effectiveness. She must undertake strategies to lead the group away from the personalization that occurs when disruptive individuals attempt to manipulate meetings.

Everybody seeks to have some role in the group process and in helping meet goals. The group leader can take many steps, before meetings, to prevent disruptions and individual domination of the process. The following is a list of ideas the group leader can use to forestall such individuals:

1. Obtain cooperation from the disrupter before the meeting by negotiating the role this individual will have.
2. Appoint the individual to a special, purposeful function and role and co-opt the person into the obligation for leadership.
3. Agree to work out any differences in a different forum.

4. Structure the session to include plenty of discussion regarding the meeting and its conduct. This discussion should focus on the participant's activities in the group.
5. Remove the disrupter-dominator from the agenda or from the meeting altogether, if necessary.
6. Indicate to the disrupting individual how that behavior appears to the group as a whole and make clear what conduct is unacceptable and the consequences of continuing it.
7. Obtain the support of the other participants on handling this individual's behavior by stiffening the others' not responding to it.
8. Place the individual's behavior on the meeting's agenda for discussion by the group as a whole.

These steps can provide some assistance to the group leader in preventing or anticipating the kinds of disruptive behavior that may have an impact on the meeting. The following are even stronger suggestions that the group leader might undertake during the meeting to help offset the disruptive individual:

1. Understand the individual's perspective and determine whether it is in opposition to the group leader's personal feelings or a broad-scale disruptive perspective and behavior.
2. Clarify by turning the disrupter's comments and behaviors into clear statements. This forces these individuals to accept responsibility for their own statements rather than interfere with the process.
3. Point out the nature of the win/lose situation in the discussion. Change roles.
4. Let the person know what the dominating behavior looks like from the leader's perspective (privately first).
5. Ignore the individual's content and input, discussing the situation with the person later.
6. Express her reaction to the individual's behaviors in terms of her own personal feelings.
7. Carry the disruptive individual's arguments to their logical, irrational conclusion.
8. Seek feedback and interaction from the rest of the group in relationship to the disrupter's behavior.

If these do not succeed and the group leader has exhausted all alternatives, she still has some extreme solutions. The leader can:

1. Remove the disruptive individual from the group membership until she can deal more effectively with the person's behavior in positive terms.

2. Create an environment for the individual that will be very uncomfortable when disruption occurs.
3. Have the group as a whole refuse to participate in the disrupter's activities.

What is vitally important is that the group leader maintain full composure and control.[12] If she allows the emotional elements to enmesh her, she loses her effectiveness in providing leadership. She must give careful consideration to the most appropriate technique to use. The first steps should involve taking the time to deal personally and directly with the offending individual. However, when first steps fail, succeeding ones must be taken to keep the group effective. The leader must never let the group become ineffective and unable to accomplish its work. Anyone who interferes with that process should not remain a group member if at all possible.[13]

The ability of the nurse manager to lead the group process is vital to her role as manager and as integrator. As indicated, in the 21st century, the role of integrator will become more and more important. The ability to manage groups, to integrate them, to provide direction and support for them, and to achieve useful outcomes will be a significant part of the manager's role.

In the context of that process, the manager who develops the requisite skills in preparing for the future will assure successful group process and a truly integrated professional organization. Then, all participants will share in decision making and acquire ownership of their outcomes, becoming a positive force for influence in the work environment.

NOTES

1. E.T. Gendlin and John Beak, III, "An Experimental Approach to Group Therapy," *Journal of Research and Development in Education* (December 1968): 19–29.

2. J.W. Pfeiffer, "Conditions Which Hinder Effective Communication," in *Handbook for Group Facilitators,* ed. J.E. Jones and J.W. Pfeiffer (San Diego: University Associates, Inc., 1973), 120–123.

3. Dean Nylin and R. Mitchell, *A Short Handbook of Staff Development and Human Relations Training* (Chicago: NTL Learning Resources Corporation, 1967), 67–70.

4. P.G. Harrison, *Learning Through Groups* (San Diego: University Associates Press, 1981).

5. W. O'Connell, *Action Therapy and Adlerian Theory* (Chicago: Alfred Adler Institute, 1975).

6. J.A. Hansen, R.W. Warner, and E.J. Smith, *Group Counseling, Theory and Practice* (Chicago: Rand McNally & Co., 1980).

7. J. Adams, ed., *Transforming Work* (Alexandria, Va.: Miles River Press, 1983).

8. Douglas McGregor, *The Human Side of Enterprise* (New York: McGraw-Hill Book Co., 1960).

9. Chris Argyris, *Management and Organizational Development: The Path From XA to YB* (New York: McGraw-Hill Book Co., 1971).

10. O.M. Walter and R.L. Scott, *Thinking and Speaking* (New York: Macmillan Publishing Co., Inc., 1973).

11. J.H. Wood, "Constructive Conflict," in J.E. Jones and J.W. Pfeiffer, eds., *1977 Annual Handbook for Group Facilitators* (San Diego: University Associates, Inc., 1977), 115–19.

12. J.E. Jones, "Dealing With Disruptive Individuals In Meetings," in *Annual Handbook for Group Facilitators* (San Diego: University Associates, Inc., 1980), 161–65.

13. J. Hackman, E. Lawler, and L. Porter, *Perspectives on Behavior in Organizations* (New York: McGraw-Hill Book Company, 1983), 327–85.

Chapter 7

The Nursing Group: Peer Process at Work

Objectives for Chapter Seven

Discuss the characteristics of the nursing group that are unique in establishing group process.

Identify the specific needs of nurses in the group process and the application of these needs to the workplace.

Outline the special character of performance evaluation in a participatory work environment.

Indicate the impact of the career ladder in performance evaluation and in providing for accountability-based practice.

Review the nursing staff role in establishing the responsibility for assuring the quality of nursing practice.

Outline the nurse's role in providing for her own and her peers' continuing education and growth and development.

7

Chapter 6 discussed the nature of working together and the interactions essential for group success. Here, the focus is on identifying ways to create strong group focus and interaction, assuring that the peer process begins to take precedence and has an impact on the direction of the institution. It is through interaction involving the professional group that the nurse manager can see the greatest results. It is through group process that participation is most clearly evident in the work environment. Without group activities and interactions, the nurse manager will be unable to achieve the goals that support the needs of nursing.

Therefore, the skills and abilities she develops in relation to good group management, especially management processes, the better manager she will become. Again, it is important to reemphasize that creating an environment where nurses can behave professionally, as discussed earlier, also is the route to creating high levels of participation and even higher levels of nursing success in the workplace.

If the workplace is to truly make a transition to a meaningful place for professional nursing practice, the character of relationships among the members of the work group must be altered. In this new relationship, the professionals must improve how they behave and interact with one another. In that new context, newer relationships are established and a specific process for achieving goals is undertaken.

THE GROUP AND ITS MEMBERS

A group is a collection or a set of individuals who must depend on and relate to one another. Nursing is a relatively homogeneous group and provides a sense of uniformity. It is, in fact, the basis upon which the nursing activity maintains its consistent identity. While nursing is both social and independent work, the primary need of the nursing group is for social interaction. Nurses form a unit of activity and of relationship. The effective leader develops the sense of uniformity and oneness that is the basis upon which group work can begin.

To do this, the nurse manager identifies strong informal leaders and develops them through her own relationship to facilitate the activities of the group. It is here that peer processes begin. As the individual identified by the nurse leader assumes more formal responsibility for representing the interests of the group, she also learns from the manager the skills that can aid peer members in the group. This does not occur, however, without the manager's first having a set of well-established skills. Nurse managers must be able to build the group consensus in order to develop peer cohesiveness. That cohesiveness is the strength of the individual nurses' desire to maintain their membership in the group. For the nurse manager, identifying ways in which to establish membership and then maintain it is important in developing effective peer processes.

When the nursing group is more cohesive, it develops a characteristic that represents values common to all members. As cohesiveness becomes stronger, the members identify with each other more readily, are more sensitive to each other's needs, and can influence one another more easily. As both personal and professional needs are addressed by the membership, a group cohesiveness is established that encourages further group interaction and satisfaction (see Figure 7–1).

Generally, a nurse becomes more interested in membership in the group when she has a specific need and determines whether this work group actually can satisfy the need. It is, of course, up to the nurse manager to identify more specifically what the need is and to provide opportunities for individuals to fulfill the need in the group. The individual needs friends, achievement, protection, help, health, fun, and interest. Through the group, she may be able to attain some of those goals. The more the individual identifies personal goals with group goals, the stronger the group is likely to become. In nursing, the more identity the nursing group acquires, the more likely it is to fulfill opportunities to meet individual needs through the group process.

Creating a Consensus

The role of the nurse manager in creating this kind of consensus is to:

1. provide opportunities for increasing the number of individual and personal needs that can be satisfied through membership with the group
2. increase the value and the meaning of these needs to every member of the group
3. help members recognize that the group will be able to satisfy specified needs

Figure 7–1 Group Identification Factors

Integration
of
Needs

Professional Needs → ← Personal Needs

Collaboration
Discipline
Coordination
Relationship
Autonomy
Communication
Accountability

Communion
Identification
Verification
Association
Incorporation
Integration

Affiliation
Socialization
Validation
Interaction
Affirmation
Involvement
Love

Group Satisfiers

4. offer opportunities to have the group gain skill and ability in filling or meeting individuals' needs
5. measure objectively the opportunities as well as the practicality of individual need fulfillment through group strategies; in that manner, the nurse manager can recognize whether the group actually does meet individual needs
6. let the members know the degree to which the group fulfills its personal and corporate objectives; each member should recognize when group goals and objectives actually have met individuals' needs and when they have not.

Identifying ways in which solidarity can be achieved in group process will be important for the manager because solidarity or cohesiveness is a primary issue. It is through the process of providing cohesiveness, that the nurse manager begins to establish a basis that can make further group action successful. Providing an open opportunity for members to verbalize whether they feel the group is or is not directed toward meeting individual goals in and of itself provides opportunities for it to begin to meet those goals. [1]

To begin to provide opportunities for group socialization, the nurse manager must be able to identify the needs of every individual on her unit. In the emerging era, a good part of the manager's work will involve understanding the personal characteristics and needs of each individual in order to provide opportunities for the nurses to find fulfillment in their jobs. Nursing professionals require some sensitivity to the needs of their personal social systems and are looking for opportunities to have those needs addressed. Nurse managers should determine from each member of the group what factors are important in working on the unit. Some needs of nurses might relate to the following factors that the work environment can provide:

- an opportunity to do a good job
- adequate salaries and opportunities for increases
- promotions
- steps to make work easier
- consistency in work
- lack of confusion
- assignment of specific titles consistent with role and responsibility
- equal and fair treatment
- open organizations
- good working conditions
- interesting and meaningful work
- job security
- recognition for work well done
- a sense of belonging, of group oneness.

These elements should give the nurse manager clues that the individual values specific things and the manager should address those that could help this nurse in meeting the organization's and the group's goals. This way, the nurse manager can identify the individual's skills, abilities and talents that can help meet the organization's needs and can enhance the nurse's development.

Personal Needs and Values

Personal needs and values also are significant. The nurse does not leave them at home when she goes to work; they remain with her on the job. It often is as important to know those needs as it is those related specifically to work. Their importance becomes obvious when the values of the individual in the work environment are the same as in her life process, whether it be at work or at home. Some of her needs might be:

- a need for accomplishment
- an opportunity to grow
- a feeling of pride in what one does
- a desire for recognition, not only for the work but for the ability and the effort that go into it
- a considered voice in decisions that affect her practice
- opportunities to exert personal authority in the workplace
- honest support and praise from those she works with and for
- opportunities for socialization and for sharing
- opportunities to learn and to be knowledgeable
- opportunities to provide association and to work together in accomplishing specified tasks
- an opportunity to make friends and keep them
- freedom from worry and from risk
- knowledge of both the expectations and the opportunities in the environment.

Although these are similar to the professional job demands and desires, they are much more personal, more intimate in relation to the nurse's needs. In meeting her professional goals, as noted, she also must be able to achieve her personal goals. The nurse manager, utilizing good assessment skills, can begin to identify issues that will help the nurse meet those goals if the manager is sensitive to maintaining focus on those needs. Through identifying, maintaining, and understanding these needs, the nurse manager can use her resources more effectively and broadly and allow them to grow in the workplace.[2]

As the group begins to take shape, members must accept some responsibilities if it is to meet their needs. Each member must know what she wants to get out of being in the group. In nursing, the practitioner may come to work, undertake responsibility for specified patient assignments, fulfill them, then leave the group and go home. If group cohesiveness is to be established, an entirely different—positive—attitude is necessary. A positive attitude is facilitated when the individual assumes responsibility for identifying the needs of the group, of others, and of herself. The group should expect and encourage the nurse to define her wants and needs and in some way develop an understanding of how the group can provide opportunities to fulfill them. The nurse manager, by looking at the role of the individual, at how it is applied, and at the group dynamics on a unit, can enable each member to recognize her specific needs and her opportunities for contributing to meeting the group's collective needs.

Helping and Loyalty

When the nurse becomes a member of the unit, the nurse manager assumes a role in helping her understand what she can realistically expect in the work and in the relationships in the group. A good manager will spend time finding out the nurse's specific needs in order to determine how the group process can best be adapted toward meeting those needs, how this can be done, and what alternatives and options are available. The nurse manager then can assess the difference between the individual's needs and the group's needs, desires, and talents. The smaller the gap, the more the integration between individual and group; the larger the difference, the more opportunity for challenges in creating cohesiveness.

The nurse manager often does not give enough of her energy or time to this role. Recognizing "fit" between the work unit or group and the individual should be an important part of her interview with any new nurse in order to make sure that there is balance and cohesiveness. Based on the new nurse's background and skill mix, the managers can provide either opportunity or constraint in the interview, depending upon the degree of fit.

As in the Japanese tradition, it is important to develop an opportunity to help members achieve a certain level of group loyalty. Group loyalty can be provided by creating a strong identity with the unit and its values, and by developing a commitment to its integrity, cohesiveness, and work objectives. This process is called bonding. It offers opportunities to develop friendships, relationships, and satisfactions, and, both informally and formally, to meet the individual's needs. These opportunities do not stop at the workplace but cross into the nurse's personal life. There is no arbitrary division between personal and workplace values and needs. Informal relationships at gatherings or social events provide opportunities for further cohesiveness on the personal level. While that obviously is not part of the work structure, it does provide an opportunity for group identification. It is at that point that cohesiveness begins to build in the group.[3]

The Role of Sacrifices and Threats

The nurse manager has further opportunities to create a cohesive, bonded environment by allowing satisfied members to make specific sacrifices for the group, refraining from behaviors such as: taking sole credit for ideas; not listening; manipulating conversation; badmouthing ideas, etc. The member who is asked to give up something of value for her group becomes both more attracted and attractive to the group. Other members can see some identification with her and her values and rewards this by increasing support. These small but meaningful sacrifices inform the group members of the individual's commitment. This enhances cohesiveness between the group and its individual members and the cohesiveness felt by the group as a whole. The more the nurse values the item she is sacrificing for the group, the more strongly she can be bonded to the group and the stronger the group feeling about its sense of solidarity.[4]

Individuals are willing to participate in a group when they believe it will protect itself from threats from outside. While this process must be handled with care, a sense of developing cohesiveness can enable the group to identify its strengths and to address such outside threats as: devaluing group work; undermining group activities; harassing group members; denegrating group ideas, etc. It is important to reemphasize that individual work groups are a part of a larger group, and there must be a place in which the two interrelate, especially in a professional environment. However, the smaller group should recognize in its own right that there are opportunities from within to help strengthen individuals and the group to confront issues that might threaten its solidarity, values, and work. The smaller group in particular has a strong interest in maintaining effective interrelationships so that it can receive support when an individual or group threat appears.

The role of the nurse manager in this process is to provide opportunities for group members to support each other so that peers may find mutual aid in problem solving, in assuming risks for perceived group problems, and in sharing responsibility for resolving issues. She must be sensitive to the possibility of developing some conflict of ideas, processes, or goals with external groups because of an overwhelming solidarity within the nurse group that leads to a feeling of group omnipotence. The us/them confrontation that may result can be damaging to both groups. While it is important to create solidarity, the nurse manager also must recognize that blind solidarity can generate serious trouble for the success of the group's work. If carefully developed, group processes and interrelationships should easily avoid both internal and external relational conflicts.

The nurse manager must provide the group with the internal tools to meet its needs. For the group to function at a peer level, the members must be brought to agreement on its purposes, activities, goals, objectives, processes, procedures, and beliefs. The nurse group must develop its rules, policies, norms, practices, and regulations consistent with those of the larger group and the institution as a whole but also specific to the needs of each member.

The work group's standards and behavioral expectations not only must be acknowledged, they also must be articulated so that each member understands them clearly. When the members accept the group's standards and principles, each one responds to them with consistency. Each person can relate to colleagues and other members of the group with full understanding of its expectations. This becomes especially important when an individual member operates contrary to the group values. That errant behavior can be identified quickly by the group, assessed in relationship to its own expectations, and adjustments made either in the individual or the group.

Peer processes and peer relations begin in this context. Without a strong, cohesive beginning point for establishing a relationship, the nursing group will not coalesce. If more attention had been paid to these needs in the past, the nursing group could have a stronger basis upon which to meet professional needs. Emphasis on the peer relations aspect of work group activity provides an opportunity for peers to establish accountability with each other. Definite accomplishments can be assigned as appropriate to group members. In this way, the manager transfers responsibility for concerns to the nursing staff and maintains accountability for coordinating and integrating peer processes.

THE NEED FOR NURSING GROUPS' SUCCESS

When personal success is linked to group success, a different set of dynamics comes into play in the work environment: Individual success becomes a basis for assuring group success. If the nurse recognizes that she can meet her own needs through the group process, that process takes on more value. It is easy for nurses to recall instances in which individuals have worked hard for the group without the slightest possibility of personal gain. Such individuals tied their personal gain to that of the group and recognized, as members, that as it gains, so do they as individuals.

Because nursing is a service group, its product is easy to identify: Positive outcomes in patient and nursing care. It is a single-item product that depends on its collective membership for its success. The work group then should be able, if focused on its own accountabilities, to pay careful heed to the quality of its joint accomplishments and to recognize that individuals' efforts support its success. Development of a strong group identity achieves this outcome and provides a basis for further group growth.[5]

On this basis, it is possible to construct a general model for guiding group process and working with professional nurses. After the nurse manager has developed the appropriate environment, staff supports and trusts have emerged, and the motivating characteristics identified previously are in place, she can establish the direction for accomplishing work. The basis of all motivation comes out of individuals' desire to contribute and to participate fully.

Having harnessed that desire, the nurse manager now must apply individual processes to the group as a whole. She must remember that a group consists of individuals coming together to meet the needs of the organization and that their own needs are the basis of successful group process. Through individual motivation, the members and the group can begin to develop interaction and communication. The work unit already should have a system allowing nurses to know what behaviors and interactions are acceptable and what kinds do not receive individual or collective rewards.

Performance stems, therefore, from a combination of the effort each individual puts into the process and the degree of successful interaction of members in meeting their needs and the group's goals and objectives. As a result of the focus on performance, nurses as individuals attain personal outcomes and as group members address collective results. The hope is that both can be achieved. Through performance, individuals participate in a renewed and rewarded way in the group process. When individual goals and group goals are congruent, levels of satisfaction are enhanced.[6]

Putting group process principles to work and stimulating individuals and the group to meet specific objectives, both for themselves and for the organization, will be challenging for the nurse manager. The needs of the organization and of the profession require that some level of congruence be established. The nurse manager will be responsible for coordinating this activity.

Group process in the professional practice of nursing is important to the organization in three major areas—performance evaluation, quality assurance, and educational development.

PERFORMANCE EVALUATION

Performance evaluation is a significant element in appraising individuals' competence and commitment to the practice of professional nursing. By accepting the responsibility of her position, the individual acquires some basic understanding of what that involves, and exercising it consistent with the agreement she makes in becoming a member of the professional staff. In a professional organization, the issue of membership is far more important than the issue of employment. Employment indicates that an individual is a part of a work group, made responsible for certain activities by the employing institution. Membership in a professional group indicates that a nurse has been selected, approved, and supported by her peers as an equal member of an entity that has defined for itself and the institution what it is and what it will do to meet the hospital's goals and needs. While there may appear to be only subtle differences in these two definitions, they are significant.

To the institution, responsibility as a professional means that the nurse brings with her certain skills, abilities, commitments, and priorities upon which it can depend. It is these assets that are vital to the success of the nursing function in any health care organization. The professionalism involved in the performance of that role must be visibly apparent to everyone. The individual who fulfills nursing accountability does so because of her own sense of responsibility to the role and to the institution, not because the institution demands it. Because of this, the professional practitioner has an a priori responsibility to address the issue of competence on a continuing basis. Competence is the responsibility of every professional nurse. It is not, as is currently held, the responsibility of the institution to validate, assure, and evaluate. In a professional organization that responsibility rests with every nurse. Therefore a peer-based competency and performance evaluation mechanism should be in place in the nursing organization, assuring both the staff and the institution that its nurses are competent and capable.

It is upon this basis that performance evaluation must be built in a professional organization. The obligation for evaluation then must shift from the nurse managers of an institution to its professional providers—in this case, nurses. Nurses, through a representative process, must exercise responsibility for (1) participating in the definition of competency, (2) defining the criteria that will determine levels of competence, and (3) performing activities on which competency will be evaluated and measured.

The key point here is the obligation of the practitioner to participate fully in all three levels of activity. The role of the nurse manager in this case is to provide the support and the system through which the professional nursing staff can undertake its process of assuring competence and evaluating performance. Therefore, performance evaluation can begin in the context of the individual's accountability for assuring that her performance will be consistent with the highest levels of measurement.

The assessment starts with the basic definition of the role of the professional nurse in the institution. Perhaps the best and most succinct definition of nursing can be found in the ANA Social Policy Statement, stated as follows: "Nursing is the diagnosis and treatment of human responses to actual or potential health problems."[7] From this definition of nursing, standards of practice or measurement then can be defined by the nursing group responsible for this definition. In this refinement, additional criteria can reflect the values of the institution in assuring appropriate nursing competence. This assurance supports the initial definition of the role. This creates a continuum that moves from the basic definition of competence, to the standards of practice, to evaluation mechanisms and additional performance criteria. This continuum provides the basis upon which a performance evaluation system is built.

It is important to recognize that, in the 21st century, integrated data bases are important. Therefore, there should be a relationship between performance evaluation and the construction of the theoretical framework for nursing practice. This in turn guides nursing practice in the institution, including the obligation to meet goals and objectives consistent with nursing mandates and the personal obligation of applying professional nursing skills to the delivery of services. This information is designed to support the delivery of care. Each element of the process plays a significant role in relation to other elements. The continuum outlines the basis for all measurement and the mechanics that will be used to implement it.

The Position Charter

The position charter or job description is a clear delineation of accountability expectations that are parallel to or consistent with the overall goals and objectives framework for the nursing organization. The specifics of the position charter should resemble those of the nursing goals and objectives. The efforts of each nurse to achieve those goals and objectives should parallel those of the organization as stated in its critical objectives. (See Appendix A.)

All position charters, consistent with the professional character of nursing, should be accountability based. Accountability statements define functions and responsibilities different from task-focused or laundry list job descriptions that identify the things the nurse is responsible for accomplishing. In the accountability job description, overall responsibilities are identified, with each activity having some measurable component in the organization that can assess the performance of that activity. Accountability based job descriptions or position charters should have the following characteristics:

1. Statements of role or function should be descriptive rather than prescriptive.
2. The responsibility for an action should be defined, rather than the description of the action itself.
3. The job description should guide the nurse in understanding the generic responsibilities of the role, rather than functional tasks to be completed.
4. The job description should reflect the character of the role through its professional delineations and mandates.
5. The job description should provide opportunities to seek higher levels of performance.

Using an accountability based format, the job description should define role expectations in all of the major professional areas. Those areas can be identified by each institution, based on its service, its values, and how its objectives describe the nurse's role. (See Appendix B.) This format provides a broad-based measure of accountability and a specific delineation of role functions and expectations. Finally, objective delineators of measurement relate to the specific items identified in the job description. This instrument is important to peers who will participate in the process, assuring that such measurability helps provide some level of objectivity and some basic criteria against which to evaluate performance.

Performance Evaluation and Objectivity

Objectivity in performance evaluation requires discussion. Much is said in nursing about providing an objective basis for evaluating performances. While objectivity, where it is possible, should be maintained at its highest level, it is important to understand that nursing as a practice is not a specifically objective undertaking. It is difficult to objectify relationships between patients and nurses or between individuals in the work group. Objectivity is achieved only when it can be applied mechanically since mechanical instruments, equipment, etc., do not have a human subjective component.

It is easy to say that nurses should be evaluated relatively objectively based on their performance. However, when evaluating human beings in a human-intensive environment, it is unrealistic and perhaps a little foolish to suggest that totally objective evaluation can be achieved. What must be recognized is that there are certain subjective values that have meaning in the workplace. Identifying those subjective values and providing opportunities for anonymity or protection of individual rights and views will be an important part of the nurse manager's task in developing an effective evaluation system.

The idea that the system must somehow be divorced from subjectivity is erroneous. It therefore is important that the nurse manager recognize that a healthy balance between subjective and objective measurement is perhaps the best she can expect. The work group also must be encouraged to accept this reality. In the development of job descriptions and evaluation tools for professionals, subjective measures will give some clear performance indexes to evaluators. The measures indicate the character of the relationship, interaction, and intervention of each nurse in the workplace and with patients.

The performance evaluation tools themselves are important. To the individual being evaluated, the tool becomes, in fact, the process. Therefore, it should clearly reflect to all members of a work group the values and ideals they hold and express. When the staff is involved in developing the tool, those workplace values and expectations tend to be expressed more clearly and reflect the values and concerns of the individual members. From that perspective, the tool does give the nurse an opportunity to see what elements in her performance are generally valued by the staff as a whole. Often the evaluation form resembles the management-developed job description and evaluation tool, even though they often have a different emphasis and a more specific focus on role expectations.

The performance criteria must incorporate all of the issues the manager feels must be addressed in terms of meeting the institution's needs. It is important that the tool be the property of the staff developing it so the nurse manager will need considerable skill to integrate items essential to meeting the mandates of the organization, either through its policies or its response to legal requirements. One way of doing this is to make the tool available to the staff and assure that it is not a "secret" process and is generally available at any time to members of the group. This will help to demystify the evaluation mechanism; it is this mystification that generates the fear and concern associated with performance evaluation.

CAREER LADDERS OR LEVELS PROGRAMS

There has been much in the literature in recent years on career ladders, levels programs, and similar systems in the nursing organizations.[8,9] (See Figure 7–2.) The intent of these programs is to provide opportunities for the professional staff to grow in ways not previously available. Many levels programs have been suc-

Figure 7–2 Career Parallel Levels Track

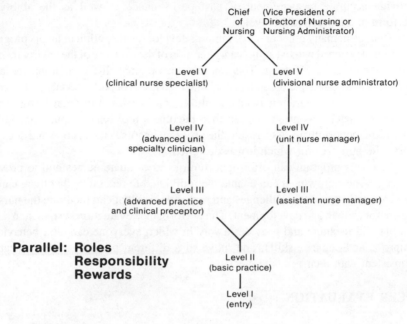

Chief (Vice President or
of Director of Nursing or
Nursing Nursing Administrator)

Level V
(clinical nurse specialist)

Level V
(divisional nurse administrator)

Level IV
(advanced unit
specialty clinician)

Level IV
(unit nurse manager)

Level III
(advanced practice
and clinical preceptor)

Level III
(assistant nurse manager)

**Parallel: Roles
Responsibility
Rewards**

Level II
(basic practice)

Level I
(entry)

cessful, some have not. The measure of success is likely to be related to several factors in the organization: the kind of nursing structure, the participants involved, the degree of participation of all those affected, and the ownership of the program.

The same rules that apply to the organization in general also apply to the development of levels programs specifically. A clinical ladder provides the opportunity for every nurse to grow in the context of her clinical practice. The ladder provides accelerating levels of opportunity and rewards to individuals who have both the time and the abilities to move through them. The fact that these opportunities are optional should in no way limit the chance of each nurse to practice at whatever level she has chosen based on her own needs, circumstances, and abilities. Making the program optional eliminates limitations; it also does not force individuals to participate in something for which they are not prepared.

The impact on performance evaluation is clear. A performance evaluation system based on one level of work may not altogether represent or respond to the growth-oriented needs of nurses or of the institution. As a result, the individual looks at the process as an evaluation of current performance. The opportunity to expand, alter, and improve performance is limited by the single level of expectations and opportunity in the organization. While there are a number of ways that this can be overcome, the success of the clinical leveling format really depends upon its fairness, its true opportunities, its relative objectivity, and its ability to provide accurate measurement of past performance as well as the ability to perform at the accelerated level.

Often, as in many other areas of nursing development, a clinical levels program has been developed without significant alteration of the structure of the environment in which the program will exist. This can hurt the program. If the environment lacks sufficient trust, participation, interaction, and high levels of professional involvement, the clinical levels program may take on the characteristics of its sponsoring entity. In some cases levels programs can then become a tool for manipulation, favoritism, and opportunism. As a result, the program becomes ineffective and does not serve the purposes for which it was designed.

The levels program can offer opportunities to evaluate nurses and to provide space for their growth. It can enable the individual to recognize that there can be rewards and additional challenges and opportunities that can facilitate the nurse's desire for growth and development. The performance evaluation system then takes on life and meaning and provides a way in which everyone can alter behaviors, improve and enhance skills, and move to a different place in the organization consistent with their needs and desires.

PEER EVALUATION

The peer evaluation process in a leveled organization needs to be placed at a higher priority in the organization's evaluation system than has been historically evident. Peers need to reflect, in the performance evaluation system, a way in which a collective appraisal of an individual's potential and ability can be conducted using performance criteria and other information. It is important to stress that this process should involve clinical peers in such a way that they participate fully in evaluating the data and evidence of a candidate's willingness and ability to move to higher levels of performance. The structure also must be devised so that the individual's interests, needs, and wants as a human being are respected. This supports the capability of the individual to move ahead. It also identifies those whose performance may suggest that they are not able to move ahead.

Sensitivity, opportunity, and the willingness of the organization and the collective peers to develop mechanisms that focus on these responses is an important corollary to the focus on the criteria for performance itself. An evaluation system that does not look at the need for sensitivity, for involvement, or for developing mechanisms that carefully and considerately share information that may either negatively or positively affect a candidate for growth, might even be dangerous to the organization.

One of the greatest difficulties an organization can face is to have a performance evaluation system that is developed inadequately. Such a system lacks a clear understanding of the mechanisms necessary to evaluate nurses sensitively and carefully or to communicate evaluation processes among peers in a way that can facilitate staff growth and, if possible, ensure positive outcomes.

An effective peer evaluation system in relation to a levels or growth development program for professional nurses must include the following:

1. Predefined criteria for measurement and performance specifically directed to the position, not the person, must be outlined and clearly understood. Explanatory statements regarding each of the criteria must be available as needed. The criteria must have some measurable elements that can be identified by the participants, as well as the evaluator.

2. The collective staff should look at the data and the evidence of standards for performance rather than whether that performance is currently evident in the practice staff. Specific criteria for measurement, and data that indicate fulfillment (or nonfulfillment) of those criteria, should be the basis for evaluation activities.

3. Data and performance criteria should be documented to the extent possible. The documentation can attest (or not attest) the presence (or absence) of skills essential to validation of performance and/or growth. While not possible in all areas, a documentation process should provide the cornerstone for building criteria for performance evaluation systems that involve a peer process.

4. Peers involved in evaluation should include some the nurse knows and some she does not. If the documentation criteria are clear, detailed, and representative of the demands of the role, then for the most part that should be sufficient for peers to make judgments regarding her performance. Peers' personal knowledge of the individual is not always essential for the evaluation.

5. The professional character of the evaluation process involving peers should be maintained by limiting their interaction with the nurse as much as possible. Where performance evaluations require direct interaction with peers, the interaction should relate specifically to some clinical obligation or task the nurse is required to do for the evaluators. The interaction and relationship, therefore, are based on a formal presentation involving a defined task rather than on any factor of personality, dress, body language, or other personal affectation.

6. A continuing evaluation mechanism must be in place so that components of the system can be reviewed and altered as required to make it more effective. The system must be subject to continued monitoring to determine where it is effective and to facilitate growth, as well as to determine where it is not effective and to make changes.

The effective peer involvement and evaluation system stems from management's belief that peers can develop such a high-level system and the mechanisms to make it work effectively. Once such a system has been implemented, management must manifest its trust by permitting the professional nursing staff the opportunity to evaluate it, alter it, and continue to develop it.

A good performance evaluation is an important element of all of the activities in the division of nursing. It is through the peer evaluation process that performance is looked at within the context of the expectations of the organization. The evaluation system should provide opportunities for each of the participants to view herself in relation to the organization and to the peers with whom she works. The system should help to monitor the practitioner's work and to delineate the opportunities, constraints, and possibilities that exist in the role.

The punitive character of performance evaluation should be minimal. If the system is effective, it provides opportunities for growing, for improving, for monitoring individual performance consistent with the mandates of the organization. Through the peer processes, it gives each individual a responsibility for assessing performance in relationship to her role in meeting group goals. The use of peers in developing the criteria that constitute the cornerstone of an effective evaluation system enhances its value and enables nurses to evaluate the individuals responsible for carrying out the care system.

The peer component of an evaluation system should not engender fear, concern, mistrust, or parochial behavior on the part of the participants. If carefully described, developed, evaluated (and amended when necessary), peer evaluation can be at least as effective as a system operated by individual managers. In a peer evaluation system, the role of the manager is to integrate, coordinate, and facilitate the process. The manager often must be the one who acts as the intermediary, the agent of the staff, in relation to providing services to assure that the evaluation system is implemented well: timing when the evaluation will occur, the dissemination of the tools, the coordination of the group process, handling the completed materials, and often undertaking the individual counseling that may be needed after an evaluation. As agent of the staff, the manager should focus counseling on results of the performance evaluation that require corrective action or improved behavior.

In this role, she supports the peers in fulfilling the obligation of improving performance and reviewing overall effectiveness of the organization. Her role should be one that does not take from staff members the opportunity and the obligation for identifying problems or concerns in any individual's performance but represents their interest through the counseling, development, and growth-oriented process.

If upon the recommendation of the nursing staff the manager must take significant corrective action or terminate a nurse, she does so with the support of the work group members. If a performance evaluation process has been developed properly, it should come as no surprise to participant or to group when an individual is found not to fit the needs of the institution or of the work group. This lack of fit usually is clear to everyone in most organizations anyway. Through an effective peer evaluation system, the nurse manager becomes a part of the group process in facilitating response to various types of situations, bringing them to their appropriate conclusion.

QUALITY ASSURANCE RESPONSIBILITIES

In the traditional organizational structure the quality assurance activity is a part of the mandate of the institution to assure that outcomes of work are as prescribed. Through quality assurance, the institution can ensure that the services it delivers are the ones the patients receive. In nursing, quality assurance generally is viewed by the staff as an additional burden that watchdogs the effectiveness of their practice in relation to process, structure, and outcome.

Quality assurance has undergone many changes since its formal adoption into nursing clinical practice early in the 1970s. It was incorporated into all nursing organizations in the delivery of their service, if only to meet the requirements of the Joint Commission on Accreditation of Hospitals.[10]

However, quality assurance is a staff process. It relates directly to how the professional staff delivers the quality services required to meet patient needs. Quality assurance therefore needs to be an integral part of the operational role of the staff and of individual practitioners. The nursing organization does not bear sole responsibility for quality assurance; the institution rightly insists on being a part of the system to assure high levels of performance. In nursing, the professional has an obligation to assure that the practice is consistent with the standards of the profession, the requirements of the patients, and the needs of the location where care is being provided.

Since the individual staff nurse is a part of the group function in the organization, the group also has a responsibility for quality assurance through defining levels of performance, setting standards of practice upon which performance can be evaluated, and specifying the response to those standards. In this context, the individual nurse is a part of the collective. She shares responsibility for the development and maintenance of the standards and the system upon which quality assurance is based. The collective nursing organization has a responsibility for the following quality assurance items:

1. developing the conceptual framework for nursing in the organization
2. defining standards of practice that can provide basic measurable criteria upon which to measure and validate performance

3. developing a system that each individual nurse must follow that will (a) identify her compliance with quality and (b) pinpoint deficits in her delivery of care that can be addressed
4. developing a mechanism for continually monitoring the effectiveness of nursing care as both a collective and an individual professional enterprise.

In the context of these major characteristics, the nurse manager should develop mechanisms at the unit level to assure that each individual nurse recognizes that quality assurance is not a function disassociated from her role but indeed is incorporated into every aspect of her work. If the nurse is to do this effectively, quality assurance must be a part of the expectations for her performance and should be written into the position charter or job description. This gives her a sense of her individual obligations and of ownership of quality assurance functions.

Functions for Nurses

The quality assurance function can be demonstrated in many ways, depending on the system in which the nurse operates, the mandates of the program, and the interaction on this issue among the professional nurse providers. Whatever the basic components of the quality assurance obligation are for the individual nurse, peers also have a major responsibility in defining a collective obligation. The nursing group must be encouraged in finding ways in which the basic activities of nursing practice also can become elements of the unit's quality assurance program. The following items could be incorporated into all nurses' quality assurance processes. The nurse should:

- participate in any one or several components of the quality assurance program in the context of the nursing process
- use assessment skills in identifying and assessing individual nursing compliance with specified standards
- undertake process evaluation of a particular nursing care event specific to patient needs and reflect that assessment against the standards defining that care
- validate her planning activity with expectations for a specific nursing intervention and reflect that in the nursing care record
- integrate the implementation and evaluation through peer observation and interaction with the planning process in quality assurance
- utilize a nursing care framework (tool) for assessing patients' perception of response to their needs as indicated by their individual evaluations

- use peer process in defining a standard of performance for a unique clinical activity; each peer will have some responsibility for evaluating individual process in relation to such criteria
- interact with the research activities of the institution and define specific roles and responsibilities for performing the functional elements of the research process (research design, data collection, evaluation, etc.)
- participate as a member of the divisional or institutional quality assurance committee in planning, reviewing, altering, and implementing all such activities that relate to the organization's goals and objectives.

These and a host of other tasks, depending on the individual institution's obligation for quality assurance, can be the responsibility of each practitioner. It must be recognized that in the peer process, quality assurance becomes a part of the role of every professional staff nurse. As a result, the staff nurse participates more fully in meeting the obligation of quality assurance. The performance evaluation system reflects this in the criteria that address quality assurance.

Obviously the structural planning element of quality assurance operates at the highest levels in the institution. Therefore, this activity should not be divorced from those of the professional staff nurse in carrying out functional parts of the quality assurance program. The professional staff should be involved at all levels of the institution in developing quality assurance. The need for a staff role in ownership of the process is evidenced through the activities directed toward its participation. The nurse manager then must assure that her professional staff members participate at all levels of the quality assurance system to ensure that the process is integrated into the operational caregiving component of their role.

Nurses' obligation in quality assurance is their participation in assuring competence, in providing an appropriate process, and in measuring it against nursing care outcomes. Since nursing in the institution is primarily clinical and focuses on these issues, it is important that professional staff members realize that quality assurance issues are not optional and cannot be undertaken at the whim or desire of each individual practitioner. It also is important for the staff to know that quality assurance is not a process that the institution goes through to meet some third party requirements. Staff members must recognize that quality assurance is the obligation of each role and is a functional, primary responsibility of the professional nurse in offering her services to patients.

The quality assurance program also is an opportunity for the nurse to recognize that the service she offers is valuable and meaningful. She realizes care must maintain a certain standard in order to remain viable. When staff members understand this viability and incorporate its ownership into their roles, they recognize their obligation to assure that their participation and contribution to the care services of the organization are fundamental to its success.

Group Monitoring of the Process

The group on any individual nursing unit thus has an obligation to monitor the quality assurance process on that unit. The nurse manager must coordinate such activities for staff members. As objectively as possible, she must compare their role with the performance criteria. When performance is an issue, the nurse manager must allow the group to deal with it and to reach collective conclusions:

- If corrective action must be undertaken, the group should identify mechanisms for doing so.
- If quality is an issue, then it must be discussed and remedied by the group.
- If individual compromises in practice are apparent, then the peer evaluation system must be effective in identifying them.
- If new standards of practice must be implemented or changes in practice behavior must be undertaken by the professional staff, then the mechanism used must assure that the alteration is implemented properly. The nurse manager in this process must accept the responsibility for assuring that these activities take place on her unit.

That does not mean that the nurse manager must assume the ownership of the group process; rather, she is coordinator, and provides leadership of the process. She compares the organizational needs in quality assurance with the criteria established to nursing its performance. She initiates the response to assure that practice is directed to maintaining high levels of care. She acts to change practice or standards with the staff as the need arises. As the agent of the staff, she becomes its eyes and ears to help integrate all of the data available on practice and leads the response that can support positive outcomes.

The expectations for individual participation in quality assurance are stated in the position charter or job description. The nurse who is responsible for assuring the quality of her own work should be clear as to the specific expectations or evidences of performance over a defined period. In a levels program or career ladder approach, she must know the particular performance expectations for quality assurance for her levels category. The evidence of appropriate participation in quality assurance rests with the individual nurse, not with the institution. She is responsible for showing to her peers in the evaluation process that she has participated fully in quality assurance activities and that the data she presents are evidence of her doing so successfully.

The ownership of responsibility and the locus of control is shared by the institution and the nurse. This sharing of relations and responsibility between organization and participant becomes more unified. The level of performance also improves because ownership and expectations rest with the individual nurse, who assumes functional responsibility for undertaking quality assurance activities. Expectation for nursing quality is the individual's as well as the institution's. Through this shared approach to accountability, a higher level of participation and interaction in quality assurance is achieved. As a side benefit, quality assurance becomes directed more specifically to care that can be measured, evaluated, and altered as necessary.

COMPETENCE AND CONTINUING EDUCATION

As in performance evaluation and quality assurance, individual practitioners have specific obligations in relation to their own competence, development, and continued growth in the professional performance of their nursing role. Most institutions have services and departments to assure that opportunities exist for nurses to seek to foster their growth. Education departments have been created to provide opportunities for nurses to achieve higher levels of competence and to maintain state-of-the-art performance in providing care.

A major problem in most institutions is whether professional nurses are willing and able to take advantage of educational opportunities. One concern is how worthwhile the education department actually is. The institution often develops educational programs to meet the needs of the organization and the staff, only to find that they are poorly attended and that the response rate and educational outcomes are disappointing.

A basic problem in that kind of situation relates to the cost effectiveness and viability of the education department. When nursing staff members are disassociated from their personal obligation for continuing education—not only to receive it but also to provide it to their peers—then they have relinquished ownership of that obligation.

When a hospital department of education assumes responsibility for nursing education, it assumes accountability for assuring learning and competence—taking it from the individual member of the nursing staff. As a result, the department becomes solely responsible and the only purveyor of education in the institution. The individual's sense of obligation for education to fulfill her professional responsibility as a nurse diminishes. As has been seen in most institutions around the country, the nurse then feels limited personal responsibility for learning or sharing as a fundamental element of her professional obligation. In most cases, this is caused by a faulty management process. Educational departments that have taken upon themselves the full responsibility for education in the division of nursing in effect have assumed that role from the professional staff members, who, by transferring ownership, have disassociated themselves from their own sense of obligation—they have been relieved of any personal educational accountability. Even much of patient education responsibilities have been disassociated from the role of staff nurse.

In the interest of time, a department of patient education has taken over that function. This has freed the nursing staff not only from the role of patient educator but also from accountability for patient education that is a basic element of the role of every professional nurse. Here again the issue is ownership. When ownership is transferred away, it goes to the individual, group, department, or service that assumes it. As a result, the nurses' responsibility for those roles diminishes and shifts to the individuals who have taken on that obligation.

In a professional participatory organization, it is obvious that the educational role must be reassociated with the practitioner of nursing. As a result, there must be a refocus or reorientation in the organization that provides opportunities for the nurse to reassert herself in relation to personal professional growth and the development of peers and patients.

Practitioners' Individual Responsibilities

Here again the nurse manager must assume leadership and integrating responsibility. It is challenging to reincorporate in the role of the practitioner at the unit level the educational responsibilities that are fundamental to her professional function. Initially, the nurse manager may have to assume the total responsibility and risks involved in assuring that this issue is dealt with by the professional peer group in each nursing unit. The profession mandates require that in development and education each professional nurse is:

1. individually accountable for her own professional growth
2. individually accountable for participating in the growth of the profession
3. individually accountable for participating in the growth and development of her professional peers
4. individually responsible for participating fully in patient education activities.

In an environment where the responsibility for professional nursing practice includes accountability for her own self-development, it is important to provide opportunities for the nurse to exercise that responsibility.

The nurse manager can do this through several strategies to help the transition from the hospital's providing educational services to nurses to practitioners' providing their own nursing education. One of the best ways is for the unit to assume responsibility for education for all its practitioners. That will focus the unit's needs for education on addressing individuals' needs. The nurse manager then can develop mechanisms with the professional staff for assigning responsibilities to individual nurses to educate their peers. In doing so, the nurse also begins to address specific needs for her own education and development as a professional. In such cases, responsibility for basic educational needs at the unit level is transferred from a centralized educational service to a decentralized, unit-base service.

The staff can be assisted in this development through the use of the institution's professional educational resources. The nurse manager can call on the services of the nurse educators in the hospital to help the professional staff in the development of educational programs—objectives, content, delivery format, and adult learning strategies. Through use of the department of education as a resource, the nurse manager begins to set up a different kind of relationship between nursing and education. The ownership of education traditionally in the hands of the department of education, is now the responsibility of the staff who are facilitated through use of its services. The education department in this relationship takes on a new character: It provides support, information, resources, and structure for educational programs that remain essentially the responsibility of the professional staff.

The performance evaluation should include the educational responsibility of the staff nurse and should be appraised as part of her professional commitment. She thus has basic accountability for fulfilling not only her educational requirements but also her continuing growth and educational competence.

The Group's Role

Through use of group process strategies as outlined, the nurse manager helps professional staff members identify their responsibilities (including educational) to each other and for the patients. Through the work group, an annual educational program calendar and assignment of responsibility can be defined at the unit level. This educational calendar provides an opportunity for each nurse to identify specific educational responsibilities and topics essential to meet the unique needs of a given nursing unit. The use of adult education principles shared with the education department can make possible creative mechanisms for activities at the unit level as a result of the group process. The educational evaluation or plan also can be part of the group's responsibility for assessing education at the unit level.

Impact of the Marketplace for Services

Depending on the needs and changes in the marketplace for health care services, nurses on a given unit may need to adjust the educational plan to make it more specifically useful to that workplace. The best way to assure implementation is to incorporate the plan into the continuing activities of the nursing unit so that it is an integral part of the functions discussed and evaluated by the staff in its collective deliberations.

Education is an important structural element of the nursing organization and therefore requires a significant amount of documentation. The documentation format or system developed must reflect individual responsibilities for maintaining that process. Each professional nursing staff member should be responsible for maintaining her own documentation regarding her professional growth, participation in the growth of others, relationship to the development of skills, and patient education. Using the institution's documentation framework, the nurse manager should have some mechanism in place for each nurse to assume primary responsibility for collection of data related to her own educational development and participation. When performance evaluations are scheduled, the nurse should have evidence of having met her basic educational compliance objectives. That puts the onus for providing the evidence on the nurse rather than on the institution.

In this context, the education evaluation at least really is governed by the individual being appraised rather than by the traditional evaluator. The evaluation format must be developed in a way that permits the individual staff member to hold ownership of that process. (See Appendix C.) The staff nurse thus becomes the moderator of the evaluation process and also the determinant of the value of her performance in relation to the established criteria. That way, she bears sole responsibility for proving her performance.

The role of the manager and of peers is to continue to validate the performance or indicate developmental needs and concerns. Only when the nurse's perception is not congruent with that of the manager and her peers is there concern over the peer evaluation process. When the nurse is not able to meet the requirements, that should become apparent to her with little intervention by management or peers.

With the establishment of a trusting and responsive environment, all of the systems that support individual accountability will provide opportunities to validate appropriate performance and to indicate where it falls short. The system gives individuals the opportunity to appraise their compliance with the established criteria. The fact that staff has established the criteria and the evaluation mechanisms and is responsible for validating performance shifts the responsibility from the management, as controllers, to a shared role with the staff. An integrated matrix of evaluation competence and peer responsibilities becomes evident. Accountability for providing evidence of competence and compliance with nursing standards to the manager and peers rests with each nurse. (See Figure 7–3.)

OUTCOMES OF PARTICIPATION

It is clear in the processes described here that the need for participation and the resultant transfer of ownership reflect a different character in the organization. When the staff is allowed to participate, then expected to fulfill the obligations of participation, it acquires responsibility that is different from that in the traditional organization. As manager and staff move toward the 21st century where professional practice will be central to nursing, major changes will occur. Organizations of the future will be decentralized and the work will be distributed over a broad base. Newer and more specialized health care delivery services will appear.

Figure 7–3 Peer Review Matrix

	Nurse Manager	Peer Level Above	Clinical Specialist
	Nursing Process	Quality Assurance	Professional Involvement	Governance Activities
Peer I				
	Client Relations	Maintaining Competency (credentialing)	Clinical Growth	Professional Contribution
Peer II				
	Staff Development	Peer Interaction	Self Assessment	Work Rewards
Peer III				
	Clinical Levels Participation	Preceptor and Orientation	Employee Update Requirements (CPR, Policy Infection Control etc.)	Benefits Use

As the services become more decentralized, accountability also will need to be decentralized at the front lines. The individual service providers—practicing professional nurses—will assume increasing accountability and with more independence, accompanied by increased ownership of their role. This accountability, together with ownership, provides an entirely new framework within which the organization must design its human resource strategies.

The nurse, as outlined here, becomes increasingly accountable in exercising her responsibilities as a professional. Within that accountability, the organizational system must provide mechanisms that facilitate interdependence, using such factors as performance, quality assurance, development, competence, and continuing growth. The value that the institution gets out of all of this is a nurse that has a clear understanding of her role and responsibilities and is committed to participate fully in the goals and objectives of the nursing organization to help meet institutional needs. She defines her obligations, she defines their measurement, she participates in their evaluation, and she assumes responsibility in validating her own performance in relation to these obligations. The result: the institution does not have simply a "nine to five" worker; rather, it has a fully committed wholly invested, involved, and valuable participant in the goals of the institution.

Participatory and group processes thus will be the mechanism of choice for the astute nurse managers preparing professional nurses to assume the kinds of responsibility they will confront. The nurse manager of the future will spend a great deal of time and energy in developing those staff members so that they can become independent and interdependent in assuming responsibilities, individually and collectively, for their nursing practice.

The key to this approach is the nurse manager. She must be prepared to assume an expanded role in staff growth and development. She must be skilled in processes involving the use of group participatory strategies, as noted earlier. The ability to share ownership in nursing management and professional processes and to develop her position in such a way that she can support the continuing growth and development of her staff all will be important to her successful transition to the new role.

To maximize nurses' ability to assume these new responsibilities, the nurse manager must provide a supportive, trusting, and open environment that permits them to undertake activities to improve their performance as well as deal with nursing issues that have an impact on the organization as a whole. Even as the nurse manager develops supportive structures, individual nurses must establish fuller accountability in their roles. In the newer era, both nurse manager and individual practitioners must change and advance together.

This balance of an open, creative, and responsive organization, with accelerating expectations of individual performance and accountability, will enable the organization to establish an environment that truly addresses the needs of professional practice in an institutional context. To the extent that the nurse manager provides leadership in opening the organization and defining individual accountability, she enhances both the meaning and the value of the nursing role, currently and in preparation for the future.

NOTES

1. Michael Shaw, *Group Dynamics: The Psychology of Small Group Behavior* (New York: McGraw-Hill Book Company, 1981).

2. L. Donaldson, *Human Resources Development* (Reading, Mass.: Addison-Wesley Publishing Company, 1978), 70–74.

3. E.F. Vogel, *Japan As Number One: Lessons for America* (Tokyo: Tuddle Publishing Company, 1979).

4. L.A. Festinger, *A Theory of Cognitive Dissonance* (New York: Harper & Row, 1957).

5. A.E. Zander, *Making Groups Effective* (San Francisco: Jossey-Bass, Inc., Publishers, 1982), 119–30.

6. E.E. Lawler et al., "Job Choice and Postdecision Dissonance," *Organizational Behavior and Human Performance,* 13 1975: 133–45.

7. American Nurses Association, *Nursing: A Social Policy Statement* (Kansas City, Mo.: ANA, 1980), 9.

8. Margaret Anderson & Mary Denyes, "A Ladder for Clinical Advancement in Nursing Practice: Implementation" *Journal of Nursing Administration,* February 1975: 16–22.

9. Ruth Colavecchio, Barbara Tescher, & Cynthia Scalzi, "A Clinical Ladder for Nursing Practice," *Journal of Nursing Administration,* September 1974: 54–58.

10. Joint Commission on Accreditation of Hospitals, *Hospital Accreditation Manual, 1985,* Standards for Nursing Services (Chicago: JCAH, 1985), 95–101.

Chapter 8

The Challenge of the 21st Century

Chapter 8

Century

Objectives for Chapter Eight

Identify the changes that will have a direct impact on both the management and practice of nursing.

Predict social changes that will affect the direction of nursing practice in the 21st century.

Discuss the need for a cost accounting framework for nursing practice and the management strategy that supports it.

Outline the business interests in health care and the changes that business involvement will bring to nursing practice.

Identify response strategies that will need to be undertaken by nursing education and administration to prepare practitioners for the 21st century.

8

This text throughout has discussed providing a framework that permits nurses to work together as peers, to collaborate as professionals, and to undertake the obligation of nursing collectively in preparing for the future. Preparing for the future, however, no longer is a long-term activity. Technology and change are moving at such an accelerated rate that the future is here before there is time to plan for it. Therefore, response and anticipation of future needs become a hallmark of the professional's ability to respond appropriately.

Within the nursing frame of reference, many changes are occurring that will have a dramatic and long-term impact on practice and its viability in the marketplace. Because of the changes in the prospective payment system and the introduction of a cost cap psychology in health care, nursing is placed in a tenuous position. As a result, nurses—even at the professional level—will need to spend a great deal of energy in the future looking at their professional role, their contribution to the delivery of care, and their marketability for expanding their services over a broader base.

KEYS TO SUCCESS

Nurses' ability to undertake concerted activities, to work together as professionals, and to characterize themselves in the marketplace as capable, highly developed individuals will be important keys to their success. Nurses do not have a tradition of representing themselves in a unified manner to the health care community and to the society they serve. The development of professionalization, as outlined in this book, relies in part on the utilization of group and collaborative strategies. This will be a key to their future success.

The ability to work as a professional team member in the practice of nursing is important. However, that must include the ability to work with groups and other members of a multidisciplinary, complex health care team. This ability must transcend any parochial and unilateral issues of nursing and focus on the health care delivery system that has an impact on all participants in, and consumers of, health services in the country. Therefore, the skills and processes cited here will have special implications for nurses as they begin to expand their frame of reference to incorporate their role with that of other health professionals in defining health care delivery for the future.

Role in Planning

Perhaps the most significant role for the future for which nurses must be prepared is their responsibility in the planning forums of health care delivery. Much of nursing in the past has been of a clinical nature. Nurses have had little input on the national and regional levels outside of the delivery of clinical services. This is where the teamwork and professional integration of nursing roles may face its first major test. Membership in a group, and the ability to assume leadership of a multidisciplinary group, will require skills and abilities in group processes and professional interaction. The opportunities are available; the challenge is to be prepared to recognize and accept them when they arise.

The nurse manager is uniquely prepared with such skills and abilities to provide leadership and direction as a part of nursing's contribution to decisions that have an impact on health care. Expanding her frame of reference from her unit to broader bases of activity has implications for the entire care delivery system and is a natural outgrowth of the demands of her role in a participatory environment. All groups demand participatory investment and relationships with the development of group dynamics that serve to support interprofessional relationships and decision making. The nurse manager is well prepared to assume leadership and take responsibility for making key decisions in groups that are deciding issues of policy and setting direction for the future of health care. Having provided both the direction and the leadership in developing nursing staff skills in professional interaction, decision making and accountability, the nurse manager is well prepared and experienced in leading broader based groups.

As the nurse manager develops skills with her peers that affect nursing practice and makes changes in the perception and the context of that practice, she begins to make a statement regarding her relationship to other individuals. When other health professionals can see that nursing professionals can interact, problem solve, and seek creative solutions to their own problems, they will incorporate nurses into the major decision-making processes traditionally reserved for those perceived to be leaders in health care delivery.

Personal and Professional Assets

The nurse manager must display these leadership assets before she will be included in the broader problem-solving process:

- She must have a strong, well-developed, personal sense of self that translates well into her relationships with others. That sense of self not only must be internalized but also must be visibly balanced in relationship she establishes with others.

- She must have problem-solving and relational skills for influencing nursing's service environment so that others may see that nurses have highly developed interactional capabilities and can seek out and resolve relatively complex problems.

- She must be able to help assure that nursing is perceived as participating with other health professionals in collective problem solving. Creating a strong status for professionals in nursing is important. Establishing an hegemonic status with other health professionals does not create a perception of collaboration, interrelationship and respect.

- She must guide nurses in understanding how to live within the context of their expectations for professional practice. These expectations must be described clearly, must be understood by all health professionals, and must be reinforced by nursing behavior and responsiveness to the responsibilities nurses have agreed to undertake.

- She must assure that nurses are familiar with broader issues related to health care. While it is important that nurses thoroughly understand practice issues, they also must include in their roles an awareness of policy, governance, economic, and social issues related to the delivery of health care services. The nurse manager's helping develop nurses' awareness of their role in relation to these issues is the beginning point for practitioners' full participation in them.

A fuller understanding of nursing's role by all health professionals in the delivery of health care services is essential. Nursing's leaders of tomorrow will have to have a solid grasp of the environment in which practitioners function. A full understanding of the implications that influence the development of health care services and the direction of their delivery is a key factor in the manager's leadership. One reason nurse leaders have not been at the heart of health care policy and economic decisions may be their lack of information and understanding regarding the impact of these issues on the delivery of nursing services. Leaders in the future cannot operate independently of such issues. The effective manager in the 21st century will have a firm grasp and understanding of these issues. She will be able to provide the insights, advice, and direction for nursing and for health care because of her thorough understanding of the delivery system. She will then be capable of moving the nursing resource to incorporate 21st century role expectations, accountabilities, and nursing care functions into nursing practice. (See Figure 8–1.)

Figure 8–1 Role Transition into the 21st Century

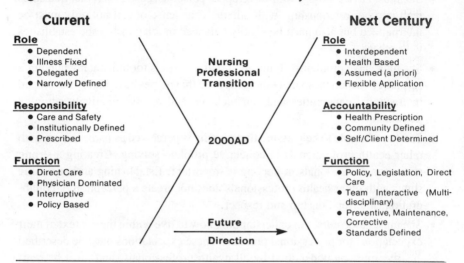

The ability of the nurse manager to provide support information and direction to her peers will be important. While she will have a special responsibility to be aware of the changes in the delivery system, she also will have an obligation to share those changes with peers and to provide leadership in advising and directing response from them in relation to specific issues having an impact on clinical nursing practice. The nurse manager therefore must be able to interpret the information she acquires as a part of her leadership development and must translate it in meaningful terms to her peers.

THE BUSINESS OF HEALTH CARE

Nurses must recognize that health care is much more than a service. While service is a major component, in the United States it is fundamentally a business. The health care delivery system operates within the context of a relatively free and open economy (congressional and legislative regulations aside) in which it must compete for resources. The advent of Medicare and Medicaid in 1965 made available many resources (particularly money) and stimulated spectacular growth in the services offered. New opportunities for the development of technology, new clinical processes, and expanding accessibility to health care resulted from federal funding of services. However, as everyone in health care is painfully aware, changes in the economy in general and in government's philosophy regarding the funding of social programs produced radical alterations in the health care system and its financial viability.

The adoption by Congress in 1982 and 1983 of a prospective payment system introduced intense competition for the dollars available for paying for services.[1] There will be a long-term impact on all clinical practice because of this major change in philosophy. It will require nursing practice in the future to be aware of the cost constraints as the industry is pushed to become more efficient and cost effective and to reduce dollar expenditures. The prospective payment system is a start in the development of control mechanisms to reduce health care services costs.[2]

The prospective payment system will have significant impact for some time into the future. While the diagnostic related grouping characteristic may not remain the basic element of accounting, it does provide a beginning framework for industry response to a cost capping approach that will be with the health care industry for some time. No longer will there be almost unlimited funds or the same commitment to the unparalleled growth of the last two decades in health care.

Nursing will feel this impact as strongly as any group. The profession has developed academically and technically since 1965. The proliferation of collegiate based programs has been a tremendous boon to the practice of nursing and to the development of conceptual thinking to guide the practice of nursing. Controls now apparent in the health care system will limit the number of dollars for nursing education for at least the next decade.

The practice of nursing and nursing management will also change a great deal in the immediate future. Focus on cost as a quality issue will become an emphasis in most health care agencies. Cost accounting methods will be introduced into the clinical areas and nurses will have to consider and evaluate the cost of care as well as the efficacy of nursing care processes. The expectation will be to render comparable levels of nursing care but in ways that reduce the cost of services. Newer and creative strategies will be used to deliver nursing care. Purely technical and costly processes once thought to be of vital importance to the healing process will be rethought and more effective self care and supportive strategies will be utilized to help the patient recover, or to accommodate the patient's health condition.

Focus on outcomes will also take on more importance in delivering nursing services. While much lip service has been paid to outcomes in the service sector, mechanisms that compare process to outcomes have not been widely utilized. In the future there will be a stronger relationship established between what the nurse does in delivering care and the impact or outcome of those processes. Since the development of costing systems in nursing will be a moot point by the 21st century, the ability to articulate specific and refined costs of nursing activity and compare them to achieved outcomes will have a direct relationship to the ability of nurses to render measurable, achievable, and cost effective care. Proving this value and effectiveness will be a basic expectation of the nursing operation. The ability to fund resources and programs will be fully based on the ability to show a cost/benefit relationship in the service.

As the nurse manager seeks to respond to the changes in the delivery system, even in using her skills in managing and developing her professional nursing group, she must be aware of what those changes are, particularly those of which she must be a part. This will help her provide leadership to her peers as they confront the issues themselves. As mentioned previously, the nurse manager's role in the future must be directed toward anticipating, planning, and preparing her nursing professional peers for assuming responsibilities they will face tomorrow.

This chapter is designed to assist the nurse manager and the professional nursing group in understanding issues that will prepare them to cope with the delivery system of the future. They must have some basic knowledge regarding the direction of that system, how it will operate in the long term, and its impact on her ability to deliver nursing services.

The business of health care will continue to grow. The nurse leader of tomorrow must recognize that, based on today's trends, the expansion will continue over the next 20 to 30 years, depending in part on (1) the baby boom-or-bust cycle and (2) the rapid increase in the older population. The expanding services will be provided in a framework different from the past. Previously, much of the growth and transition, both in technology and service, was generated by the government. Congress continually seeks to rein in the government's share of spending. However, private investment will continue to expand, particularly through the growth of multihospital systems.

With the expansion, controls also will begin to change in the delivery system from government to the private sector. Business principles and methods of operation are in the ascendency, with tremendous long-range impact on the delivery of care.

Nurses must understand that hospitals will be stimulated more and more to operate as businesses, to look carefully at their costs, and to make changes to assure their viability to survive. Because of the need to offset tightened government funding, new approaches based on business principles will take over.

Inpatient services already are declining and no longer will be the primary focus of health care because they are too expensive and inappropriate to the needs of many consumers. Traditional inservice care will be offered in other settings that are less expensive, faster, demand fewer resources, and allow patients to resume their own lives earlier. Again, the focus is cost savings—but now the focus is on continued improvement in the delivery of services.

The implication for nursing is clear. Sixty-six percent of the nurses licensed in the United States practice in inpatient facilities. The shift to alternative services poses the question for nursing leadership: Are nurses positioned inappropriately to confront the future? Nurses in institutional settings must begin to address the issues of declining patient days and reduced utilization of inpatient services and determine the most effective transition in practice to assist in addressing this issue.

Nurse managers' ability to change from inpatient alternative services can help assure the viability of practice.

Nurses are the most flexible of health care providers and should be able to make the transition from inpatient to alternative services relatively easily. Nurse managers can provide opportunities for nurses to practice in such other settings as clinics, agencies focusing on health care, rehabilitative environments, ambulatory care, educational, and a host of as yet unconceived services to the public.

Participating in marketing, in strategic planning, in assessing the environment for the utilization of appropriate nursing services for both their viability of those services and their economic rewards will be essential to the management role of the nurse leader of the future. This will help assure the continuing development and growth of the profession away from narrow, rigidly described practice.

Therefore, the skills essential to the nurse manager of the future, and to the nurse leader even in the clinical setting, will be different from those valued in the past. Operational skills will continue to be important (as discussed earlier). Human relations skills will be central to the success of any service. The nurse manager also will need to develop insights and abilities in:

- strategic planning
- marketing
- clinical relationships
- cost-containment strategies
- alternative revenue provision
- case mix (cost accounting management).[3]

The nurse manager must have the ability to manage fiscally like her peers in other industries and will be expected to enhance and expand such skills. To the extent that the nurse manager and clinical leader of the future are familiar with the economic realities and the practice parameters that are involved, nursing is well served. If the nurse manager does not accept or understand those realities—and soon—nursing will feel the constraints in the policy, political, economic, and, finally, practice context. The reduction of financial resources for nursing will result in limiting opportunities to participate in decisions that affect practice and, ultimately, cuts in the nursing work force and its viability in delivering health care services.

COST ACCOUNTING FOR NURSING

One of the hottest topics in nursing management is cost accounting for nursing services—providing a basis for determining their value so that they can be evaluated and, in the final analysis, directed to generating revenue. It is hoped that the issue becomes a long-term practice reality. One of the important components of developing the viability of nursing is to determine its value and contribution to the delivery of health care services.

In an economic framework, the value, productivity, and revenue capabilities of any service or product are absolutely essential to the success of the business. Without addressing these issues, the business leaves a large portion of its management structure unaddressed. This is essentially what has occurred over the past half century or more in nursing. Nursing has not been looked at in the context of its value and contribution to the institution as a whole. The nonrevenue-related approach to the costing of nursing services has served to disadvantage the hospital over the long term as to the fundamental value, contribution, and cost characteristics of such services. Without addressing that particular issue, hospital viability in relation to its primary practitioner has always been questionable.

That no longer will be true in the future. Mechanisms are being developed to identify the cost characteristics of nursing. This is being done primarily by others not specifically familiar with professional practice characteristics of nursing. Time and its value to the delivery of services will be the cornerstone of the costing system. Time is what nurses offer, just as does any other professional. It is what nurses do in that time that constitutes its value. A time-based costing system must be developed to assign specific dollar values to the time normally spent in delivering each service. Since quantifiable characteristics are essential for costing and revenue production analyses, time that can be clearly quantified will be an essential component of a cost-based value for nursing.

This cost-based value will be based on all the services nurses offer, so that their cost characteristics can be identified clearly in any setting at any time. Pinpointing the kind, nature, and specific services provided, and allocating those factors in the time frames they require, will give a basis for costing nursing in a realistic and relatively uniform way. Most of the costing systems that will be used in the future will have a strong time base.

Along with the cost-based systems will be the need to develop a cost accounting management process for nursing as the financial management system of choice in the future. Like any other business, nursing delivers care to specific service accounts, which have clearly identifiable characteristics in relation to practice, use of materials and resources and human resources. Analysis of nursing management and leadership in the context of those cost accounts will provide a framework for assessing and evaluating such roles. It also will generate a whole system of evaluating the processes of delivering care in terms of their costs. Tying the mechanics of care to the costs and combining the resources and the management strategies to evaluate those costs will provide the base line for establishing a revenue framework for determining the value of the contribution of nursing services to the institution's viability.[4] The cost accounting process will continually develop and refine this mechanism so that all processes in nursing will relate to the accounts in which practitioners offer services.

BUSINESS AND INDUSTRY INTERESTS

Because business and industry share such a large portion of the costs of delivering health care services, they will have a stronger interest in reviewing their programs and the services they obtain from the system. They are developing a host of competitive and creative payment strategies. For example, they are moving to shift a larger portion of payment to the consumers of the services. Alternative programs to reduce the overall cost to industry are being developed or expanded, such as health maintenance organizations (HMOs) and preferred provider organizations (PPOs). In the latter, businesses give certain providers preference because of their ability to offer a high level of quality services at costs lower than providers in general. Consumers are willing to participate in the preferred arrangements because their payments will be less, as they will be to the business or industry. Consumers not participating of course will pay more for health coverage.

Individuals will find numerous new options in health insurance programs. They also will find that their employers are more interested in how the consumers use businesses' health care dollars—how they are consumed and what the business can do to help consumers use them more judiciously.

Development of creative responses to funding health care will continue for years to come. Questions for nurses are (1) What is their role in the provision of these new services? (2) What is the impact of preferred arrangements on nursing practice and the availability of nursing services? (3) Where does nursing play a significant role in policy decisions affecting the delivery of care in these new arrangements? All of these must be addressed somehow by nurses as they confront the transition in the 21st century.

The industry will address unusual and creative response strategies to higher costs and less government involvement in health care over the next few decades. Business interest in health care will continue to grow. In fact, health care will model business strategies that operate in other industries. Since a large portion of the health care dollar comes from the business community, they will be anticipating a higher level of influence over how those dollars are spent and will themselves become involved in the delivery of services. This is already apparent to a limited extent in preferred provider arrangements and health maintenance organizations. Corporate health services and employee directed health services centers, wellness services, community centers will all be addressed by the business community.

Insurance companies, traditionally slow to respond to creative approaches to delivering services, will quicken the pace to respond to newer and inexpensive ways of rendering services. There will be more interest on payment of preventive services, diagnostic, and rehabilitative services. This will have an impact on reducing long term expenditures of illness service dollars. Newer and creative arrangements with employers for paying for services not traditionally covered, which will have a net result of reducing utilization of the more expensive illness services, will continue to expand. Even payment for professional services from psychologists, podiatrists, physical and occupational therapists, nurse clinical specialists, cardiac rehabilitation specialists, etc. will be covered in ways not previously anticipated, especially if such services keep people out of hospitals.

Insurance companies will also keep trying different ways of paying for inpatient hospital services. Some will model the processes undertaken by the government. Others will seek newer ways of paying either by contract with specified hospitals who agree to special payment conditions or to preset cost limits. Some will even develop their own health care systems with specified services and payment structures.

The key in the future will be creativity and cost effectiveness. Nurses will be utilized in creative and cost effective ways. The challenge for nurses will be to provide the industry ways in which they can be utilized in new and creative ways. Historically, nurses have filled roles that have often been prescribed by others for them. While the industry is changing, opportunity exists for nurses to create and develop roles that give evidence of needed service. Areas of wellness, health maintenance, care and council of the aged, healthy lifestyle education from childhood to retirement etc. provide just some of the cost effective services that can not only reduce illness and cost, but can provide a long-term basis upon which solid healthy lifestyles can be developed.

TRANSITION FROM ILLNESS TO HEALTH

Another significant change in the delivery system is the slow social transformation away from focusing on illness toward focusing on health or wellness. Health obviously is much less expensive than illness. If structures and strategies can be developed that continue to facilitate this change in the focus on health, the outcome will be fewer costs related to illness. Maintaining health, therefore, becomes a central issue in the delivery system. Nurses can play a major role in providing services that maintain health. Participating in that transition will be an important part of the leadership role of nursing in the future.

In the past, nurses have been located at the terminal end of the delivery system: They have been exposed to patients when illness has occurred already. Nurses' roles have been primarily in the healing process. However, true healing occurs before illness begins. A major responsibility of nursing in the future will be to focus on preventing illness, maintaining health, and changing those life-style conditions that have contributed to illness.[5]

Here again, opportunities for growth in nursing practice are unlimited. With the shift away from inpatient care, a number of alternatives are available in ambulatory service centers, health care corporations, free-standing surgical service centers, emergency medical and diagnostic centers not located in a hospital, community nursing centers, home health care, and educational services established specifically for business. All of these provide almost unlimited opportunities for nursing practice in a framework other than their traditional one. These also involve nurses' responsibility to the new delivery system.

It must be remembered that if a new service or setting is to be valued, it must provide opportunities for those who need it to use it and for it ultimately to be economically rewarding. This is more than just a transition in care delivery—it is a social transformation. Even the traditional power equations in the delivery system are changing. Physicians are no longer occupying as much of a central focus or role in making decisions that affect health care delivery. There now is much broader participation in such decisions. This will continue.

No one provider of health care services will have a corner on determining the direction of the marketplace or the utilization of services. Since business and industry have become involved, they also are sharing in decisions that will affect the direction of health care into the 21st century. The power relationships in the system are rebalancing themselves. The medical model no longer is alone at the heart of the care system because it represents an illness-based approach to delivering services.[6] The health-based approach means involving persons other than the primary illness care provider (the physician).

This new balance, of course, will continue to require broad nursing input. Nurses must make a concerted effort to perpetuate this social shift and to assure that their participation in this change provides for the profession's successful transition to the future.

Because of other changes in society, especially those that relate to the role of women, there is a political shift that encourages changes in the way health care is provided: the new health-based system. Nurses must anticipate the direction of change and make responses that will assure their full participation in the process.

- Work at the policy level to incorporate health teaching at the very earliest levels of social education. Beginning with preschool, health-based behaviors should be taught, and by nurses.
- Become involved in the initiation of policy, legislative programs, and the implementing of practice changes in transportation safety, environment, human relations, and social and domestic issues, especially those related to social violence.
- Give evidence that nursing practice that focuses on psychological and emotional implications and responses will affect the health of the consumer and improve the healing processes.

- Be involved directly in areas that focus on the promotion of sound and purposeful health practices. Nurses must analyze consumers' behaviors and promote changes that will move emphasis from illness-producing to health-maintaining conduct.
- Change nursing's focus in part from inpatient bed-related care to services that address health-related issues in the community, in the workplace, and in the home. As appropriate, as strategies for marketing and planning improve, and as medicine shifts its sights, nurses must participate in reducing their numbers in the inpatient area but broaden their practice in others. Additional educational preparation will enable them to have greater impact.
- Participate more fully in the political, planning, administrative, and legislative process, in the development of health policy, and in assuring the maintenance of a transition to a health-based care system.
- Work with executives in the private sector to develop approaches to delivering health care that is cost effective and specifically health related.
- Increase the number of nurses involved in private enterprises directed toward facilitating health, such as private nursing businesses, community nursing centers, nursing health education, and other revenue-producing entities that help assure the profession's economic viability.
- Provide leadership in designing health-based systems that address the needs of an elderly and continually aging population. This population is an appropriate group with which nursing can address wellness activities to help to maintain older persons' activity and health. This is a relatively underserved group in relation to teaching health practices. It constitutes an ideal example for demonstrating, that nursing practice can provide meaningful help in health care delivery.

JOINT VENTURE HEALTH CARE SERVICES

One trend in the marketplace is the integration and collaboration involving health care resources in ventures that can be mutually beneficial to all participants. Joint venturing will continue to grow. Joint ventures encourage participating in the risks of delivering specific health services with the hope of sharing in the resultant revenues. They provide opportunities for individuals and groups to invest in a project that can produce value to the users and to the health professionals participating.

Nurses need to understand the mechanisms of joint ventures and the relationships essential to make them successful. Joint venturing with physicians, with other health professionals, or with hospitals provides a framework for nurses to offer specific services of value to consumers that can provide rewards to the nursing professionals as well as to those with whom they collaborate. Nurses will find almost unlimited opportunities in joint ventures: health and nutritional services with dieticians, physical and rehabilitative services with specialists in those fields; health and exercise programs with exercise physiologists and other rehabilitation specialists; psychiatric services with psychiatrists, psychologists, social workers, and other behavioral-oriented professionals.

These ventures and services are alternatives to the hospital. The utilization of office space, other facilities, home health mechanisms, patient ambulatory care settings, day care settings, and other kinds of alternative sites provides a broad base for health professionals looking at joint venturing. Institutions find that joint ventures with health professionals provide continuing economic growth. Nurses need to focus on participating in joint ventures in which their services and skills will enable the new entities to offer cost-effective and meaningful care. Nurses could establish joint ventures with other nurses to serve consumers with care that may not be physician related in centers that may not be linked directly to hospitals or other traditional settings.

INFORMATION AGE

As society moves into the 21st century, information becomes even more abundant than it is now. The information will be complex and highly detailed. Most health care systems will develop integrated data bases rather than spreadsheet management processes. These data bases will permit services to centralize all information that relates to their specific functional elements. Financial information will be integrated with clinical data, clinical data with statistical data, and so on. Computers already constitute an important component of services delivery and will become increasingly so, providing opportunities not available to nurses. Data bases will help in making decisions that can have a substantial impact on the delivery of nursing services.

Computer use in the delivery of clinical services also will grow. In diagnostic technology and the application of diagnostic processes they can reduce error in subjective decisions. They also will facilitate patient health assessments, therapeutic recommendations, and integration of services to help clients and consumers make their own decisions regarding their health and possible therapeutic processes.

Computers are becoming more user friendly, reducing or eliminating much of the fear or uncertainty associated with their technology. Nurses will find them much more in keeping with the new era than with the traditional situation. No nursing practice will be able to exist without computer resources. Nurses thus must become familiar with computers and with their technology.

Computer technology will be applied increasingly in the improvement of clinical services. Examples include:

- the use of laser technology in reducing the time and trauma related to surgical intervention
- the use of computerized diagnostic technologies
- the use of special radiological procedures that use low-risk levels of radiation to produce high resolution in clinically specific diagnostic outcomes.
- their use in therapeutic and supportive technologies directly utilized by nurses
- the use of highly computerized intensive care delivery modules, expectable in the next decade
- the use of automatic and computerized monitoring of every functional component of the human process.

The danger is that nurses will become machine managers and forget that their primary role is to support the process of healing. They will need to be able to integrate patients' needs with the new technologies.

New technology also will have significant ethical implications for the future. The nurse will have to assume more and more the role of mediator in ethical and life-altering decisions involving patients and technology. The nurse in this setting will have to provide information, support the therapeutic process of family involvement, help the patient and health professionals make decisions that will have an impact on the use of technology, and assist in their application and their evaluation.

Improving technology will have major implications for issues related to the quality of life. Consumers' increasing participation in decisions on the kind and quality of life they lead will involve the nurse of the future. Patients will need to have the kinds of information and support necessary to assist them in looking at their own life needs, life processes, and self-determination in regard to using technology and services. This will be true even when the quality of life provided might not be consistent with the moral values of those to whom that life support is addressed.

These and many other issues related to the application of technology will become a part of the role of the professional nurse of the future. Nurses cannot be insulated from the realities of the progress of technology. As it becomes more and more complex, their involvement will increase in (1) the technology assessment process of the institutions, (2) the ethics committees on the use of these technologies, and (3) how technology is applied and integrated with the human system principles and processes. Such involvement will be demanding, yet essential. Preparation for such roles will be continuous, beginning at the basic levels of nursing education and continuing as a process of lifelong learning and adaptation throughout the nurse's career.

PREPARING TO REACT POSITIVELY

If nursing is to be able to react to these radical changes in the health care delivery system, what kind of basic responses need to be undertaken? This question arises when considering all of the issues involved. When looked at collectively, they seem overwhelmed in their complexity and their numbers. Indeed, how should nursing be prepared to respond when some of the best minds in health care are struggling to determine the appropriate response to many of these changes that are occurring at an accelerating rate? In preparing for the future, what kinds of responses can be anticipated? What kind of preparation is needed by nurses if they are to be ready to respond appropriately?

The nurse must be prepared to deal with such issues in her day-to-day practice. The very nature of practice will be altered drastically. Nurses must anticipate these changes and incorporate them into their work.

A NEW SCRIPT FOR EDUCATION

A good place to begin obviously is with the basic preparation of the professional nurse of the future. While many changes have occurred in the educational framework, continuing adjustment will be essential. The basic curricula of nursing schools across the country will have to be reoriented. The current curriculum is designed to utilize health-based principles, which is commendable and should continue. However, new courses on some of the new variables must be included.

Since the practitioner of the future is not going to be "bed bound," different types of practice will emerge. The nurse must prepare for responsible roles in the community and in institutions that will offer a whole range of alternative services. Nursing schools will have to revise the focus of their philosophy dramatically. This will require a shift from an illness-based health care delivery system to one that is wellness based. All this will create significant demands on the design of nursing education programs at the undergraduate level.

A trend toward baccalaureate education will have to be accelerated. The practitioner of tomorrow not only must be technically prepared to cope with the broadening information base but also must be prepared at the professional level to make judgments independent of other health practitioners, requiring insight and skills beyond those of today. Even those now prepared in baccalaureate programs are not fully ready to meet the realities and the demands of the future, including an expanding marketplace that will depend upon primary services generated by the practicing nurse herself.

Traditionally, this training has been available at the graduate education level. Graduate education will continue to be important but the new era will need far more practitioners than the graduate system can currently supply.

Graduate education will need to focus on nursing leadership, which is growing at an accelerating rate. The graduate level should provide preparation for leadership. While many schools offer such a course track, they also must provide education for broader skills in leadership, political process, group management, interdisciplinary relations, health care economics, and a host of related topics.

Nursing will not reach parity with other health care services at the graduate level until its curriculum is directed toward issues other health care leaders find in their curricula. When nurses become competent to discuss and relate to the issues in a political, social, policy, and economic framework, they will participate in the forums where these issues are discussed and where the decisions are made. Until then, nurses will always be subject to carrying out the decisions of others who traditionally have held the authority.

Transitions similar to those in health care are occurring in society at large. Nurses are not the only leaders who are being asked to make adjustments in their behaviors, in their information base, and in their style of practice. Business, industry, labor, and government leaders also are being required to make significant changes as society moves to meet the accelerating standards of living, better education, and higher levels of expectation from the populace.[7]

The changes in nursing reflect the larger trends in the reorganization of society. Health care is reorganizing itself, and a parallel revamping of practice behaviors will be necessary as it begins to respond to the social and economic changes.[8] This reorganization will have a dramatic impact on nursing practice, so the professionals must be prepared, not only to practice in the new environment but also to cope with the new challenges.

Nurses of tomorrow must be prepared with skills in independent decision making, interdependent relationships, problem solving, collective action, group process, and the full range of management information strategies that traditionally have been available only to institutional management. Today's management-level information will have to be expanded to the practice levels. Higher levels of complexity will develop and nurses not only must be able to deal with them but also must be able to interpret them to benefit the patients receiving care and the practitioners providing it.

Therefore, undergraduate nursing education, at some level, will need exposure to such topics as health care economics, management of human resources, community needs assessment, peer governance, health care agencies, systems management, cost control, cost-effectiveness strategies, and cost accounting. While the complexity of these programs will vary, all practitioners at the undergraduate level should have some exposure.

At the graduate level, the curricula of all nursing-related programs must expand substantially in the areas of policy and economics. So, too, must education for leadership in group practice, health policy formation in governance, and the regulatory process. These nurses need to be taught to strategize and to anticipate, through the use of appropriate forecasting mechanisms, the trends and issues that soon will become a part of the health care delivery system.

Many trends and issues will have an impact well beyond the year 2000. Some of these relate to the future utilization of human resources, their availability, and the kind and quality that will be needed. The structuring of health care regulations, payment systems, finance, social philosophy, and ethical issues are among the trends and strategies that will have to be dealt with. Indeed, the health care delivery system is dealing with these issues now and will continue to do so well beyond the year 2000.[9]

LEADERSHIP IN SERVICE

Nurses already out of the academic environment and into service are concerned about their ability to deal with the future and the issues involved in preparing for it. Obviously, professional nurses must constantly remain aware of the changes in the delivery system, adjusting their own practices as they occur. There also is a strong need to provide leadership for the nursing services provided. Nursing will require creative management and administrative leadership more than at any time in its history. This means that nurse managers must be prepared for their role. To be prepared by both education and experience calls for exposure to the theories and processes that influence the delivery of services. Thorough knowledge of the activities currently undergoing transition in the health care delivery system, and understanding their meaning, value, history, and potential are part of preparing the practitioner to confront the changes that lie before her.[10]

Continuing education in the areas mentioned earlier also will have to be applied to the role of the practitioner currently operating in the health care system and to the nurse manager who is providing leadership. The nursing managers' at all levels in the institution understanding of economic, social, policy, and business strategies will help incorporate the department's activities into those of the institution as a whole. If nurses expect to provide leadership with their peers in health administration, they all must have the same information base, using the same data, the same strategies, and the same marketing trends. When institutions that employ nurses make changes, the nurses can provide leadership when they are informed and thus can anticipate the timing of the moves and the use of nursing resources in applying them.

Nurses must look at the health care delivery system from the viewpoint of their value to it. They also must come to understand that nobody responds for nursing unless nursing does so for itself. No other health professional is looking out for the interests of nursing practice in the delivery of services. It is nursing's responsibility to assure those who operate and those who participate in health care delivery are always aware of the impact and the value of nursing in developing services and expanding them to meet consumers' needs. It is nursing's responsibility to validate for other health professionals that nursing has a significant contribution to make. This contribution must involve economic, social, and policy factors. In institutions where nurses have not been a part of policymaking, the framework must be altered to permit nursing to be involved at the highest levels of decision making.

Nurses need to be involved not only at the administrative level but also at the board and community levels in decisions that have an impact on the distribution and delivery of health care services. Nurses constitute the largest single group of health care providers in the United States. For this country to benefit economically and socially, nursing's services must be well utilized. No practitioners are better prepared or more available to provide creative and cost-effective health care services than are nurses.

But nurses need to be positioned to articulate their position, and they need leadership to get them there. Leadership in health care service is vital, but not in a narrowly focused nursing-related sense; leadership in nursing must be broader than it has been traditionally. Nursing leaders must move beyond the framework of specific applications and look at practice in the broader area of health care.

If nurses do not expect to make social policy affecting their role, no one else will, either. If nurses do not see themselves involved in the legislative and political processes that fund health care, others will not either. If nursing's point of view is to be heard in the establishment of broad policy and governmental decisions, then nursing must be present in the forums where those decisions are made. It is nurses' responsibilities to insist that they be there, not the responsibility of others to ask them to participate. Nurses must participate by virtue of their contribution and their ability to benefit the health care delivery system, the institution, or the services involved in meeting health care needs. (See Figure 8–2.)

Preparation in the practice of nursing management must be at the graduate level. Administration of nursing services must incorporate into its educational base issues that deal specifically with economics, finance, social policy, collective decision making, governance, and professional strategies. These functional components will provide an excellent background for nursing leaders in any institution to participate fully, and to provide opportunities to share her information with her leadership individuals so that they also may take part.

It no longer is appropriate for the only truly powerful nursing management individual in the institution to be the nursing administrator, nor for the nursing administrator to be the sole representative of the profession's interests in an institution, a region, or even nationally. Power, authority, responsibility, and involvement must be broadly based in the nursing organization regardless of how large or how small it is, so that all its members have a share and an investment in the processes that affect their services. The manager of the future will participate with her peers in providing direction and sharing responsibility in meeting health care needs for consumers.

Figure 8–2 Health System Focus 2000 A.D.

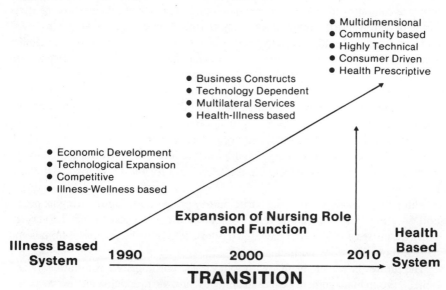

- Multidimensional
- Community based
- Highly Technical
- Consumer Driven
- Health Prescriptive

- Business Constructs
- Technology Dependent
- Multilateral Services
- Health-Illness based

- Economic Development
- Technological Expansion
- Competitive
- Illness-Wellness based

Expansion of Nursing Role and Function

Illness Based System   1990   2000   2010   **Health Based System**

TRANSITION

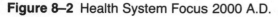

Finally, nurses must be brought into the mainstream of decision making affecting clinical practice. They no longer can be isolated from the realities of the health care system and be taken care of by managers who assume responsibility for the delivery of services. This responsibility must lead the transition to the new era so that practitioners are slowly and carefully incorporated into the decision-making process. Involvement and participation at all levels of the organization provide nurses opportunities not only to be well informed but also to make decisions that have an impact on their practice and its growth. Before the profession can expect to be included in the institution's highest echelons it first must bring its own practitioners fully into the processes that have an impact on their nursing.

Obviously, practitioners at the outset will not be skilled in making decisions and in undertaking strategies using principles and processes of group management. This text has been devoted to assisting management individuals in developing their own insights and skills in relation to group processes so they can share these with their practitioners. Through this text and others, that focus on the management of groups, and the use of strategies, nurse managers and practitioners together can help to develop the skills necessary to make appropriate decisions for the delivery of nursing services.

Nurses have much to contribute. The health care delivery system has depended on nurses for almost a century. There is no indication that that will change now.

However, for the era ahead, the quality of nurses' contributions and their dedication to accelerating levels of service require a new and deepening investment in the future of health care by nurses from every setting. Nurses will need to be involved and participate in health care delivery in a way never anticipated before the 1980s. To the extent that they are willing to contribute and to participate as peers with each other and with other professionals, the system will be enhanced.

It is through participation in the management system, in the clinical system, in the community, and in every forum where health care issues are deliberated that nurse managers will provide meaningful services. Meaningful health care means something different in the 1980s, and even more so in the 1990s and the year 2000 than it has in the previous century. Health must be looked at as a priority in society. Nurses must be prepared to provide the leadership for the move toward the new health care system.

Through skills acquired in the participatory process, through sharing as peers, collaborating, and confronting each other on issues related to the delivery of services, nurses will be better prepared to work with other health professionals and to face those issues in the future.

The future, however, begins with today. The participatory commitments and beliefs, group management skills and abilities, and the practicing nurses' response to the challenges ahead provide an unlimited vista of opportunity. All opportunity begins with the first step. Nurses must take that first step.

NOTES

1. P.L. 92–248, Tax Equity and Responsibility Act of 1982 (TEFRA), requiring prospective payment to hospitals, etc., and P.L. 98–21, Social Security Amendments of 1983, requiring Medicare to shift to prospective payment system based on diagnosis related groups (DRGs). 14, no. 2.

2. Roxanne Spitzer, "Legislation and New Regulation," *Nursing Management* 14, no. 2 (February 1983): 13–17.

3. Barry Moore, "Survey Shows CEO's Priorities Are Changing," *Hospitals* 58, no. 26 (December 16, 1984): 71–74.

4. William Riley and Vicky Schaefers, "Costing Nursing Services," *Nursing Management* 14, no. 12 (December 1983): 40–43.

5. Alvin Toffler, *The Third Wave* (New York: William Morrow & Co., Inc., 1980), 251–52.

6. Norman Cousins, *The Healing Heart* (New York: W.W. Norton & Co., Inc., 1983).

7. John Naisbitt, *Megatrends* (New York: Warner Books, Inc., 1982).

8. Leah Curtin, ed., *DRGs: The Reorganization of Health* (Chicago: S-N Publications, 1984), 193–269.

9. Arthur Anderson & Company and the American College of Hospital Administrators, *Health Care in the 1990s: Trends and Strategies* (Chicago: Arthur Anderson and Co., 1984).

10. Lyndia Flanagan, ed., *One Strong Voice: The Story of the American Nurses' Association* (Kansas City: American Nurses' Association, 1976), 123–288.

Critical Objectives of the Nursing Division

Critical Objective I: Nursing Performance
Provide quality nursing care to the patient.
Standards:

a. An individual nurse-client relationships is entered into upon admission, with a specific understanding between nurse and client of the client's plan of care.
b. A nursing assessment and care plan is completed with each client, organized in the problem-oriented format with measurable care objectives identified.
c. The primary nurse (nurse admitting the client) is accountable to the client for the 24-hour plan of care. Specifics of care are identified and implemented in collaboration with appropriate other health professionals.
d. Periodic nursing audits (process) indicate that nursing care provided has met the objectives identified in the nursing plan of care. At the termination of the care plan, the outcome of the nursing care is measured against the objectives identified in the plan of care.

Critical Objective II: Planning Performance
A continuing planning system is utilized to ensure effective use of resources in meeting short-term and long-term objectives.
Standards:

a. All planning includes clearly identified objectives and standards utilizing all available information.
b. Long-term plans reflect the long-term objectives of the Division of Nursing identified through forecasting mechanisms, outlining advances in nursing practice and technology, and changing social conditions.
c. Planning is based on accurate projections of personnel, materials, and financial resources four quarters in advance. Plans are reviewed quarterly

and revised as necessary, with consideration toward achieving objectives within the cost framework identified for them.

d. Unit budgets are planned for four quarters in advance by the unit's Nurse Manager within the constraints of nursing and unit objectives. Departmental budgets are reviewed quarterly and submitted to the Nursing Administrator. The annual nursing budget is submitted to the Hospital Administrator by the Nursing Administrator for approval prior to its submission to the hospital board.

Critical Objective III: Leading Performance
Maintain a working environment that encourages professional growth through nursing research, education, and practice, resulting in quality nursing care and personal satisfaction for nursing practitioners.
Standards:

a. Decisions are made at each level of accountability in the organization, utilizing a decision-making model.
b. The Nurse Manager of the individual unit is ultimately responsible for the nursing activities and personnel in the department and is accountable to the appropriate Nursing Administrator.
c. Individual nursing practitioners are directly accountable to the client for the nursing care they provide in accordance with the objectives of the Division of Nursing and the individual department.
d. Each nursing department maintains a continuing inservice education program designed to meet the educational needs of its nursing practitioners. Advice and service for educational programs is obtained from the Department of Education.
e. All nursing research conducted in the Division of Nursing is coordinated by the Council on Nursing Quality Assurance, Division of Nursing. All nursing departments cooperate and collaborate with nurse researchers to the extent that such research does not affect individual nursing care adversely.
f. All positions in the Nursing Division are filled by the most suitable candidates available who meet the criteria and objectives for the position, regardless of any other factor.
g. Performance appraisal is a continuing process, with individuals appraised against identified individual objectives and departmental objectives. The professional nurse is peer appraised for her/his clinical practice, using developed standards of nursing care.

Critical Objective IV: Organizing Performance
All work is organized and related so that effectiveness and personal satisfaction are maintained.

Standards:

a. The organizational chart reflects professional relationships as well as the communicating mechanisms.
b. Decisions are made at the lowest possible level.
c. Position descriptions and objectives are maintained for all nursing positions in order to facilitate advice and service in the most expeditious manner.
d. Patterns of organization are reviewed and updated periodically in order to accurately reflect actual organization and communication mechanisms.
e. The organization of the Division of Nursing represents a commitment to shared governance at all levels of the division.

Critical Objective V: Controlling Performance
Results will be measured against objectives, with consideration given to acceptable exceptions. Corrective action is implemented immediately where varianaces are not within acceptable limits.
Standards:

a. "Results measured against plans" is undertaken at all levels of the nursing service organization.
b. A time frame is established (quarterly) for corrective action of all unacceptable variances.
c. All exceptions outside acceptable limits of variance not corrected within an acceptable time frame are reported to the Nursing Administrator with recommendation for corrective action.

Sample Management Position Charter

DIVISION OF NURSING SERVICE

Unit Coordinator
ICU/CCU

POSITION CHARTER

Critical Objective I: Nursing Performance
The unit coordinator is primarily responsible for planning, organizing, leading, and controlling nursing practice within the ICU/CCU nursing unit of Your Hospital and is directly accountable to the Director of Nursing.
Standards:

a. Standards of care will be based on the [State] Law regulating the practice of professional nursing, the American Nurses' Association Standards of Nursing Practice, and the Nursing Policies and Procedures of Your Hospital.

b. A patient classification system will be implemented using validated numerical indicators and clinically specific criteria to categorize patients according to their need for care.

c. A nursing care plan will be implemented using the nursing process in a problem-oriented manner. A nursing care plan will be completed on every patient admitted to the intensive care unit and will be reviewed and updated every 24 hours.

d. Unit coordinator is primarily accountable for the care and safety of all patients while in ICU/CCU.

e. The unit coordinator of ICU/CCU will plan a nursing care approach for her staff by utilizing the patient-centered care concept.

f. The unit coordinator will expect the professional nurse to be accountable for nursing care given using the patient-centered care concept.

g. The unit coordinator will expect those physician orders questioned to be double-checked with her or whomever is delegated as coordinator when orders jeopardize or endanger the safety of patients.
h. The unit coordinator of ICU/CCU is directly accountable to the Director of Nursing for quality of patient care given within the unit.
i. The unit coordinator will want to see defined scheduled nursing audits performed in ICU/CCU that measure intensive medical-surgical or coronary care in order to determine if care given is in compliance with quality nursing according to law, practice, and the ANA.

Critical Objective II: Planning Performance
The unit coordinator in ICU/CCU has 24-hour accountability for planning nursing service to ensure effective use of resources in meeting short-term and long-term goals.
Standards:

a. Learn to plan and to manage by objective system (MBO, Bailey Claus).
b. Participate with the Nursing Division in defining annual goals and objectives, breaking down to quarterly goals and objectives, and assisting nursing administration in meeting these goals and objectives. Monitor quarterly goals and objectives, set time frames, and make a statement that objectives have been met or exception statement that they have not been met.
c. Participate with staffing coordinator with assignments of nursing staff for short-term and long-term planning in staffing for the ICU/CCU. Utilize man-hour reports daily, weekly, monthly, and annually as a tool for the ICU/CCU in identifying staffing deficiencies as well as specific staffing problems.
d. Participate in the formulation of the budget for nursing resources, equipment, and supplies essential to meeting the needs of the intensive care unit with the assistance of the Director of Nursing. Budgets for the intensive care unit will be sumitted four quarters in advance and will be consistent with the overall goals and objectives for the Nursing Division of Your Hospital.
e. The unit coordinator in ICU/CCU will establish time frames in collaboration with other departments and nursing staff for the performance of specific objectives.

Critical Objective III: Leading Performance
The unit coordinator in the intensive care unit is responsible for maintaining a working environment that encourages professional activities and personal growth that results in quality nursing care and personal satisfaction for professional nurses.

Standards:

    a. The unit coordinator in the intensive care unit encourages an environment in which decisions are made at the lowest possible clinical level, utilizing the Bailey Claus model (decision analysis/rendering framework) established by the Director of Nursing.

    b. The unit coordinator in the intensive care unit creates an environment that will stimulate professional nurses to seek and utilize resources that are available, including medical social workers and other personnel, and is ultimately accountable for the nursing activities of personnel in the unit.

    c. The unit coordinator in the intensive care unit will provide for continuing inservice education and standards in the unit to meet the educational needs of the intensive care personnel. Advice for inservice educational programs is obtained from the assistant director of nursing, quality assurance, and educational coordinator.

    d. The unit coordinator in the intensive care unit will cooperate and collaborate with nurse researcher as approved by the Director of Nursing.

    e. The unit coordinator in the intensive care unit will communicate as requested by the director of nursing to interview competent candidates for professional nursing positions in the unit.

    f. The unit coordinator in the intensive care unit is responsible for evaluating the professional nurse, licensed practical nurse, and nursing assistant, and appraising each for clinical practice in the unit.

    g. The unit coordinator in the intensive care unit will make use of the nursing and institutions communication channels to help identify problems and objectives in order to solve problems, implement objectives, and evaluate.

Critical Objective IV: Organizing Performance
The unit coordinator of the intensive care unit will support, give advice, and direct the organizing of the work in the unit effectively and efficiently and meet the goals of the nursing organization.
Standards:

    a. The unit coordinator of the intensive care unit will report directly to the Director of Nursing regarding all matters of organization, work, and related matters about the unit and will have direct response from an administrative level in regards to problems that may occur.

    b. The unit coordinator, as a leader, is accountable for all work organized and methods of work as clearly stated in her position charter.

    c. The unit coordinator will utilize leadership skills of other individuals in the unit to assist in organization of work more efficiently.

d. The unit coordinator of the intensive care unit will support her professional staff members by assisting them in making decisions that affect the care of patients, thus allowing them to make decisions regarding their own practice.

e. The unit coordinator will assist in interdepartmental problem solving and complete responsibilities, tasks and relationships with other areas of the hospital in order to work together effectively for the completion of work.

f. The position charter will be reviewed once a year in regard to its content so that it states clearly what is expected of the unit coordinator and her position in her role.

Critical Objective V: Controlling Performance

The unit coordinator is responsible for the appropriate fulfillment of tasks and responsibilities in the unit and is responsible for the quality of work and cost of work.

Standards:

a. There are defined goals and objectives, as well as exception reports when these goals cannot be met.

b. The unit coordinator is responsible for appropriate discipline and following of hospital policy and procedures in the unit by the staff.

c. Evaluations and monitoring mechanisms are undertaken in ICU/CCU to evaluate the quality and kind of nursing care by means of retrospective audits, process audits, critical evaluations, and other means or mechanisms.

d. The unit coordinator of the intensive care unit communicates clearly all tasks, responsibilities, and expectations of the nursing staff, assuring nursing staff understanding before staff acceptance is obtained.

e. The cost of patient care is monitored and reviewed monthly through the hospital Monthly Operating Report, which will contain human resources costs and operational costs. These are reviewed by the unit coordinator of the intensive care unit to determine if they are consistent with the budget, and variances from standards are investigated.

f. The unit coordinator participates in developing the annual budget for the unit. Patient cost is kept to a minimum to ensure the cost-effective delivery of nursing care.

g. The unit coordinator has controlling of cost as a continuing responsibility.

h. The unit/coordinator takes appropriate corrective action as necessary in regard to employees or expenses, either through disciplinary process (policies and procedures, and nursing standards) or through management of departmental costs. Discipline is administered consistently and fairly. Peer processes are utilized where established.

Sample Clinical Levels: Position Description and Performance Review*

REQUIREMENTS

Level II

- Current Georgia professional registered nursing license.
- Completion of 90-day probationary period in current position.
- Two years of experience in a hospital setting.

INSTRUCTIONS TO LEVELS APPLICANT

A. **Preparation of Packet**
   Contact a Levels resource person for orientation to your packet. A list of these people can be found in the front of the Parallel Levels Notebook on each unit or contact any Assessment Panel member, Level II staff nurse, or Clinical Nurse Specialist.

B. **Organization of Packet**
   All materials submitted should be:
   a. labeled with applicant's name
   b. organized in logical sequence
   c. typed or written legibly
   d. placed in bound notebook

C. **Case Study**
   a. contact Clinical Specialist for a case study when packet is well under way
   b. may utilize appropriate resource people during assessment phase

---

*For the materials as adapted in Appendix C, acknowledgment is given to St. Joseph's Hospital Parallel Levels Committee, Atlanta, Ga.

    c. complete remainder of nursing process independently
    d. document according to hospital standard (APIE [assessment, plan, implementation, evaluation] format) for charting
    e. seek feedback regarding case study from Clinical Specialist after Assessment Panel reviews applications.

D. **Completion of Peer Evaluation and Chart Audit Form**
The applicant will:
    a. select peers to complete forms
    b. Distribute and collect appropriate forms
    c. orient evaluators to form, including instruction sheets on how to complete forms.

E. **Completion of Skills Checklist**
The applicant will submit an up-to-date skills checklist appropriate to the area where the majority of practice occurs plus a general nursing skills checklist.

F. **Completion of "Verification of Completion of Criteria" Form**
When the need for evidence of participation in a particular activity is anticipated and documentation is not readily available, e.g., when participating in data collection for audits or research or when completing peer evaluations, utilize the "Verification of Completion" form [next]. Complete the form and obtain the signature of the responsible person who has requested or been involved in your participation.

VERIFICATION OF COMPLETION OF CRITERIA

Checklist number and criterion:

Date of Activity:

Activity/Evidence: Describe how your activity met each criterion:

Date	Authorized Signature, Position

REQUIREMENTS CHECKLIST — LEVEL II

Current licensure _____
Degree(s) held/year(s) _____
National Certification _____
Years of Experience _____
Years of Experience in Speciality _____

Specialty Courses:

_____
_____
_____
_____
_____
_____

1. Letter of intent _____
2. Completed case study _____
3. Last annual evaluation in current position _____
4. Peer evaluation forms (3) _____
5. Self-evaluation form (1) _____
6. Chart audits (3) plus 2 additional patient names _____
7. Skills checklists (2): general and specialty _____
8. CPR certificate _____

Documentation of the following:

9. Eighteen education contact hours _____
10. Attendance at 75 percent of staff meetings _____
11. Participation in governance activities _____
12. Participation in peer evaluation process _____
13. Participation in patient care conferences _____
14. Definition of and submission of one quality assurance
    or research problem per year _____
15. Collection of data for quality assurance or research _____
16. One peer education program conducted per year _____

LEVEL II JOB DESCRIPTION

Performance Criteria

A. Professional Growth

1. Participates actively in a committee and maintains 75 percent attendance record, or
   a. Participates in nursing governance practice activities.

2. Performs nursing practice independently.

3. Utilizes the health care team member appropriately in delivery of nursing care.

4. Demonstrates effective communication skills through a comprehensive verbal report and clear, concise charting.

5. Incorporates new standards into nursing practice.

6. Develops and evaluates own goals for professional development.

Performance Is Satisfactory When:

1. Participation in nursing committee is evidenced by official attendance record or Verification of Completion of Criteria (VCC) form, or
   a. Participation in governance activities is evidenced by VCC form or copy of standard written or revised or copy of inservice report form.

2. Independence in nursing practice is evidenced through peer evaluation forms.

3. Utilization of health care team members is demonstrated by audit of care plans.

4. Demonstration of communication skills is evidenced through chart audit and peer evaluation forms.

5. Incorporation of new standards into practice is evidenced through peer evaluation forms and/or audit of care plans.

6. Development and evaluation of goals for professional growth is evidenced through written self-evaluation.

Rating Scale

1	2	3	4	5	N/A

7. Is available to serve as a preceptor or supervises new staff/students on the unit.

8. Assists in the development of and conducts one unit inservice per year.

9. Earns 18 continuing education contact hours:

   a. Hours in excess of the minimum requirement may not be forwarded to the next calendar year.

   b. Contact hours from the Governance Councils will comprise no more than 25 percent of minimum requirements. (No other committee meetings will be counted.)

   c. Contact hours may include teaching an in-hospital or community project related to nursing. Not to exceed six contact hours (one hour taught = two contact hours).

   d. Six contact hours may be earned in an academic program toward a nursing degree (one semester hour = 15 contact hours) (one quarter hour = 12.5 contact hours).

7. Preceptorship to students/new staff is evidenced through peer evaluation forms and/or written evaluations of student nurses/new staff.

8. Participation in unit inservice is evidenced by inservice report form.

9. Attainment of 18 education contact hours is evidenced by certificates of completion, official attendance records, or VCC forms.

	Rating Scale				
	1	2	3	4	5	N/A

LEVEL II JOB DESCRIPTION

Performance Criteria

Performance Is Satisfactory When:

10. Attends 75 percent of unit staff meetings.

10. Attendance at 75 percent of staff meetings is evidenced by VCC form.

11. Participates in the peer evaluation process.

11. Participation in peer evaluation process is evidenced by the VCC form.

B. Clinical Teaching

1. Develops individualized teaching plans for a specific patient/family.

1. Development of individualized patient teaching plans is evidenced through audit of care plans.

2. Initiates and conducts one individual patient care conference per year.

2. Initiation and conducting of a patient care conference is evidenced by inservice report form.

C. Self-Assessment

1. Identifies and begins setting long-term goals.

1. Identification of long-term goals is evidenced by written self-evaluation forms.

2. Demonstrates appropriate insight into clinical role.

2. Insight into clinical role is evidenced through parallel self-evaluation and peer evaluation forms.

3. Considers choices for clinical direction.

3. Identification of clinical direction is evidenced by self-evaluation form.

_____

_____
_____
_____
_____
_____

_____

4. Supports the hospital philosophy, participating as a team member and showing courtesy, respect, and concern for the needs of others.

4. Support of the hospital philosophy is evidenced by peer and self-evaluations.

D. Nursing Process:

1. Performs a comprehensive nursing assessment as the data base.

1. Performance of comprehensive nursing assessment is evidenced by audit of nursing admission assessment form and progress records.

2. Establishes a comprehensive problem list and determines appropriate priorities.

2. Identification of a comprehensive problem list and priorities is evidenced by audit of problem list and care plans.

3. Develops patient care plans reflecting complex nursing actions based on a holistic approach.

3. Development of patient care plans reflecting complex nursing actions and development of standard patient care plans is evidenced by audit of care plans.

4. Collaborates with patients, family, and other health care team members in establishing short-term and long-term goals.

4. Collaboration with patient, family, and health care team members in establishing goals is evidenced by audit of care plans.

5. Develops specific discharge plans utilizing health care team members.

5. Development of specific discharge plans is evidenced by audit of care plans.

6. Implements designated plan of care.

6. Implementation of designated plan of care is evidenced by audit of flow sheets and progress record.

LEVEL II JOB DESCRIPTION

Performance Criteria

7. Validates level of nursing skills.

8. Revises the comprehensive care plan as necessary based on evaluative criteria.

E. Quality Assurance/Research

1. Defines and submits one research or quality assurance problem per year.

2. Collects and compiles data.

3. Incorporates quality assurance/research findings into practice.

Performance Is Satisfactory When:

7. Validation of skill level is evidenced by completion of general and unit-specific skills checklist and annual CPR update.

8. Revision of comprehensive care plan is evidenced by audit of nursing records.

1. Definition and submission of one research or quality assurance problem a year is evidenced by written problem forwarded to Quality Assurance Council.

2. Compilation and collection of data is evidenced by documentation with collector's name or VCC form.

3. Incorporation of approved research/quality assurance findings is evidenced by audit of care plans and peer and self-evaluation forms.

Rating Scale					
1	2	3	4	5	N/A

Job Description continued

Employee's Summary:

Evaluator's Summary:

Developmental Goals:

_____

Employee's Signature

_____   _____
Date   Department Head

QUALITY ASSURANCE/RESEARCH GUIDELINES FOR LEVEL II PACKET

Problem Identification

1. The problem identified will have a nursing-specific focus (although it may be a part of a multidisciplinary study).
2. The problem identified should indicate a discrepancy between what is currently evidenced in nursing practice and what is idealized in nursing practice.

3. The idealized nursing practice will be evidenced in some objective standard, rationale, or process found in the literature. The literature is any text, standard, journal, or reference.

Summary
Problem finding can be accomplished in three basic steps:

1. Originate a question, identify what it is you want to know.
2. Specify why you want to have this particular question or issue answered or addressed.
3. State the question so that a specific single, measurable nursing care activity can be addressed.

Format for Problem Identification
The following questions must be answered by the Level II applicant in order to meet Level II criteria for problem identified:

1. What is the problem? Contrast it to the perceived total ideal practice situation.
2. How does the problem have direct effect on *nursing* practice?
3. How do you perceive the problem arose?
4. What will happen if the problem continues as currently described?

Presentation of Problem

1. When the problem has been written, the Level II applicant will place the problem on the agenda of a unit staff meeting and other committees as appropriate.
2. The Level II applicant also is required to forward a copy of the problem to the Quality Assurance Council through the appropriate Quality Assurance Council representative. Completion of these activities will satisfy meeting the criteria for problem identification.

Data Collection
The Level II applicant must give evidence of participating in the data collection process by:

1. Submitting a copy of the list of data collectors maintained by the principal quality assurance investigator, OR
2. Submitting a VCC form signed with an authorized signature.
3. The applicant must participate at least annually in data collection.

	Less Than 80%	80-85%	86-95%	95-100%

LEVEL II SELF-EVALUATION

A. Professional Growth

1. Performs nursing practice independently.

   a. Demonstrates ability to utilize nursing process in health care delivery.

   b. Makes nursing diagnoses and formulates nursing plans on patient assignments.

   c. Evaluates patient outcomes and makes appropriate changes in plan.

2. Demonstrates effective communication skills through a comprehensive verbal report and clear, concise charting.

   a. Gives pertinent and concise reporting describing patient's reponse to medical and nursing plans of care.

   b. Utilizes nursing process tools (flow sheets, care plans, Kardexes, problem list) according to standards.

3. Incorporates new standards into nursing practice.

4. Is available to serve as a preceptor or supervises new staff/students on unit.

   a. Serves as a preceptor to new staff and students when requested.

   b. Supervises new staff/students.

	Less Than 80%	80-85%	86-95%	95-100%

LEVEL II SELF-EVALUATION continued

B. Self-Assessment

1. Demonstrates appropriate insight into clinical role.

   a. Recognizes own capabilities and limitations (utilizes appropriate resources).

   b. Practices within the scope of these capabilities and limitations.

2. Supports the Mercy philosophy, participating as a team member and showing courtesy, respect, and concern for the needs of others.

C. Research/Quality Assurance

1. Incorporates research/quality assurance findings into practice.

Level II Self-Evaluation continued

Individual's Strengths:

Areas for Growth:

Success in Current Role:

Long-Term Goals:

_____   _____
            Date   Employee's Signature

PEER EVALUATION GUIDELINES

You have been asked to complete a peer evaluation of your nursing colleague. To make this process worthwhile and valid, guidelines are provided.

The peer evaluation process takes time. Please allow yourself ample time to become familiar with the forms and format and to collect your thoughts about your peer. If there is a particular area you feel the need to address, but it is not included on the form, please place your comments on the last page under the appropriate heading, or on the reverse side. Any item that you feel is important enough to include is a vital part of your colleague's growth process. If you are having difficulty with phrasing comments, please seek assistance from a resource person.

Peer evaluation is an important responsibility in every profession. After all, who has more first-hand information regarding clinical performance than our colleagues with whom we practice every day?

LEVEL II PEER EVALUATION

A. Professional Growth

	Less Than 80%	80-85%	86-95%	95-100%
1. Performs nursing practice independently.				
a. Demonstrates ability to utilize nursing process in health care delivery.				
b. Makes nursing diagnoses and formulates nursing plans on patient assignments.				
c. Evaluates patient outcomes and makes appropriate changes in plan.				
2. Demonstrates effective communication skills through a comprehensive verbal report and clear, concise charting.				
a. Gives pertinent and concise report describing patient's response to medical and nursing plans of care.				
b. Utilizes nursing process tools (flow sheets, care plans, Kardexes, problem list) according to standards.				
3. Incorporates new standards into nursing practice.				
4. Is available to serve as a preceptor or supervises new staff/students on unit.				
a. Serves as a preceptor to new staff and students when requested.				
b. Supervises new staff/students.				

B. Self-Assessment

1. Demonstrates appropriate insight into clinical role.
   a. Recognizes own capabilities and limitations (utilizes appropriate resources).
   b. Practices within the scope of these capabilities and limitations.
2. Supports the Mercy philosophy, participating as a team member and showing courtesy, respect, and concern for the needs of others.

C. Research/Quality Assurance

1. Incorporates research/quality assurance findings into practice.

Level II Peer Evaluation continued

Individual's areas of strengths:

Individual's areas for growth:

_____
Signature/Date

CHART AUDIT INSTRUCTIONS

Your nursing colleague has selected you to perform a chart audit as part of his/her requirements to move up the clinical ladder of St. Joseph's Parallel Levels Program. The Chart Audit portion of these requirements looks at the professional nurse's ability to document nursing process. Please refer to your Parallel Levels Manual for clarification of the criteria you are being asked to evaluate. Also, in the front of that manual is a list of resource persons you may consult to answer additional questions you may have.

The numbers across the top of the sheet refer to Chart #1, Chart #2, etc. Make a check (✔) under the chart number if documentation is present. If documentation is not present, mark an "0" (deficient) in that column. Mark "N/A" (not applicable) when an item would not be expected to be present in that particular chart. This one Chart Audit Form will be used by all three auditors. Each auditor will sign and date this form.

Thank you for your participation in the Levels Program. If you anticipate applying for promotion yourself, for your own record, please complete a "Verification of Completion of Criteria" form and have your colleague, who has requested the audit, sign your form.

APPLICANT'S NAME:_____

AUDIT OF NURSING RECORD
LEVEL II

Professional Growth   1   2   3

1. Utilizes the health care team members appropriately in delivery of nursing care.
2. Demonstrates effective communication skills through a comprehensive verbal report and clear, concise charting.
3. Incorporates new standards into nursing practice.

CLINICAL TEACHING
1. Develops individualized teaching plans for a specific patient/family.

NURSING PROCESS
1. Performs a comprehensive nursing assessment as the data base.
2. Establishes a comprehensive problem list and determines appropriate priorities.
3. Develops patient care plans reflecting complex nursing actions based on a holistic approach.
4. Collaborates with patients, family, and other health care team members in establishing short-term and long-term goals.
5. Develops specific discharge plans utilizing health care team members.
6. Implements designated plan of care.
7. Revises the comprehensive care plan based on evaluative criteria.

⯅ - Affirmative
0 - Deficient
N/A - Not Applicable

RESEARCH   1   2   3

1.   Incorporates research findings into practice.

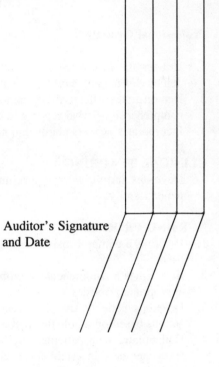

Auditor's Signature
and Date

Submit the following information on two additional medical records for possible
audit by Levels Assessment Review Panel:

Chart #1   *Chart #2*
Patient's name   Patient's name
Discharge date   Discharge date
Primary diagnosis   Primary diagnosis

✔ - Affirmative
O - Deficient
N/A - Not Applicable

NURSING SKILLS CHECKLIST A

	Have Never Done	Have Done Previously	Review
Applications			
Cold			
1. Ice caps			
2. Compresses			
Hot			
1. Warm soaks and packs			
2. Compresses (sterile-nonsterile)			
3. Heat lamp			
4. Bed regulation			
Catheters			
Insertion of retention			
Nonretention catheter			
Catheter care			
Removal of catheter			
Cardiopulmonary Resuscitation			
Collecting Specimens			
Stool			
Routine urine			
Clean catch urine			
Sputum			
24-hour urine			
Culture			
Urine			
Sputum			
Throat			
Dressings			
Sterile dressing change			
Use of Montgomery straps			
Ace bandages			
Burn net			

	Have Never Done	Have Done Previously	Review
Drug Administration			
Oral			
Intramuscular			
Intravenous			
Enemas			
Fleets			
Soap suds			
Rectal tube			
Examinations (assisting with)			
Rectal exams			
Vaginal exams			
Pap smear			
Physical exam of patient			
Intake			
Gastric feeding			
Calculation of intravenous intake			
Output			
Emptying Foley catheter bag			
Use of Urimeter			
Emptying of Gomoco suction bottle			
Emesis			
T-tube			
Wall suction			
Intravenous Therapy			
Irrigations			
Nasogastric			
Inhalation Therapy			
Humidity			
Steam			
Aerosol			

	Have Never Done	Have Done Previously	Review
Oxygen Administration			
Mask			
Cannula			
Face shield			
Restraints			
Posey			
Limb			
Leather			
Special Procedures			
Admission of patient			
Vaginal irrigations			
Gastric feeding			
Application of elastic hose			
Sitz bath			
Isolation technique			
Clinitest–Acetest			
Postmortem care			
Passive range of motion exercise			
Insertion of Dobbhoff tube			
Suctioning			
Oral			
Traction			
Crutchfield tongs			
Pelvic			
Bucks			
90-90			
Extremity			
Cervical			

NURSING SKILLS CHECKLIST B

	Have Never Done	Have Done Previously	Review
Dressings			
Burns			
Dermatologic			

	Have Never Done	Have Done Previously	Review
Collecting Specimens			
Spinal fluid			
Abdominal fluid			
Thoracic fluid			
Diagnostic Tests (preparation)			
Clinical Lab			
X-ray			
Radioisotopes			
EKG			
EEG			
Blood gases			
Cytology			
Pathology			
GIDU procedures			
Enemas			
Medicated			
Irrigations			
Gastric			
Colostomy			
Murphy drip			
Intravenous Therapy			
Regulation of parenteral fluids			
Blood administration			
Volu-trol with medications			
Hyperalimentation			
Piggyback fluids			
IVAC controller and pump			
Suctioning			
Nasal pharyngeal			
Tracheal			

	Have Never Done	Have Done Previously	Review
Special Procedures (assisting with)			
Lumbar puncture			
Paracentesis			
Thoracentesis			
Tracheostomy care			
Insertion of chest tubes			
Special Equipment			
Stryker frame			
Alternating pressure mattress			
In-bed scales			
Lapidus pad			
Doppler			

NURSING SKILLS CHECKLIST C

	Have Never Done	Have Done Previously	Review
Equipment			
K thermia			
EKG monitor			
Rotating tourniquets			
Inhalation Therapy			
Ambu bag			
Respirator			
Suctioning			
Endotracheal			
Thoracic pump			
Chest bottles and tubes			
Special Procedures			
Central venous pressure			
Defibrillation			
Peritoneal dialysis			
Intracranial pressure checks			
Checking defibrillator			

Related References and Further Readings

Abell, Phillip. "Hierarchy and Democratic Authority. In *Work and Power,* edited by T.R. Burns, L.E. Carlson, and V.H. Rus. Beverly Hills, Cal.: Sage Publications, Inc., 1979, 141–71.

Alward, Ruth. "Nursing Administration in Crisis." *Nursing Forum* 19, no. 3 (1980): 243–53.

American Academy of Nursing. *Magnet Hospitals' Attraction* and Retention of Professional Nurses. Kansas City, Mo.: ANA, 1983.

American Hospital Association. *Role, Functions, and Qualifications of the Nursing Service Administrator in a Health Care Institution.* Chicago: AHA, 1979.

––––––– . *Profile of the Nursing Service Administrator Revisited.* Unpublished report. Chicago: AHA, 1980.

American Nurses' Association. *Standards of Nursing Practice.* Kansas City, Mo.: ANA, 1973.

––––––– . *Standards for Nursing Service.* Kansas City, Mo.: ANA, 1974.

––––––– . "Code 9." *Code for Nurses with Interpretive Statements.* Kansas City, Mo.: July 1974.

American Society for Nursing Service Administrators. *Preparation of Managers: Informational Bulletin.* Chicago: ASNSA, February 1979.

Archer, S.E., and Goehner, P.A. *Nurses: A Political Force.* North Scituate, Mass.: Wadsworth Health Sciences Division, 1981.

Argyris, Chris. *Interpersonal Competence and Organizational Effectiveness.* Homewood, Ill.: The Dorsey Press, 1962.

Ashley, JoAnn. "About Power in Nursing." *Nursing Outlook* 21, no. 10 (1973): 641.

Athos, Anthony, and Coffey, Robert. *Behavior in Organizations: A Multidimensional View.* Englewood Cliffs. N.J.: Prentice-Hall, Inc., 1968.

Baker, Constance. "Moving Toward Interdependence Strategies for Collaboration." *Nurse Educator* (September-October 1981): 27–31.

Bennis, Warren G. *Beyond Bureaucracy: Essays on the Development and Evolution of the Human Organization.* New York: McGraw-Hill Book Company, 1973.

Bennis, Warren G., and Benne, Kenneth. *The Planning of Change.* New York: Holt, Rinehart & Winston, Inc., 1976.

Berne, Eric. *Games People Play.* New York: Grove Press, 1964.

Beyers, Marjorie. *Leadership in Nursing.* Wakefield, Mass.: Nursing Resources, Inc., 1979, 1–6.

Blair, Eunice. "Needed: Nursing Administration Leaders." *Nursing Outlook* 21, no. 10 (October 1973): 641.

Blake, Robert, ed. *Perception: An Approach to Personality*. New York: The Ronald Press Company, 1951.

Blake, Robert, and Mouton, Jane. *The Managerial Grid*. Houston: Gulf Publishing Co., 1964.

Blazeck, Alice, et. al. "Unification: Nursing Education and Nursing Practice." *Nursing and Health Care* (January 1982): 18–24.

Bracken, Ruth and Christman, Luther. "An Incentive Program Designed to Reward Clinical Competence." *Journal of Nursing Administration* 10 (October, 1978): 8–18.

Cartwright, Dorwin, and Zander, Alvin, eds. *Group Dynamics: Research and Theory*. Evanston, Ill.: Row, Peterson, 1960.

Chopna, Amorjit. "Motivation in Task-Oriented Groups." *Journal of Nursing Administration* 5 (January-February 1973).

Ciancutti, Arthur; Fabric, Bruce; Wardell, Judy; and Covale, Elizabeth. "Creating Harmony Between Supervisor and Nurse." *Supervisor Nurse* 7, no. 8 (August 1976).

Colton, Margaret. "Nursing Leadership Vacuum." *Supervisor Nurse* 7, no. 10 (October 1976): 29–37.

Council for Graduate Education in Administration for Nursing. Invitational Conference, Proceedings. Atlanta, April 28, 1978.

Cowart, M.E. "Teaching the Legislative Process." *Nursing Outlook* 25 (1977): 777–80.

DeLoughery, G. and Gebbie, K. *Political Dynamics: Impact on Nurses and Nursing*. St. Louis: The C.V. Mosby Company, 1975.

Douglass, Laura Mae, and Bevis, Mem Olivia. *Nursing Management and Leadership in Action*. St. Louis: The C.V. Mosby Company, 1983.

Drucker, Peter F. *Management: Tasks, Responsibility, and Practice*. New York: Harper & Row, Publishers, Inc., 1973.

———. *Management*. New York: Harper & Row, Publishers, Inc., 1974, 130–58.

Duffy, Mary, and Gold, Nancy. "Education for Nursing Administration: What Investment Yields Highest Returns." *Nursing Administration Quarterly* 4, no. 9 (September 1980): 31–32.

Durbin, Ellen, and Zuckerman, Selma. "Legislation Affects Nursing Practice." *Nursing Administration Quarterly* (Spring 1978): 39–50.

Erickson, Eva. "The Hospital Nursing Service Administrator." Ed.D. diss., Columbia University, 1972.

———. "The Nursing Service Director 1880-1980." *Journal of Nursing Administration* 10, no. 4 (April 1980): 6–12.

Estok, James. "Socialization Theory and Entry Into the Practice of Nursing." *Image* 9, no. 1 (January 1977): 13.

Fielder, Fred. *Improving Leadership Effectiveness*. New York: McGraw-Hill Book Company, 1976.

Ganong, Warren, and Ganong, Joan. "Reducing Organizational Conflict Through Working Committees." *Journal of Nursing Administration* 2 (January-February 1972): 6–12.

Goodrich, Nancy. "A Study of the Competencies Needed for Nursing Administration." Ed.D. diss., George Washington University, 1981.

Haddad, Amy. "The Nurses' Role and Responsibility in Corporate Level Planning." *Nursing Administration Quarterly* 5, no. 2 (Winter 1981): 1–6.

Hersey, Paul, and Blanchard, Kenneth. *Management of Organizational Behavior: Utilizing Human Resources*. Englewood Cliffs, N.J.: Prentice-Hall, Inc., 1982.

Hersey, Paul; Blanchard, Kenneth; and LaMonica, Elaine. "A Situational Approach to Supervision." *Supervisor Nurse* 7, no. 5 (May 1976).

Herzburg, Frederick. *Work and the Nature of Man*. New York: World Publishing Company, 1966.

Huckabay, Loucine. "Point of View: Nursing Service and Education; Is There a Chasm?" *Nursing Administration Quarterly* 3, (Spring 1979): 51–54.

Johnson, J.C. "The Educational/Service Split. Who Loses?" *Nursing Outlook* 24, no. 3 (April 1980): 412–15.

Jongewood, Dorothy. *Everybody Wins: Transactional Analysis Applied to Organizations*. Reading, Mass.: Addison-Wesley Publishing Company, 1973.

Kanden, Mark and May, Ken, eds. *Directory of Nursing Regulations and Guidelines*. Towson, Md.: National Law Publishing Corp., 1980.

Kelman, H.C. "Compliance, Identification, and Internalization: Three Processes of Attitude Change." *Conflict Resolution* 2 (March 1958): 51–60.

Kiesler, Charles; Collins, Barry; and Miller, Norman. *Attitude Change: A Critical Analysis of Theoretical Approaches*. New York: John Wiley & Sons, Inc., 1969.

Law Regulating: The Practice of Registered Nursing. Olympia, Wash. Board of Professional Nursing, 1974, 5–9.

Lenninger, Madeline. "Leadership Crisis in Nursing." *Journal of Nursing Administration* 4 (March–April 1974): 28–34.

Levenson, Aaron. "The Challenge of Personal Growth." *Supervisor Nurse* 8, no. 11 (November, 1977): 66–67.

Levinson, R.K. "Knowledge of Professional Nursing Legislation." *Nursing Times* 73 (October 1977): 674–76.

Lewin, Kurt. "Frontiers in Group Dynamics: Concept, Method, and Reality in Social Science: Social Equilibrium and Social Change." *Human Relations* 1, no. 1 (June 1947): 5–41.

Likert, Rensis. *New Patterns of Management*. New York: McGraw-Hill Book Company, 1961.

———. *The Human Organization*. New York: McGraw-Hill Book Company, 1967.

Lun, Jean. "WICHEN: Implications for Nursing Leaders." *Journal of Nursing Administration* 9 (July 1979): 11.

MacPhail, Janetla. "Promoting Collaboration Between Education and Practice." *Nurse Educator* 5 (May 1976): 19–21.

Maslow, Abraham. *Motivation and Personality*. New York: Harper & Row, 1954.

Matejski, Myrtle. "Politics, the Nurse, and the Political Process." *Nursing Leadership* (March 1979): 31.

Mayo, Elton. *Human Problems of an Industrial Civilization*. New York: The Macmillan Company, 1933.

———. *The Social Problems of an Industrial Civilization*. Boston: Harvard University Press, 1945.

McGregor, Douglas. *The Human Side of Enterprise*. New York: McGraw-Hill Book Company, 1960.

McNeil, Jo. "An Administrator's View of Staff Education Needs." *Nursing Outlook* 27, no. 10 (October 1978): 641–45.

Mink, Oscar; Shultz, James; and Mink, Barbara. *Developing and Managing Open Organizations*. Austin, Tex.: Learning Concepts, Inc., 1979.

Naisbitt, John. *Megatrends*. New York: Warner Books, Inc., 1982.

National League for Nursing. *Some Statistics on Baccalaureate and Higher Degree Programs in Nursing—1969*. New York: NLN, 1979.

———— . *Characteristics of Graduate Education in Nursing*. New York: NLN, 1974.

———— . *Masters Education in Nursing*. New York: NLN, 1980.

Newcomb, Thomas. *Social Psychology*. New York: The Dryden Press, 1951.

"Nursing Administration: Directors for the Future." Instructional Conference Proceedings. Boston University School of Nursing, November 3–4, 1978.

"On the Scene at Saint Joseph's Hospital: Developing a Shared Governance Model for Nursing." *Nursing Administration Quarterly* 7, no. 1 (Fall 1981).

Oren, Dorothea. *Nursing: Concepts of Practice*. New York: McGraw-Hill Book Company, 1971.

Peters, Thomas J., and Waterman, Robert K. *In Search of Excellence*. New York: Harper & Row, Publishers, Inc., 1982.

Porter-O'Grady, Tim. "The Nurse Administrators' Role in Cost-Effective Facilities Planning." *Nursing Administration Quarterly* vol. 3 no. 1 (Fall 1978): 67–73.

———— . "Budgeting for Nursing." *Supervisor Nurse* (August 1979): 35-38.

———— . "What Motivation Isn't." *Nursing Management* 13, no. 12 (December 1982): 27–30.

———— . "Bylaws: An Expression of Self-Governance." In *Perspectives in Nursing, 1983–85*. New York: National League for Nursing, 1983, 122–127.

Porter-O'Grady, Tim, and Jisu, Kanri. "Creating a Professional Organization for Nursing." *Nursing Facilitator*. American Nurses' Association, (November 1983).

Porter-O'Grady, Tim, and Finnigan, Sharon. *Shared Governance for Nursing: A Creative Approach to Professional Accountability*. Rockville, Md.: Aspen Systems Corporation, 1984.

Poulin, Muriel. "Study of the Structure and Functions of the Position of Nursing Service Administrator." Ed.D. diss., Columbia University, 1972.

———— . "Nursing Service: Change or Managerial Obsolescence." *Journal of Nursing Administration* 4, no. 2 (August 1974): 40.

———— . "Foreword." *Nursing Administration Quarterly* 3, no. 4 (April 1979); ix.

———— . "Education for Nursing Administration: An Epilogue." *Nursing Administration Quarterly* 3, no. 4 (April 1979): 45–51.

Robey, Marguerite. "A Method of Designing a Competency-Based Education Program to Prepare Nursing Service Administrators for Complex Health Care Institutions." Ed.D. diss., Columbia University, 1977.

Rotkovitch, Rachel. "A Clinical Component in Education for Nursing Administration." *Nursing Outlook* 27, no. 9 (October 1979): 668–71.

———— . "The Nursing Director's Role in Money Management." Journal of Nursing Administration 1, no. 10 (November/December 1981): 13–16.

Rowland, Howard, ed. *The Nurses' Almanac*. Rockville, Md.: Aspen Systems Corporation, 1978, 57–62.

Schaeffer, Marguerite. "The Knowledge Worker." *Journal of Nursing Administration* 7, no. ' April 1977): 7–9.

ᵇn, Edgar. "Management Development as a Process of Influence." In *Behavioral Concepts in ᵃgement,* edited by David Hampton. Belmont, Cal.: Dickinson Publishing Co., 1968, 110.

Sims, Henry. "Leader Structure and Subordinate Satisfaction for Two Hospital Administrative Levels: A Path Analysis Approach." *Journal of Applied Psychology* 60, no. 4 (April 1975): 194–97.

Spitzer, Roxanne. "The Nurse in the Corporate World." *Nursing Management* 12, no. 4 (April 1981): 21–24.

Stevens, Barbara. "Education in Nursing Administration." *Supervisor Nurse* 8, no. 3 (March 1977): 19–23.

_____ . "Administration of Nursing Services: A Platform for Practice." In *Administration Present and Future*, National League for Nursing. New York: National League for Nursing, 1978.

_____ . "Power and Politics for the Nurse Executive." *Nursing and Health Care* 1, no. 11 (November 1980): 208–12.

Stogdell, Ralph, and Coons, Alvin, eds. *Leader Behavior: Its Description and Measurement*, Research Monologue no. 88. Columbus, Ohio: Ohio State University, Bureau of Business Research, 1957.

Taylor, Frederick. *The Principles of Scientific Management*. New York: Harper & Bros., 1911.

Toffler, Alvin. *The Third Wave*. New York: William Morrow & Company, Inc., 1980.

Wade, L.L. "The Neoteric Model." *Human Organization* 10, no. 26 (Spring/Summer 1967): 40–46.

Werner, June. "Joint Endeavors: The Way to Bring Service and Education Together." *Nursing Outlook* 28, no. 9 (September 1980): 546–50.

Whetstone, William. "The Nurse Administrator: A Study in Perceptions of Competencies Needed for Management Effectiveness." Ph.D. diss., University of Pittsburgh, 1977.

Whitte, John. *Democracy, Authority, and Alienation in Work*. Chicago: The University of Chicago Press, 1980.

Index